# CAREER VEER

# CAREER VEER

## How to Position Yourself For a Prosperous Future

### WILLIAM C. HOUZE

**McGraw-Hill Book Company**

New York   St. Louis   San Francisco   Bogotá
Guatemala   Hamburg   Lisbon   Madrid   Mexico
Montreal   Panama   Paris   San Juan   São Paulo
Tokyo   Toronto

1 2 3 4 5 6 7 8 9 FGR FGR 8 7 6 5 4

ISBN 0-07-030482-3

LIBRARY OF CONGRESS CATALOGING IN PUBLICATION DATA

Houze, William C.
  Career veer.

  Includes index.
  1. Vocational guidance.  I. Title.
HF5381.H687  1985      650.1′4      84-14393
ISBN 0-07-030482-3

BOOK DESIGN BY PATRICE FODERO

*For*

PAUL GILLETTE—author, coach, and friend
(and a successful cluster specialist
long before I coined the term)

*and*

GINNY—critic, motivator, and wife
(who clusters, quite successfully,
in her own special ways)

# ACKNOWLEDGMENTS

I salute my partners in our executive search business, Mary Shourds and Jim Montgomery, for their patience and forbearance while I was researching, drafting, and editing this book.

My thanks go to Madeline Cunningham, then my administrative assistant, for her after-hours typing, proofing, and processing of the early chapters.

I am indebted to two of my sons: to Bill III, for his suggestions on organization of the material, and to Vic, for his firsthand experiences as a budding entrepreneur.

I gleefully acknowledge support from scores of Paul Gillette's students—in the Master of Professional Writing program at the University of Southern California, and in his private workshop—for their questions, criticisms, ideas, and (occasional) cheerleading.

Finally, I pay tribute to Ken Stuart, my editor at McGraw-Hill; Ken liked what he saw of the early concepts and worked with me to make them better.

# CONTENTS

INTRODUCTION     xi

CHAPTER 1:    THE COMING BOOM?     1

CHAPTER 2:    THE WAY IT IS: MURK, MORASS, AND MUDDLE     7

Chapter 3:    THE WAY IT WAS: YOU CAN'T GO HOME AGAIN     21

CHAPTER 4:    THE WAY IT WILL BE: SHOCK WAVES FOR THE UNPREPARED     31

CHAPTER 5:    CAREERS IN LIMBO     57

CHAPTER 6:    TO SPECIALIZE OR NOT TO SPECIALIZE?     97

CHAPTER 7:    THE CLUSTER SPECIALIST     109

CHAPTER 8:    ORGANIZATIONAL CULTURE: FIT THE MODE OR HIT THE ROAD     131

CHAPTER 9:    THE ASSESSMENT PROCESS     155

CHAPTER 10:    CAN YOU AFFORD TO BE YOUR OWN BOSS?     179

CHAPTER 11:    DECISION TIME     201

CASE DISCUSSIONS     243

EPILOGUE     263

INDEX     265

# INTRODUCTION

This is a book about the future, about change, and about the *new way* for men and women to build successful careers.

It is designed to provide the thoughtful reader with the essential tools for taking the *career veer* by becoming a *cluster specialist;* it supplies those tools required for building and sustaining an enjoyable, rewarding career in the new order of things.

This new order, especially America's transformation from its heavy industrial base to its new role as world leader in supplying information, knowledge, and certain services and technologies, has been described in various ways by numerous authors in recent years. Naisbitt's *Megatrends,* Cetron's *Encounters with the Future,* and Toffler's *The Third Wave* are the most provocative of these books, and they go a long way toward helping us understand the world of tomorrow.

The *Career Veer* builds upon those excellent works and is an important extension of them. It reveals why the two career roles familiar to all of us, the *traditional specialist* and the *traditional generalist,* are no longer sound career choices for most people.

The book cites the advantages of becoming a *cluster specialist*, the ideal role for most individuals, whether blue-collar or white-collar. The cluster specialist is the man or woman who works effectively, at reasonable technical depth, in a small number of technologies, crafts, or markets *having one or more unifying relationships.* This is, for most of us, the best way to function:

- It reduces and minimizes the hazards which accompany change.
- It gives us a reasonable chance to continue learning and growing in our chosen work.
- It provides more satisfaction from our work because, as cluster specialists, we rely more on our broad aptitudes, attitudes, and skills than on detailed knowledge.

The book points out, in great detail, certain hazards which threaten career progress for men and women who cling to the old career roles of traditional specialist or traditional generalist:

1.  *Becoming too much of a **specialist** can be dangerous.* Your specialty can be rendered obsolete by a new invention, by foreign competition, or by some other external cause. Or the rate of change in your specialty may become so great that you just can't keep up. One day you realize that the new concepts and skills belong to the recently educated specialists, one of whom may soon leapfrog (or replace) you.

2.  *Becoming too much of a **generalist** can be dangerous.* As the rate of change increases, your position of "jack-of-all-trades" can be threatened. More new "trades" emerge every month, and breakthroughs occur every week in each of your old "trades." You know less and less about more and more, and the need for your services may soon be questioned (even by you!).

This book is about *you*—you and *work*. It helps you reexamine the work you do today, and more importantly, it offers previews of the different kinds of work you may choose or be forced to do in the years ahead. This book is for those who prefer to *choose* their work and to shape their own careers. Essentially, this is a *planning* and *action* book. It helps you assess your present career situation, formulate goals, and work toward achieving those goals. In nontechnical language and by pertinent case histories, it shows you how to position yourself for the future.

The observations and recommendations in this book are drawn from my 33 years of experience in recruiting, evaluating, and helping develop executives, supervisors, professionals, technicians, factory and clerical employees. During my fifteen years with General Electric's high-technology businesses and my seven years on Rockwell International's corporate staff, I often served as career counselor for men and women, at all levels, who were *career conscious*. One way or another, they had become aware of the importance of assessing and planning their careers:

- Some were bored with their work or frustrated in their dead-end assignments.

- Others were continuing their education and were eager to apply recently acquired knowledge and skills to a new job.

- Some were on formal, long-term management training programs, concerned about their next assignments and their value as stepping-stones to a career goal.

- Others were returning from military service or an international assignment, and exploring career options.

- A chosen few had been identified by top management as those believed to have high potential for rapid movement toward the very top layers in the corporation.

- A few were "problem employees," recommended

for counseling by their managers because of poor performance, negative attitude, and so on.

But most were average men and women, good employees who wanted to "get ahead." They were also willing to do something to get ahead. They dedicated time, effort, and, in some cases, money to help prepare themselves for future work, which they expected would be more interesting, more rewarding and, in itself, preparation for other work even farther up the pyramid.

Some of these accountants, supervisors, secretaries, engineers, executives, technicians, machinists, and managers did very well in their "career planning" efforts. Others did not.

Over the years, I began to detect some points of commonality within each group. Generally, those who were unsuccessful had become either overly specialized or overly generalized; most of the successful men and women had avoided both of those extremes.

Another factor was the types of businesses in which these people worked. Many of the high achievers had moved into businesses which were newer, smaller, and relatively unstructured. The tendency in the other group was to remain in those businesses which were established, stable, and relatively safe.

Case histories of successful and unsuccessful people are contained in the later chapters of the book. The names and other personal data have been changed, but the stories are typical—so typical, in fact, that you may recognize yourself or several of your acquaintances.

For eleven years, I have been an executive recruiter. As co-founder of one of America's better known search firms, I am retained by corporations to identify and evaluate external candidates for middle- and upper-level management positions. They hire me to help them with their staffing because there are no internal candidates qualified for the job. How can this be? Why are they not qualified?

A number of reasons exist, including inadequate managerial experience and poor communication skills. But all too often it's: "Louise is a good employee, but she is just too *narrow*—she gets too bogged down in the details of cost projections (or structure analysis, or market research, or inventory control, etc.) to see the big picture. This position requires a more *balanced* person." Sometimes it's the opposite extreme: "Frank is a good employee, and he knows as much about this company, especially its history, as anybody here. But he doesn't have expertise in much of anything; he's too shallow in several key aspects of the job."

The preceding two paragraphs were about candidates for positions paying $75,000 per year and up. But there are similar concerns about candidates for lower-level positions. As I "talk shop" with my corporate clients, I detect a growing concern about how a given job will *evolve* and thus what its future requirements might be. Candidates are being assessed on a different scale than in the past; the questions asked go deeper than how he or she will perform during the first year on the job. Employers are showing interest not only in those skills which apply to the given job, but also to related skills. I also see growing concern for other things: the ability to communicate with and work with other people, and for characteristics such as flexibility, adaptability, and survivability. In other words, employers are beginning to seek embryonic cluster specialists.

The last half of this book contains the how and where of becoming a cluster specialist; those chapters will answer your questions. So why didn't I start the book there? Why shouldn't you start reading *there?*

The sequence was established deliberately because I want your questions to be your best questions, not merely the first ones that may occur to you. Remember, I had quite a few years of recruiting and counseling experience before I began to grasp the importance of the cluster concept.

Time is critical; the concept of the cluster specialist is more important than ever. The forces of change—technological, economic, social, and political—are already re-shaping the requirements for successful career planning in the new economy. The time to prepare for the future is now. Today is the day for you to begin planning and implementing your personal preparation program to become a cluster specialist. Who knows? You may be further along than you think you are!

CHAPTER 1

# THE COMING BOOM?

## OVERVIEW

This is a book about the future, about change, and about the
new way for men and women to build successful careers.
These three elements are interwoven tightly, but many of
their critical connections are not apparent to the casual
observer. Although most people realize that the future will
be different from the present, few are aware of the extent of
that difference. Fewer still understand how the rate of
change, ever increasing, is affecting career *paths* and career *roles*. Yet the signals are everywhere, especially in our
fluctuating economy.

For far too long, large sectors of the American economy
and much of our national spirit have been mired in malaise.
Major portions of the economy have been recessed, depressed, contracted, or stagnated, depending on one's
point of view. But one fact emerges clear and unchallenged:
Despite unusually hard times, some sectors of the economy
have been and are radiating growth, profitability, and un-
precedented potential. Economic health varies by:

*Region.* Businesses in California and New Hampshire
are generally healthier than those in Illinois, Michigan, Pennsylvania, and Ohio.

*Industry.* Chemicals, basic metals, and textiles dodder
in the doldrums while financial services, personal
computers, and office automation products flourish.

1

*Company within industry.* The *Wall Street Journal* prospers as the *Washington Star* fails; International Harvester teeters on the brink of bankruptcy but John Deere remains sturdy.

*Organization within company.* Rockwell's aerospace and defense electronics divisions expand while its automotive and industrial valve businesses decline; American Can augments its financial services organization as it reduces the staff in its older businesses.

*Employee within an organization.* Many organizations have eliminated or deemphasized certain specialized activities such as acquisition analysis, strategic planning, and employee counseling. Generally, employees with narrow specialties are laid off while the organization retains workers who can perform several duties.

Many ask, "When will things get better?" This is an understandable question, but not the right question. It fails to address the fundamental issues, and it ignores important signals of impending change. *The internal inconsistencies of our economy are trying to tell us something.*

The question of *when* the new economy will come is less important to the future well-being of millions of Americans than are the critical questions of the *which, where,* and *how* of the new economy. More specifically:

*Which* technologies, industries, and companies will lead the way?

*Which* jobs will be in greatest demand?

*Which* skills, aptitudes, and attitudes will be required?

*Where* will the new career opportunities be?

*How* can we prepare ourselves for them?

Make no mistake: Our economy has begun to turn around. It has done so dozens of times since the financial panics of Revolutionary days. We have seen seven recoveries just since the recession of 1948–1949. The 1981–1983 recession is the eighth since World War II; the eighth recovery began feebly in 1983 and gathered strength in 1984. There will be a robust new economy growing from the current recovery, but with it will come a different environment, one brimming with change of all types. We shall see a markedly different economy from the one we enjoyed before the 1981–1983 recession. In the new economy, *selective prosperity* will prevail, much as it did during that recession. Selective prosperity means that the new economy will contrast sharply with the upswings that followed our nation's other downturns. Those recoveries generally put things back much as they had been and, with few exceptions, the nation soon resumed "business as usual."

It won't be that way this time! The new economy will also hasten the demise of already stagnant industries, backward-looking corporations, and obsolescent jobs. Steel, autos, plastics, chemicals, rubber, and other "blackstack" industries may improve, slightly and temporarily, as part of the spillover from selective prosperity and from protective tarrifs. But soon they may be in even greater jeopardy than during the recent recession. Further, the more hidebound a company, the greater its chances for extinction. For example, America's steel industry dates from the robber baron days of the mid-to-late nineteenth century; so do the railroad industry and the industry that serves our nation's needs for instant communication from one distant point to another. The chronological ages of the three may be about the same, but only one is young at heart.

Steel companies, generally, are in great jeopardy. The situation alone is bad, but even worse is their game plan for recovery—higher and tighter protective tariffs coupled with reduced labor costs. Such action may help in the short range, but steel's real problems remain largely unaddressed. The railroads' condition is even worse, and their game plan seems to be one of pleading for more subsidies, lower labor costs, and higher fares. In other words, these backward-looking companies are still addressing the wrong problems and with the wrong remedies.

On the other hand, forward-looking AT&T (and its even younger-at-heart competitor, IBM) have also encountered threats in the courtroom and in the international marketplace. Each of these companies has developed imaginative new business strategies and has taken bold steps to preserve its vitality and thus continue its growth.

Failures will occur while other businesses move ahead briskly, especially those majoring in the newer/higher technologies of electronics, information, and services. Some of these harbingers of tomorrow are already with us; others will have appeared by the time you read these lines. Still more will emerge in the days ahead, and at an accelerating rate.

But the same familiar basic career paths will carry over into the new economy. Most of us will either be a worker, a supervisor of workers, a staff professional, a manager of resources, or an entrepreneur. There will still be the occasional opportunity to take a different path or to return to one previously followed.

The big change will be in career *roles*, rather than *paths*. Today most of us are either a **traditional specialist** or a **traditional generalist**. In the years ahead, some of us may still be trying to play one of those old roles. But the more alert will have been the danger signals and will have taken the career veer!

The **career veer** is a role change, a departure from ever-deepening specialization and ever-widening generalization. It is based on a new concept, the **cluster specialist**, which is defined briefly in the Introduction and explored in detail in later chapters. This role change requires your becoming attached to and involved in a particular group of technologies, crafts, or markets, preferably those having high potential for future growth. It may also require some attitudinal change, especially where attitudes affect your ability to communicate with and work with other people.

Becoming a cluster specialist may be somewhat risky; although the concept is gaining acceptance every day, many employers still are not quite ready for it. Besides, what if you select a wrong cluster? But, as we shall see, the future holds even greater risk for those who insist on clinging to either of the two established alternatives: traditional specialist or traditional generalist. For most of us, the era of those traditional roles is drawing to a close; the cluster specialist is an idea whose time will soon be upon us.

This, then, is not only a book about the future, change, and the new careers—it is also about *you*. It is a guide for ambitious men and women, risk takers who

- Can feel the winds of change, and want to ride those winds, rather than be buffeted by them.
- Are willing to begin *now* to prepare themselves for an exciting and rewarding future.

# Chapter 2

# THE WAY IT IS: MURK, MORASS, AND MUDDLE

Ours is a schizophrenic society: We are lurching toward the future at the same time that we clutch at the past. We are attracted to the future because we believe, generally, that it holds the promise of better conditions for most human beings. But we also fear the future because we know so little about it and because we suspect that the costs will be high for those anticipated better conditions.

Our feelings about the past are also ambivalent. We remember the good times, reflect with pride on our society's achievements, and are pleased that so many of us have enjoyed the American Dream. But we know that in recent years things have been going wrong and we are not sure who is to blame.

One thing is certain: Few Americans are happy with the current state of affairs. These are troubled, unsettling times brought about by powerful forces which sometimes work together and sometimes work against each other. Many Americans believe that these forces, whether intrinsically evil or benign, are beyond their capacity to understand and accommodate. Still, though most of us are basically aware of the manifestations of the backward/forward tug-of-war, we believe that, in the main, the forward forces will prevail, just as they have so many times before.

John Naisbitt is president of a consulting firm which analyzes critical trends for major American corporations. He is also author of the best-seller *Megatrends: Ten New Directions Transforming Our Lives.* He sums it up this way: "As a society, we have been moving from the old to the new. And we are still in motion. Caught between eras, we experience turbulence. Yet, amid the painful and uncertain present, the restructuring of America proceeds unrelentingly."

Looking at our current condition from a longer-range perspective, James Martin, who wrote *The Telematic Society*, observes: "Humankind is poised midway between the beasts and godlike powers of communication."

As a management consultant, my observation post is closer to the action. I perceive not only that American business is experiencing fundamental change, but also that the *rate* of change is increasing. Business is moving rapidly from the familiar products and traditional management practices of a "blackstack" economy. The direction is toward an *information society* consisting of new technologies and new services, the new products to support them, and revised managerial techniques. This new society will require from each of us not only a new group of skills, but also new attitudes toward learning and toward understanding and working with each other.

# THE TIES THAT BIND

The forces that help hold us to the past are mainly *social* forces—habits, customs, and established ways of looking at things and getting things done. Some of these flow from our major institutions, such as church, school, and family. Who hasn't been forced to memorize idealistic poetry, or endure work-before-play lectures, or been urged to "try and try again"? Some habits, of course, are self-imposed, for reasons of psychological comfort: We begin smoking, wear our hair a certain way, and join the organization approved by our peers. We conform to the norm (or conceal our conduct) to avoid intense social pressures from friends, relatives, and colleagues.

*Political* forces, especially those exerted by governmental bodies, corporations, unions, and clubs, can also tether us to old patterns and established power structures. ("Register at your post office!", "We must not close the Bremerton Naval Shipyards!", "Preserve the landmarks!", and "Remember! the name of the game is profitability.")

*Economic* forces can also restrain. Much of our basic system of prices, payments, and rewards for goods, services, and performance is based on supply and demand, and looks forward rather than backward. But in some instances, the basic system has been tampered with. The artificially high wages paid assembly line workers in the automotive industry did not come about because of a shortage of skilled workers, nor were they based on objective evaluations of job content. Rather, they were caused by the economic power of the unions, coupled with management's willingness to pass on the excess costs to the captive customer. As a result, many unfortunate autoworkers found themselves trapped: they longed to do more interesting, more demanding, more satisfying work, but were unwilling or unable to leave a high-paying job. They realized, deep down, that nowhere else would their time, training, and skills command such a pay level. They were restrained and, indirectly, so was the consumer.

Surprisingly, *technological* forces can also haul us backward, or at least keep us from moving forward. Technologies determine, to a large extent, which goods and services can be made available, at what cost, and how they will be produced, distributed, and replaced. Once technology has led to a good product, such as an incandescent light bulb, certain elements of the technical community become intensely dedicated to making that light bulb better, year after year after year. These incremental improvements are, in the main, beneficial; but think about what might happen if those same resources were applied to the development of a totally new, completely different type of light-generating product.

Of these four, the social forces have the strongest ties with earlier years. Most of us understand that habits, customs, codes, and rituals are rather difficult to part with. What we underestimate is our capacity for **selective retrovision**; we tend to recall more positives than negatives as we periodically escape daily pressures by reflecting on days gone by.

---

# FORWARD MOTION

Ironically, the same forces that are holding us back, social, political, economic, and technological, are also propelling us forward. Of these, technology exerts the greatest leverage; indeed, technology is a major contributor to our current schizophrenia.

Steve Jobs is the youthful cofounder and chairman of the board of Apple Computer; not surprisingly, Jobs is a forward-looking technologist. As he sees the state of things, "We are now in the midst of a revolution that is of the same magnitude and power as the industrial revolution of the 19th century. It is changing our society, our skills and the character of employment in the United States. This revolution is driven by advances in electronics, transforming the contemporary world from an industrial to an information society."

The effects of this awesome revolution have been made even greater by interaction with other forces, especially domestic and worldwide economic forces. At the same time that some welders of refrigerators and ranges are replaced by computer-controlled robots, other welders are laid off because their companies are losing sales to foreign competition, and still others because fewer appliances are needed as fewer housing units are started.

The interplay of these four forces has brought us to our present condition: an economy, indeed an entire society, suspended between two eras.

# BETWIXT AND BETWEEN

On the one hand, businesses in America are failing at an increasing rate, faster than at any time since 1932. Government agencies and private concerns such as Dun & Bradstreet keep track of these events and publish periodic reports. A D&B study showed that 31,334 industrial and commercial business failures occurred in 1983, up from 25,346 during 1982. We hear excerpts of similar reports on the evening television news, and we are disturbed. Next morning we read that an old-line company, whose products were household staples for our parents, has agreed to become part of a conglomerate we've never heard of. Our discomfort increases.

Most of us aren't aware of the other part of the story. Our nation has many more companies doing business today than it had in 1932; obviously, a higher number of this larger base could fail without, *in itself,* becoming a cause for great national concern. Businesses fail every year and for a variety of reasons, not the least of which is that starting or running a business is, by its very nature, a risk-taking endeavor. Yet, year in and year out, tens of thousands of new incorporations are registered *each month.* In 1983 a record number—600,400—new corporations were registered, and this does not include partnerships or sole proprietorships.

Every day many new businesses open their doors, offering us new products and improved services. Your next visit to a heatlh foods store for a pound of pumpkin paté could turn into quite an event. You rush in, only to discover that the store is now a retail outlet of personal computers. Soon you have an unexpected problem: You can't decide between the Apex III (with its educational games and PDQ telecommunication attachment) and the Omicron IV-A, which, of course, features color graphics and tutorial programs in conversational Mongolian.

We know, many of us from painful personal experience, that unemployment is still too high. Although lower than in 1981, factories continue to close, some permanently. A commonly accepted estimate is that, since 1978, 1 million jobs have disappeared and will never come back. But most of these ex-employees will not disappear for quite some time, and neither will their need for work.

Well-meaning business executives, labor leaders, and government officials are attempting to think ahead, trying to figure out how to modernize plants and retrain workers. But I am not optimistic about the outcome of these activities. Neither is the Northeast-Midwest Institute, a think tank specializing in economic research. Their bottom-line is that neither business nor government is adequately prepared for the task of retraining displaced men and women.

A prominent politician has proposed that former auto and steel workers be trained as computer operators. But what will those jobs be like one or two years after training? Will new training programs be required? Will those jobs exist at all? Following the Watts riots of 1967, a concerned federal government trained hundreds of young inner-city men and women—to become elevator operators! As I see it, these well-intentioned efforts have little chance of success because they try to apply *yesterday's* remedies *today* to the problems of *tomorrow*.

Unfortunately, there is (and there may continue to be) far too much hard-core unemployment. The social and economic problems are complex in that sector of our society where, for one reason or another, so many men and women are inadequately prepared to cope with the demands of the job market. But overall, the situation is positive for the future:

- The same technologies and products which are eliminating old jobs are creating new jobs, new opportunities (computer companies have an insatiable need for ingenious men and women to create, produce, market, and service new software and hardware products).

- Employment is increasing in the newer technologies (word processing and electronic funds transfer) and in the service sectors (financial and information services).

- Skilled sales personnel and sales managers are in great demand in the newer sectors (personal computers, telecommunications, and full-service savings and loan institutions).

- American businesses, unions, and workers are beginning to understand the realities of worldwide competition.

# MEANWHILE, BACK AT THE OFFICE

Not all of the problems and opportunities are on the factory floor; office personnel are also affected by the conflicting forces surrounding us. Clerks, technicians, and recent college graduates have been terminated, and many competent professionals and middle managers have been let go. The latter is surprising, because these are the categories that management usually holds on to when work becomes slack.

My own firm's primary business is executive search and evaluation. We are retained by corporations large and small to help identify and evaluate a small number of highly talented men and women as candidates for a given executive position. Because we are well known nationally in the business community, we receive large numbers of unsolicited résumés. The point here is not that the résumé count has increased somewhat during the last thirty six months, which it has, or that we are favorably impressed by the "higher-quality" men and women whose résumés we now receive, which we are. The significant fact is that most of these higher-quality people are not unemployed. But they have decided to test the market, very discreetly, because they are confused and perhaps frustrated. They feel blocked where they are, they sense that their fast-track careers have slowed to a walk, and they can see few career opportunities in their companies, their disciplines, their professions. These are corporate executives, middle managers, and staff professionals, successful people earning from $60,000 to $200,000 per year, and they are pessimistic about their potential for future success. Their assessment of their future may well be correct, but such is not the case all over. Our view of the business world enables us to see many of their counterparts continuing to do well, very well, in other industries, other companies, and other regions of the United States.

Middle managers, those above the first supervisory level but below the vice-presidential level, are particularly prone to panic, and not totally without cause. The pyramidal form of traditional organizations dictates that few will ever attain executive rank and, as years pass, males especially experience the crisis that psychologist David Levinson refers to as "mid-life transition." Although a variety of pressures may contribute to this "middlescence," career blockage is the greatest. Such people know that change is required, but to what? And how? They can easily contrast their situations with those of younger, less expensive, and more recently trained managers. They themselves make those contrasts and ask themselves the hard questions regarding promotion, demotion, and retention.

In most cases, they remain with their companies and try to accept the fact that their careers have peaked. But many middle managers are being terminated, nudged into an early retirement for which they are generally not prepared. The "golden handcuffs" that kept these managers with Company X during the 1970s have been replaced by the semi-gold watch. Some of them hide in despair or strike out blindly and plunge into an ill-conceived business venture. Others think and act creatively and analytically, often positioning themselves better than they were before Company X became an ex-employer.

## DUAL CAREERS?

Dual-career families have been on the scene for quite some time. A relatively recent phenomenon is the *reverse* dual-career family; here the wife is the principal or sole wage earner. She might be a professional or paraprofessional in a small but booming company, or perhaps an executive secretary or attorney in a mature corporation. Her husband earns $14.50 an hour as a carpenter, when he works. Since 1981 most of his hours are spent lounging at the union hall, reading "Help Wanted" ads or puttering at home until his wife returns, excited about plans for the office party.

Or she might be holding two jobs: typist and cocktail waitress, while her husband answers ads, cleans the house, and cares for their children. Together, they economize and do their best to preserve the family and their sanity until "things get better," which to them means until his job opens up again on the assembly line at Pontiac, or in the mill at Bethlehem, or on the run from Memphis to Mobile.

While they are counting pennies, another couple, same age, city, and formal education, are scattering pesos in Acapulco and debating whether their next vacation should be in Williamsburg or Montreal. Their dual careers are humming right along! He's the star personal computer sales representative in a small chain, but most of his sales are not to the walk-in prospective buyers who enter the store and are divvied up equally. He develops additional prospects, off-hours, by conducting free seminars for schools and professional societies. Needless to say, he is planning to open his own store.

She is an independent contractor with five years of word processing experience. She takes her own Porta-Tech to her clients' offices when their machine is down or when they need additional help for a few days. Most weekends she carries home their overflow work, processing it on her Magna-Tech in what had once been the third bedroom.

So what do we have here? Some people are in dire straits, desperate trouble; others are prospering and planning to do even better. What's happening in America?

---

# CHANGE

What we are hearing throughout America is the cacophony of change—the death rattles of the old order clashing discordantly with the uncertain squeals of the new. And we are so enmeshed in today's problems, and so enslaved to the "yesterday way," that we have lost sight of tomorrow and that promise of better conditions for most human beings.

But the future is approaching, faster and faster, and it will be a bright one for those willing to meet it halfway. People willing to take forward steps will be in good company; they will have powerful helpers: the forces of technology, society, politics, and economics. The impact of these forces is, of course, even greater when they act in concert, as they have done in Nashua, New Hampshire. Many articles have told the story of Nashua's conversion from a shrinking center of decadent industries to a burgeoning hub of new tech/high tech endeavors. A few highlights:

- The state has no income tax, no sales tax, and a business tax that is modest. This pro-business climate is enhanced by state-issued, tax-free municipal bonds that provide companies with a means of borrowing capital at reasonable rates.
- Only about one-eighth of New Hampshire's work force is unionized. Without commenting on the pros

and cons of unions per se, it is reasonable to assume that employers are not saddled with the unnecessary costs, delays, and frustrations associated with restrictive work practices and the loss of management rights.

- In 1972 about two-thirds of all New Hampshire employees worked in the textile, shoe, or apparel industries. In 1984 that same fraction was employed in electronics, instrumentation, and metals.
- Nashua's unemployment is substantially better than the national average and way below the figures for major metropolitan industrial centers.

Some metropolitan areas such as Phoenix, Dallas, Albuquerque, and Boston have been attracting new ventures for several decades. Others are now trying (some desperately) to emulate these growth centers. But let's consider the large industrial metropolis, chock-full of steel mills or automobile factories or rubber plants or railroad yards. Can a Detroit make a Nashua-type turnaround? Will an Akron be able to do it? Should a Youngstown even try?

Or consider the plight of Rhode Island, a very small state with very big economic problems. Over half of its workers are employed in declining or vanishing industries, and its average manufacturing hourly wage ranks forty-eighth among the nation's fifty. Its better-educated people have been deserting the state for interesting and rewarding jobs elsewhere; many of them have found opportunity in nearby New Hampshire and adjacent Massachusetts.

In June 1984 Rhode Island residents rejected, resoundingly, the proposed Greenhouse Compact. This was a seven-year, $250 million plan for implanting and nurturing new businesses in robotics, gerontology, thin-film technology and similar fields of promise. It was a complex plan that would have provided for research greenhouses, new product creation, new business innovation, loans to fledgling enterprises, and skills training. Will Rhode Island have a second chance to participate in the new order of things?

The resistance to change in the industrial areas mentioned—in many of their industries, companies, workers, unions, and political organizations—will prevent change in the foreseeable future. The best hope for these beleaguered zones is that technological forces will prevail there. And they *will* prevail, if not in these former work centers, then elsewhere. Technology generates jobs, but only in those environments where technology can flourish. That means favorable conditions for the burgeoning businesses, and favorable conditions begin with positive attitudes.

# ON THE MOVE

The geographical movement of jobs and workers continues to gain momentum. This migration began in the 1950s, with mills abandoning New England for southern states having more favorable business climates and fewer unions. Other industries followed and soon a few of the new tech/high tech companies joined the shift to the sunbelt. Motorola chose Arizona to build its semiconductor and government electronics businesses; General Electric started its computer business there, as did Sperry its airborne electronics division. Florida, partly because of Cape Canaveral, lured a number of prestigious names: Honeywell, Harris, GE, and Martin Marietta. Colorado attracted IBM, Storage Technology, TRW, and Hewlett-Packard. The 1980 census revealed that for the first time in America, more people (about 10 million more) were living in the south and west than in the north and east. And this shift did not occur just because of retirees' preference for shuffleboard in the sun: It was based on economic growth already there and the belief that there is more growth to come. So again we see a nation in dichotomy; old industries and cities shriveling, others straining to outgrow each other.

# LOOKING FORWARD

As we contemplate the future, we should realize that it will be a "different kind of different." Until now, most futures have differed from their pasts merely by a degree or two. This was because the rate of technological change was slow. For example, some 137 years elapsed between the Somerset steam engine and that of James Watt in 1765; and the vacuum tube was king for about forty years until rendered obsolete by the transistor in 1947.

There weren't as many high-impact inventions in earlier years, and most inventions had little relationship to the few others that surfaced. But technology has a way of feeding on itself, growing and spreading geometrically. Today the velocity and breadth of technological advances is almost beyond comprehension. Specialists are unable to remain current, even in their own narrow fields. A breakthrough here opens distant as well as nearby doors. Inventions tumble over each other as they leapfrog their way to the marketplace.

Let's look at a few examples in the field of computers:

*Speed.* Computer operating speed today is about 200 times faster than in 1965.

*Size.* Computer size has been reduced markedly during the same period. The personal computer that I place at my feet in seat 22-A has roughly the same computing power as did the huge mainframe computers of only twenty years ago. But that isn't all. It can also function as a word processor and when linked to a printer, prepare business and personal correspondence—even the manuscript for this book.

*Costs.* The price of key components of computers is declining, year after year: logic devices at an annual rate of 20 percent, memory devices at about 35 percent per year.

And these electronic miracles are just the beginning. Soon to come is the optical computer, which will replace the transistor and electronic currents with beams of laser light. Computational speed will increase enormously; it may be 800 times the speed of today's fastest computers.

What we are about to see, and we are seeing bits and pieces of it already, is the revolution which Steve Jobs described. It will make our future almost totally different from that which we have known. There will be new value systems and a new work ethic marked by different concepts of leisure and responsibility. Our reward systems will seem strange to us, and we will perform our work in radically different environments. And in those environments, we will be both products of, and contributors to, those same four forces of change.

This book is concerned primarily with career alternatives and how to get ready for a prosperous future. Those careers will not exist in a vacuum; they will reflect all the properties and facets of the new age, the one we are lurching toward while still clutching at the past.

It's important that we learn as much as we can about that future and how it affects us. This foresight will help each of us determine how to function most effectively in that new order.

# LOOKING BACKWARD

But first a temporary but essential diversion: We are about to make a 180-degree turn to the rear! This trip is necessary; if we are to appreciate what we *can* become, we must understand from whence we came. Let's devote a few minutes to that earlier revolution.

# Chapter 3

# THE WAY IT WAS: YOU CAN'T GO HOME AGAIN

## WOULD YOU WANT TO?

It is April 1685 and things are about the same in Merrie Olde England as they were this time last year—and the year before, and the year before that. In fact, nothing much new has happened since sister Marian became a domestic in the vicar's manse at Tottenham. You haven't seen her in three years; Tottenham is forty miles away, maybe more, and that's too far to travel. Five years ago, brother Will became apprenticed to Blodgett, the village ironsmith; you see Will some evenings at the Spotted Swan listening gap-jawed to the tales of Old Ned, who was twice to the colonies as an able seaman before his accident.

This summer will mark the tenth anniversary of your service to Lord Ashford. Just as your father and his father did, you tend the animals and work the crops at Chelmsford Manor. In winter, you work only sixty hours a week, but more in the spring and as many as seventy-two hours in the summer. The days are longer then, and the overseer takes advantage of the additional light to find more things for you to do.

Your work requires a goodly amount of muscle power, and the tools you use in your daily chores are the same kinds of tools that your father used. In fact, the sickle and plow are the very ones he used. The overseer is demanding but fair; he likes your work, most of the time. He says that this August, after your tenth year, he will speak to the master about your service award, maybe even a quarter-acre in the common ground for you to call your own.

You enjoy the Sabbath, if not the services. There is time to rest and to trade stories with other men, some of whom walk to Chelmsford from nearby villages. Conversations are about the weather, crops, taxes, the new sheriff, the goings-on of royalty, the latest miracle (always in a distant shire), and when the next war will come and with whom. Your wife says that the womenfolk generally talk about the same things but also discuss children, disease, and witch-craft.

Another nice thing about the Sabbath is the opportunity for a man to travel. Sometimes you walk, or even ride one of the overseer's horses, to a neighboring village and back. One day you might even be able to go to Downington, to the market or the fair, stopping overnight at a village that looks very much like your own.

Women, of course, do not travel much. Your wife, Gwen, has never been more than three miles from Chelms-ford, and neither you nor she understands how Marian got that job with a vicar some forty miles away. But Gwen doesn't want to travel; she enjoys her spinning and her gossiping with the ladyfolk. And she still sings in the evenings, but not as much as she did before little Tommy died last year at age 2.

Venison is plentiful, but it has been a dreary winter and heavy spring rains have delayed the planting. Everybody knows that this will mean a shorter growing season and smaller shares for tenants and tillers. The juggler you saw last week in the manor great hall said that he had heard in Melton Mowbray that London has a lot of bad sickness again this year, that the dead carts are busy every day all over town. You shuddered when you heard the news, but then you were glad to learn that it isn't the Black Death coming back again—or is it?

It is April 1685 and things are about the same in Merrie Olde England as they are in France, Ireland, Russia, the Lowlands, Spain, Italy, Germany, and all those other nations that are beginning to supply the stock for the colonial melting pots of America.

1685—just another year for most of the men and women who lived it. Had they been asked, many would have speculated that a hundred or two hundred years later, conditions would be much the same for their descendants.

The fact that they would have been very wrong in such a projection is not important. The fundamental reason for the error, however, deserves our thought; there might be a message here for us, three hundred years later.

In essence, these late-seventeenth century men and women visualized little, if any, future change because they were *ignorant*. A host of factors, only one of which was the lack of formal education, made them unaware of most of the events and forces, especially scientific/technological and social, that were occurring in their lifetimes and that had occurred in earlier generations. Furthermore, they were unaware of the relationships between those forces, and how those relationships would lead to substantive change. Is it possible that we, three hundred years later, are similarly unaware and unprepared to contemplate our future?

---

# STEAM: PRESSURE BUILDING

In 1628, Edward Somerset, an English engineer, invented the first steam engine. It was a crude device, but it demonstrated that large amounts of steam could be generated by machine. Somerset, of course, was not the first person interested in steam. In A.D. 60, Hero (of Alexandria) reported on a number of recent inventions, one of which we would categorize today as a miniature or toy steam turbine.

Across the North Sea from Somerset lived the Prussian physicist Otto von Guericke. His interest was not in steam but in the possibility of creating vacuums. In 1650 he constructed the first air pump and used it to evacuate air from various containers. In 1654 at Madgeburg (where, coincidentally, he was burgomaster) Guericke demonstrated, in a most practical way, the power of a vacuum. Two teams of draft horses, 16 in all, could not pull apart two metal hemispheres joined only by the vacuum sealed within them.

Meanwhile, back in Scotland, unfortunate men and boys were forced to work long hours in the coal mines. Working conditions were abominable, especially when the water level began to rise in the tunnels. Misery mounted and production dropped off as larger and larger bucket brigades worked feverishly to bail out the workplaces. But in most cases, once the water really began to rise, the mine was forced to close, shaft after shaft, abandoning huge deposits of the much needed resource. Although the mine operators did not know it, a *vacuum* was needed to remove the water.

# A MACHINE, A PRINCIPLE, A NEED

England now had a crude, but working, model steam engine; Germany had an air pump and the ability to create a vacuum. In Scotland, the owners of the coal mines were in deep financial trouble and their serfs/slaves were in misery.

Things began to come together in the 1680s when Denis Papin, a French physicist, began conducting experiments with Robert Boyle in England and Christian Huygens in Holland. In 1683 he built the first pressure cooker; this device compressed, within a closed vessel, steam that had been superheated. Papin and his associates survived that tricky feat because they had fitted the vessel with a safety valve, complete with a movable weight. (This valve was itself a remarkable advance in the evolution of the machine; it stands as the progenitor of automatic control mechanisms.) Papin then built a steam engine that was larger than Somerset's and installed it in a ship. He was unsuccessful in his attempts to propel the ship against the wind, but his engine incorporated a concept that is still with us today: a compressor/piston moving within a cylinder.

Soon thereafter, Thomas Savery, an English inventor, produced a new steam engine. It was sufficiently different that he was awarded a patent in 1698 for his "engine to raise water by fire." The Savery engine sprayed cold water on the outside shell of the hot boiler, thus producing condensation and a partial vacuum. His engine did pump water but only from shallow pits; it was ineffective at the depths required in most mines.

The first truly successful steam engine was introduced in 1705 by Thomas Newcomen. His arrangement had the cold water injected into the steam-filled boiler, thus producing a powerful vacuum which depressed the piston. Atop the engine, Newcomen's rocking beam tipped up and down with the travel of the piston. By 1712 his design and machinery had been improved to the point that Newcomen engines were removing water from deep mines.

Thomas Newcomen had put it all together: He combined the principle of the vacuum and the kinetic energy of steam and applied them to the solution of a major economic and social problem. True, his engines burned large amounts of coal to produce the vacuum that lifted the water so that more coal could be extracted. But they were a commercial success for decades until rendered obsolete by the improved designs of James Watt in 1765. Watt is commonly (and incorrectly) referred to as *the* inventor of the steam engine and "father" of the industrial revolution. He was, however, a truly remarkable man. His engine was considerably more efficient than Newcomen's, and his designs lent themselves readily to additional applications such as powered tools, the locomotive, and the tractor. His addition of a governor to his engine was the earliest example of an automatic feedback system, the core of today's "closed-loop" cybernetic/robotic system.

But James Watt, as did Newcomen, Savery, Papin, von Guericke, and Somerset, benefited from the ideas, questions, models, successes, and failures of others. Watt saw farther and more clearly than others because "he stood on the shoulders of giants," a phrase used by Newton (and by Einstein, three centuries later) to explain the "break-through" process in science and technology.

But were these giants and their ideas, questions, models, successes, and failures visible to most men and women of 1685? Of 1735? In large part, no. Whether living on farms, in villages, or in large cities, most people tended to be preoccupied; they were so self-involved that they were ignorant of the forces gathering around them.

Of course, not all forces that were beginning to move seventeenth-century England toward the Industrial Revolution sprang from the relatively simple science and tool tinkering of the day. The future of the men and women of 1685, and that of their descendants, was also being shaped slowly but surely by events social, political, and economic. The following occurrences are seemingly unrelated. Yet many became linked in various and subtle ways, and each helped move Western society toward the new era:

- Blaise Pascal, a teenage French mathematical wizard, invents an adding and subtracting machine in 1642.

- In 1643, the New England Confederation is formed, the first union of English colonies in America.

- Six years later, an iron works in Saugus, Massachusetts, is producing eight tons of high-quality iron each week. This production rate is made possible by new blast furnaces, a refinery forge, and skilled workers recruited from England.

- London's population, despite the plagues, has grown

to about 350,000 by 1650; about one of every seventeen English residents is now a Londoner.

- The Navigation Act of 1651 provides impetus to England's shipping and shipbuilding industries.

- In 1657, tea is introduced to Londoners, both as a refreshing drink and as a panacea for almost everything except the plague. The brisk tea trade increases England's need for round-the-Horn sailing vessels and for products which support the shipping industry.

- By 1658 the deforestation of England is almost complete, and coal can be extracted only from shallow pits or those few deep mines whose shafts remain dry. Wood is still needed to produce charcoal, essential in the carbonizing and smelting of iron for tools and weapons. The Newcastle mines expand and produce about one-half million tons in 1685, a fifteen-fold increase over the tonnage of 1654, but cannot meet demand.

- In 1662, the Royal Society for the Improvement of Natural Knowledge is established in London. Two years later it urges the planting of potatoes as a hedge against famine.

- New Amsterdam becomes New York in 1664. More and more Londoners now smoke tobacco to ward off the Black Death, and Virginia plantations strain to meet the increasing demand.

- Isaac Newton, abandoning plague-ravaged London in 1666 for the comparative safety of the countryside, invents the calculus so that he may develop and explain his concepts of gravity.

- In 1672, England antagonizes her American colonists by tacking import taxes on goods transported *from one colony to another* in America. There are now about 50,000 men and women residing in the colonies.

- Parliament passes the Habeas Corpus Act in 1679; Hugenots begin manufacturing silk in the Carolina Colony.

- In 1681, the first bank checks are issued in England. The Atlantic Ocean and Mediterranean Sea are connected by France's Languedoc Canal, a project begun eighty-eight years earlier.

- Anton van Leeuwenhoek invents an improved microscope in 1683. He discovers living organisms in scrapings from his teeth and thus advances the germ theory of disease.

- In 1688, Lloyd's of London begins as a society to underwrite shipping risks.

- Three years later, the colonies' first paper mill begins production in Pennsylvania. England's John Locke argues for a "social contract" between man and monarch.

- In 1692, Pascal's adding and subtracting machine is rendered obsolete by an invention of von Leibniz, a German philosopher and mathematician. This new device can multiply and divide as well as add and subtract; it also mechanizes the complex trigonometric calculations used in celestial navigation by merchant and naval vessels.

- England's total population is about 6 million; about half of these men and women still work on farms. But Norwich and Bristol are now cities of about 30,000, and York and Exeter have each grown to about 10,000 inhabitants. About one in twelve English residents now lives in London, a city of about 500,000 people.

- By 1693 many merchants and merchant bankers, made wealthy by the growth in shipping, are financing the modernization of mines, investing in land, and reinvesting in the shipbuilding industry. They form the basis of modern capitalism and, as a new aristocracy of wealth, begin replacing the guilds and the feudal lords as important power blocs in English society.

- The Bank of London is chartered in 1694 and its notes soon become official tender for debts public and private.

- In 1696, Newton and Locke persuade Parliament to revise and standarize the nation's coinage. The first insurance company dealing with property risks opens its doors.

- Savery's steam engine ("the miner's friend") begins pumping water from near-the-surface coal pits in 1698.

- In 1699, Parliament passes the Woolens Act, forbidding the American colonies to export wool and woolen cloth "to any place whatsoever." London, with 550,000 residents, is now the largest city in Europe, but the American colonies are growing rapidly. In this, the final year of the seventeenth century, Boston and Philadelphia each have about 12,000 residents and some 5000 people live in New York. The total population of the colonies is now about 260,000, roughly one-half the size of London.

I have mentioned only a few of the important events that occurred in the Western world from 1642 through 1699. But that chronological sample displays a wide variety of human thought, purpose, action, and achievement.

The power of hindsight is often exaggerated except, of course, by Monday-morning quarterbacks. Most of us assume that a review, however cursory, of prior events reveals what should (and should not) have been done by those who made those earlier decisions and performed those actions.

Any one of these individual events could be scrutinized in detail and its merit debated. In retrospect, should Parlia-

ment have passed the Woolens Act or chartered the Bank
of England? Should Papin have been more persistent in his
attempts to build a steamship? Why didn't Newcomen build
a locomotive?

Such speculations might be enjoyable, but they miss
two cardinal points:

1.  These seemingly unrelated events did not occur in
    isolation; most of them influenced, or were influ-
    enced by, the others. Together, for good or for evil,
    they propelled society toward a new beginning.

2.  Most seventeenth-century people were unaware of
    most of these events until long after they had oc-
    curred. They were, therefore, largely unaware of
    the events' interrelationships and the resulting im-
    petus for change.

Another historical certainty: those events not only carried England, Europe, and the colonies into the eighteenth
century, they also pulled those societies, economies, and
individuals from the feudal/guild way of life. The events
pushed them, ready or not, toward the greatest change that
human beings had experienced to that time—the Industrial
Revolution.

One thing that we do *not* know for certain: How ready is
American society, its economy and citizens, for the next
big change, the one that is already under way? On the one
hand, we are much better educated today, and we benefit
from instant communication. Conversely, much more is
happening today. Events now come at breakneck speed,
and the interrelationships, although often observable, are
complex and difficult to assess. How prepared, therefore, is
America for its new beginning?

No less important, how prepared are *you*?

# CHAPTER 4

# THE WAY IT WILL BE: SHOCK WAVES FOR THE UNPREPARED

I hope that you are well prepared: equipped by talent, training, knowledge of self, and experience to succeed in the new order. I hope also that your definition of success is broader and of longer range than simply avoiding the next layoff or winning the next promotion. Those could be important to you, of course, but they are merely single events. The *successful you* is continually planning and replanning your career, alert for signals of change while working effectively to achieve, one by one, the milestones enroute to your career goals.

How well prepared for the future do you think you are? One good way to find out is to perceive, as clearly as possible, what the future will be like for those of us who will work in America's factories, offices, homes, schools, shops, and other centers of employment. To see clearly we must observe objectively, putting aside our biases and preconceived notions of what the future *should* be. We must also recognize that the future is already partly with us; portions of our tomorrows are already portions of our todays.

31

# THE FACTORY OF THE FUTURE

FMS, shorthand for **flexible manufacturing system,** is already upon us, or at least upon the Japanese. And its acceptance there has come quickly since the concept was imported from the United States in the late 1950s. But the speed with which Japanese companies have improved and installed robotic systems has raised the inevitable *who* questions—those raised by the emergence of all new technologies:

- Who will benefit from the breakthrough?
- Who will be replaced by the new process?
- Who should be trained/retrained for the new jobs created?
- Who will lead the new industry by developing better, more sophisticated models?
- Who will provide the best service to customers?
- Who will become the most cost-effective producer?
- Who will dominate the worldwide market?

In some 200 modern Japanese factories industrial robots are now producing, with great precision and at very low cost, a variety of machined and welded parts. These parts are later assembled, often by other robots, into products such as electric motors, diesel engines, machine tools, solar cells, and (naturally) other robots—in short, automation.

But some may say that we have had automation in the United States for years; that duplicating lathes, profiling milling machines, and numerical tape-controlled tooling have been in our factories since the 1950s. So what's new?

Almost everything! That's the short answer. The detailed and technically correct answer would weave its way through several books the size of this one.

Neither of these extremes is appropriate for our purposes. So let's summarize by glancing at the major differences as they exist today between a typical flexible manufacturing system (FMS) and the typical level of automation in most American factories.

The FMS:

1.  Is an *integrated* system. It begins with product design and carries through all machining, welding, and inspection processes, and ends with delivery to the shipping area.

2.  Can also include many assembly and subassembly operations, processes which until recently were considered extremely difficult to automate.

3.  Is readily adaptable to both "soft" and "hard" automation. That is, an FMS is as cost-effective in small-batch, low-volume production as it is in those high-volume runs which were once regarded as *the* essential element for justifying investments in automation.

4.  Has, as its first step, product design. This is done by CAD (computer-aided design) backed by CAE (computer-aided engineering). The engineer draws product designs directly on the screen of a computer linked to the manufacturing system. The designs are completed, verified, and released to production rapidly and inexpensively. Similarly, subsequent design changes can be placed in the system with little delay and at small cost.

5.  Uses only new machine tools and accessories. Startup costs can be high but, once under way, FMS is much more cost-effective than are piecemeal attempts to refurbish individual machine tools of an earlier era.

6.  Is largely self-contained. It operates, usually on three shifts, without production employees and with very few production-support personnel.

By way of contrast, a typical American factory producing machined metal parts depends on a system which:

1. Uses a loose collection of independent and, at best, semiautomatic machine tools and devices. (These tools are quite similar to the ones that I, as a machinist trainee, learned to operate in 1950.)

2. Is incapable of assembling parts automatically.

3. Is geared primarily to "hard," high-volume production runs.

4. Cannot begin production until after many sequential steps have been taken in product design. These include conceptual sketches, basic design, detailed drafting, design checking and approval, and blueprinting. Finally, these are converted into simplified sketches, "exploded" drawings, and detailed procedural instructions for the production machine operator and assembler. Worse yet, when it becomes necessary to modify an engineering design, the production line is idle until the design changes are worked through all the sequential steps.

5. Uses outmoded or, at best, refurbished machine tools. Even when an American corporation opens a new manufacturing facility in the Sunbelt, the standard practice is to fill it with production equipment not needed in the company's older plants. Sometimes this practice can be cost-effective; usually it is not.

6. Uses a large number of production and production-support employees, usually on one or two shifts. These employees perform many tasks which are unnecessary with an FMS.

This difference in the number and types of employees required to operate these two radically different types of manufacturing systems is important. It matters, of course, to the employees and employers involved and to those who will purchase and use the end products.

But it is also important to the rest of us. The "factory of the future" is one main point of reference for us as we try to grasp the *enormity* and *velocity* of change, as we try to visualize the new job market, and as we begin planning that new career.

A Japanese factory using FMS can generate the same amount of production as a Japanese factory using a conventional system, and it does so with 75 to 90 percent *fewer* employees. And the 10 to 25 percent who are required in FMS perform different kinds of tasks than do those employed in conventional production systems.

We have already seen how CAE and CAD can render unnecessary many of the professional and semiprofessional duties required in the design of the product. Replacing many of these designers, drafters, and checkers is the "on-line" designer equipped with a light pen and other new, computer-related design tools. These tools enable the engineer to project creations directly onto the monitor for instant review and modification. When satisfied, he or she loads them into the memory of the CAM (computer-aided manufacturing) controller for the start of the production cycle.

The CAM controller commands a robot in the raw stockroom to load specific material on a delivery cart. It then orders that cart to deliver these castings, forgings, or pieces of bar stock to a specific workstation by following a specific magnetic pathway (usually a cable embedded beneath the surface of the shop floor).

By these commands and operations, the CAM controller and the automatic cart have replaced several employees, including a stock clerk, an industrial trucker, and perhaps an expediter or production clerk.

As soon as the raw material arrives at the workstation, it is loaded in the machine, positioned precisely, and subjected to multitool machining processes. The machined part may then be transported automatically to other workstations for robotic welding, in-process inspection, and subassembly, thus eliminating the need for several more human beings.

But what about the shop supervisors? Where are they, and what are they doing while all this is going on without human effort? Well, the supervisors are there, directing the work and making sure that things go smoothly. But they are a different kind of supervisor; not at all like those who yelled when I made a mistake and praised my good work with their silence. In fact, the supervisor has become an "it"—an *electronic* supervisor—a programmable computer with a keyboard terminal in the heart of the FMS, which can, if necessary, be reprogrammed by a technician to change the amount and types of parts being produced that hour.

Final inspection is rigorous. It is performed by a special "camera" with preset silicon chips that measure all critical surface finishes and dimensions against established quality standards.

The manufacturing processes are so designed that all, or almost all, parts will be machined so reliably that they will meet those high standards. But the camera is a tough inspector and will signal a technician as soon as a deviation is detected. The technician will then determine the cause of the unacceptable work, shut down that particular workstation, and reroute the work flow until the faulty workstation has been repaired.

The acceptable work is speeded on its way by a robotic crane, which releases the finished work from the inspection station and positions it securely in an automatic cart. The cart then delivers it to the shipping area, where another crane . . . and on the process goes.

An estimated 250 flexible systems similar to that just described are already working in Japan, a nation where the total number of industrial robots is about 25,000, four times the number for all of Europe. Most of the Japanese robots and flexible systems are in factories which produce machine tools and other industrial products. But Japanese producers of consumer electronics goods such as radios, television sets, and home computers are now racing toward FMS installations.

In contrast, America has only about 8000 robots and a mere handful of FMS lines. Our nation has, until recently, shown surprisingly little interest in taking the plunge. It costs money, often scarce money, to automate a factory, and our obsession with short-term financial measurements tends to discourage such investments in the future. Besides, several highly regarded American corporations have reported bad experiences with robotic installations. They have been disappointed with the cost-benefit ratios of their investments, and they usually lay the blame on equipment failures, inadequate software, or militant union resistance. (What they don't report is that the *underlying* reason for their disappointment may have been their own unreasonable expectations. Or applying the "right" equipment to the "wrong" process, or having incompetent engineering and maintenance staffs, or trying to skimp on their investment by inserting two or three new, high-powered devices into their creaky, cranky production system.)

Overall, our nation's pace toward the automated factory has been midway between snail and tortoise. But several factors are now causing American business executives to rethink their modernization plans:

*Worldwide competition.* The pressures and threats of competition have increased.

*Technical success.* Japanese systems have achieved this while maintaining cost-effectiveness.

*Positive experiences.* GE, GM, and several other blue-chip corporations have had good experiences with limited FMS applications in their domestic installations.

*User/supplier potential.* GE is betting huge resources on robotics and FMS, not just as a user but also as a *supplier* of CAE/CAD/CAM, robots, and total systems to industry. So are IBM and GM.

*Antiquated tools.* About one-third of America's machine tools are at least twenty years old, the most outdated tooling array of any major free-world nation.

*Sources of supply.* America, for decades the world leader in machine tool technology and production, is now a poor third to Japan and West Germany. (We now import more machine tools than we export.) We originated numerical controlled machines thirty years ago, yet only about 5 percent of our tools today use even that primitive technology. The concept of FMS began in our machine tool centers of Cincinnati, Cleveland, and Milwaukee, but the idea was *implemented* in Japan, several years after the Japanese purchased their first industrial robots from us in the late 1950s. Japan is now beginning to return FMS to America, and with a vengeance. Yamazaki, a maker of numerically controlled machine tools, has had several spectacular FMS lines operating in Japan for several years. It recently installed an FMS production line in its new northern Kentucky machine tool plant. This boomerang of our own technology is located just across the Ohio River from the headquarters of Cincinnati Milacron, *the* former world leader in machine tools—a company now trying to play catch-up.

So what does all this mean? Quite simply, it means that robots and FMS, or versions thereof, are already on their way into our way of life. The changes, gradual at first, will accelerate as America moves toward the factory of the future (or as GE's robotics marketeers term it, "the factory *with* a future"). Of course, the total transformation will take many years, and some projections by robot enthusiasts may never come to pass. But we are beginning to leave the Model T stage of robotics. Fundamental change is on its course and a decade or so from now we will look back and marvel at the speed of the conversion.

We will also then see that although many workers will

have been displaced by these automated processes, many new jobs will have been created, especially in the design, sale, programming, maintenance, and repair of industrial robots and their systems.

# DUES, DONT'S, AND "PROBABLIES"

A story widely circulated in industrial relations circles of the 1950s went something like this: An auto industry executive was proudly displaying the new line of automatic cylinder-block boring machines to Walter Reuther, then president of the United Auto Workers. "Just look at those beauties, Walter," he crowed. "They are hardworking, efficient, and dependable. And they don't pay one cent of dues to your union!"

To which Reuther is said to have retorted, "And they don't buy any of your cars, either!"

Today we know that although automated systems don't buy autos, they will probably require a multitude of behind-the-scenes goods and services to produce, sell and install them and to keep them operating efficiently. And because human beings will supply these goods and services, many people will probably need training.

A debate launched in the 1950s is still going on and probably will for years to come. It has to do with whether robots and other forms of automation will create as many, more than, or fewer jobs than they eliminate. The jury is still out on this question, but my experience tells me that automated processes will probably create a huge number of jobs—new and different jobs—and that there will probably be thousands of training and retraining programs—some bad, some good.

National Education Corporation, the world's largest and fastest training company, has been gearing up for the anticipated demand for technical and vocational training in robotics and programable controllers. It is already featuring new courses in pneumatics and hydraulics to go along with revised courses in electronics and microprocessors.

H. David Bright, president and CEO of NEC, sees the situation this way: "Robotics and controllers are part of the emerging technology we hear about every day. Industrial needs for training in this field grow greater each week. . . . Changes in technology tend not to reduce the number of jobs, but to raise the level of skills necessary to do those jobs that are created by automation. Machines are able to do the work, but our society needs *people* to repair those machines and they need to be trained in the skills to do so. This is the future of vocational training."

# THE INTEGRATED OFFICE

Although some of us will work directly in the new factory system, the chances are that many more of us will be engaged in office work. This work could, of course, be in support of shop-floor activities. We would then be using computer systems to help us plan, monitor, maintain, and redirect the output of raw materials, capital goods, or consumer products.

Or we could be in a different kind of company, helping our employer supply a valuable service, either to end users or to other supplier organizations in the information/communication/service economy.

Or we could be running our very own little business enterprise, providing services or goods responsive to the needs of the new society.

In any event, most of us will be working with new office machines and systems. We will perform our work in new physical and social environments. In fact, some of us are already working in some of these settings; the rate of change in America's offices is much greater than in its factories.

But we are not yet working in the "office of the future" (or in related concepts such as the "automated office," the "electronic office," the "paperless office," or "the integrated office")—not yet, not quite.

The term **office of the future** has been used, misused, and abused for a decade. It's an intangible phrase, but catchy enough to have captured the attention of many different kinds of people. The problem with it is its fuzziness. It can mean almost anything that you or I want it to mean. (The same is true, incidentally, of many other descriptive phrases: oil glut, modern capitalism, Middle America, Greenwich Village, working class, rational conservation, Paris fashions—to name but a few.)

For the past ten years or so I have probed at this futuristic concept. I am now aware of several rational ways in which we can view tomorrow's office as we attempt to learn more about what it is, what it will be, and what our career roles in it might be.

A good way to begin is by taking time to recognize that the office we know *today* is merely a modified version of a *yesterday's* projection of the office of *tomorrow*. A typical case involves a well-known word processor/printer. Someone had a good idea (perhaps even a prototype) for a new text-editing and processing system and "sold it upstairs." There it was repackaged, renamed, and rushed to market ahead of the potential competition. Two years later that same system (now redesigned to correct operational problems and reengineered to take advantage of the latest chip technology) is recognized as the keystone of today's state-of-the-art office. But today is soon to become another yesterday, and tomorrow there will be a new idea.

Another way to deal with the concept is to recognize that because the office of the present is always changing, the office of the future is also certain to change and to keep changing. This recognition leads us to the realization that, as its name suggests, the office of the future will always be "out there," always ahead of us.

Yet another approach is to view the office of the future as a *way of doing things* rather than as an assemblage of high-priced, fast-paced pieces of equipment. That's the perspective of John Connell, head of Office Technology Research Group and America's leading advocate for the future office. "It's a *process*," he says, "an attempt to improve productivity in the office." Clerical employees, please note: Connell is, of course, interested in ways to help you become more productive. But his greatest concern and largest problem is helping managers, supervisors, and staff professionals increase *their* effectiveness. His reason is largely economic; these are the people responsible for about two-thirds of the total costs of American offices. Yet, as a group, they have been largely ignored in earlier attempts to improve productivity.

Enough for now on the office of the future. Although the concept (perhaps under a different name) deserves our thoughtful attention, let's put that name aside temporarily.

With respect to other names for the same general idea, some practitioners prefer "automated office," "electronic office," or "paperless office." These, unfortunately, are at least as vague as "office of the future." Further, they have an image problem; their very names cause them to be rejected, out of hand, by those office workers who are either uninformed or misinformed.

The word **automated** creates horrendous mental pictures, such as:

An office area dominated by machines, conveyors, and monitors—a setting almost as mechanistic as that of an FMS

A large percentage of America's 50 million office workers being replaced by robots

The few surviving office workers being subservient to the machines and forced to perform tasks which require no human judgment or decision making

The word **electronic** means arcade games and home entertainment to the younger generation, but to suspicious office workers it means beeps, burps, and blinks. It means staring at, and being watched by, unfriendly screens, monitors, and tubes. Everybody "knows" that those strange sights and sounds cause eyestrain and headaches. They may also be responsible for employees becoming bald, or obese, or . . . and so the rumors fly.

The word **paperless** doesn't threaten job security, physical health, or emotional stability. Nor does it position us as "mechanoids" forced to perform routine tasks at the pleasure of our machine masters. But the very idea of an office *without* paper does boggle the mind. It's as if we were expected to drive the Indy 500 pace car without a steering wheel, or enjoy a seven-course gourmet dinner with no utensils, or scale Mt. Everest without the aid of ice axe and Sherpas. In a paperless office how does one jot down an unlisted phone number? For that matter, what takes the place of the phone book? And what has become of our good friend and trusted informant, the computer printout? (Yes, that's the same stack of paper we hated intensely only a few years ago; it seemed so alien and threatening at the time.) Without paper, how can the boss be protected legally in that European export deal? Or scribble a reminder to pick up a pound of salami and a dozen roses? How can I, an employee, be sure that the boss will appreciate my writing skills? Or remember the date for my performance appraisal? For that matter, how will anybody remember anything?

I have seen the mere mention of the words *automated, electronic,* and *paperless* draw mixed reactions from workers in many conventional offices. For the most part, the reactions have ranged from complete confusion and far-flung fright to rapid rejection and unbridled unwillingness.

But it doesn't have to be that way, nor should it be. In fact, it seldom is—in the real world. Let's look again at the word processor, a new entrant in American offices but whose acceptance has grown rapidly since 1978. Most typists who have tried to do so have made a successful, although not necessarily easy transition from the typewriter to the word processor. They are now glad that they had the opportunity and that they made an honest effort to keep an open mind, to learn the different processes, and to acquire the new skills. What to them was once a big unknown, or a manipulative monster, soon became a valuable tool—a beautiful instrument with which to work, experiment, and learn. Now their only worry is about replacement—not for themselves, but for the machine. You see, this model has been in the office for almost two years now, and a friend on the tenth floor has a new Super Eight. The Super Eight has several new features, one of which enables the friend to . . .

I have encountered at least a dozen other labels which hardware producers, consultants, and users have tried to attach to the new office; none of these labels has stuck. But there is a relatively new one which shows promise of becoming *the* descriptor: the **integrated office**. The origin of the term is hazy, but systems suppliers are now beginning to use it to describe how their new products can be connected to function as an integrated system.

But despite the different names people apply to the new office, they talk about it in surprisingly similar fashion. For example, consider these comments of equipment and systems manufacturers, of major users of the new products, and of leading consultants in the field:

- "Office integration should be viewed as a network of computer and communication systems designed to improve access to information and enhance human communication. Its goal is to help people work more effectively, not to replace them with intelligent robots."
- "Total office systems are . . . company-sized tool chests that provide office workers the electronic tools they require to accomplish their jobs."
- "Office automation is people using technology to manage and communicate information more effectively."

- "It should meet the needs of four specific areas: document management, decision support, personal support and organizational communciations."
- "It helps people collect, compose, analyze, store, recall, reformulate and distribute information."
- "A major function of office automation is putting vital information at an office worker's fingertips."
- "It is designed to make your work life more productive, more interesting, even more enjoyable."
- "So what starts out to be a better way to type, is in reality a better way to do business. And *that's* what 'office automation' really means."
- "Many kinds of human endeavors can be carried on only in a face-to-face mode. . . . Some issues can't be resolved in a letter, over a tube or a telephone. Communication includes body action and looking the other person in the eye."
- "Office automation includes a variety of tools to support office work. These tools may be applied in two ways. First, they may be used to improve the *efficiency* of routine, well-structured administrative processes. . . . Second, office automation today may be used for 'value-added' applications . . . that increase the *effectiveness* of managers and professionals."

These descriptions provide us with insight. Running through them are several common threads that merit our attention:

1. *Information.* Office automation is concerned with information—making more of it available, and to more employees, for their use in performing their work.
2. *Systems and networks.* Office automation involves not only new machines but systems and net-

works which communicate with each other, within and between offices.

3. *Job creation.* In the office (as opposed to the factory) automation eliminates very few, if any, production jobs, especially those above the billing/file clerk level. On the broad scale, it may create more jobs than it eliminates.

4. *Efficiency and effectiveness.* It can increase the efficiency and effectiveness of office workers: clerical, professional, and managerial.

5. *Productivity and interest.* These new technologies are merely new tools for office workers to use to become more productive and, perhaps, more interested in their work.

6. *People.* The human factor will be an essential element in any form of the new office.

7. *Communication.* The exchange of information and ideas between people will be at least as important as it was in yesterday's organization.

There are many points of difference between factory and office automation. At this point we will explore only two: the nature of the work which *must* be performed and the nature of the work which *can* be performed.

In the factory, the "must" factor is the only one that matters. The completed work must meet quality and reliability standards, it must be produced at an agreed-upon cost, and it must be delivered to the customer on schedule. Conventional factory systems have always attempted to meet these three "must" requirements. All any FMS can do is improve the manufacturer's chances of meeting them in worldwide markets that are becoming more demanding, more competitive each year.

Factory work, then, tends to be regulated and standardized. Once the processes are established, the production line grinds out the product of the moment until it's time to change the setup and begin to grind out a different product. Not so in the office. True, a few highly repetitive new office tasks resemble somewhat the product world of the factory. These usually exist in the operations division of a bank or an insurance company. Each day, data pertaining to thousands of claims, premium notices, and account statements are entered by keyboard into a huge computer. Those processing jobs *are* routine; for many employees the work may become boring, perhaps even demeaning.

These conditions, too, shall pass. In the office, just as in the factory, those processes most likely to be automated are those that are labor intensive and highly repetitive. My projection is that before long a form of OCR (optical character recognition) will take over most of these mechanistic duties, much as OCR devices are now doing for cashiers in progressive supermarkets.

For the most part, however, office work is not routine. Rather, it varies from worker to worker, from desk to desk, and from time to time. It also differs from factory work in that most office employees, regardless of job classification, can modify the product *as they work on it* and thus improve its value to the end user. The secretary can devise a better way to display the graphics or may elect to tap one of several international data banks to verify, refute, or amplify a critical bit of information. The financial analyst can explore several different mathematical models rapidly, even devise new models, while striving for the best possible answer to the question: Should we acquire Rasputin Robotics? Even the manager can be creative! He or she may introduce several shortcuts in a process or think of a way to ensure that the London office understands the footnotes.

Perhaps a better way to grasp the differences between factory and office automation is to reread the comparisons between a flexible manufacturing system (FMS) and a conventional manufacturing system. Following that, we can consider the differences between conventional office practices and those made possible by the new office products and systems. For example, let's look at a typical office routine, the preparation and distribution of a large number of letters that contain large amounts of identical words and sentences.

The situation is this: Sam Salamander, the vice president of marketing for Convoluted Corporation, is headquartered in Chicago. Sam wants to send letters to all 150 of the corporation's sales engineers. His main purpose is to announce the general 10 percent increase in sales quotas for the coming year, but he also wants to convey some motivational thoughts. He dislikes form letters and insists that each of the 150 letters be personalized, where appropriate, to that man or woman. His secretary, Susan, is assigned the project.

In a conventional office (that is, one using the best of non-word-processing typewriters) the secretary must type each of the 150 letters individually, even though most of their content is common to all. Modern offices have equipment that enables the secretary to accomplish the vice president's objective faster, easier, more economically, and with greater precision. Thus the secretary can direct her attention to more interesting responsibilities, perhaps drafting and presenting the plan for the next semiannual meeting of district managers.

But in the meantime, Sam's letters must be dealt with, and with the equipment at hand. Here is the letter to the sales engineer in Phoenix. This man has eight years' experience with the company and has met the vice president on several occasions.

Mr. H. L. Prestwick
3007 North 7th Avenue
Phoenix, AZ 85062

Hi, Hal!

I've just returned from Convoluted's annual executive meeting in Honolulu. A detailed account of that jam-packed business session will be in the quarterly newsletter, but I wanted to make sure that you and district manager Tim O'Neill had the important highlights as soon as possible.

Briefly, our business picture looks brighter than ever, and all the officers were enthusiastic about the new P-19 model. As our Chairman phrased it, "The P-19 will knock the socks off the competition, especially in the upper price range!"

He's right, of course, and that started me thinking about you and the Central Arizona territory. The P-19 should be a "natural" for big sales to companies such as Arizona Amalgamated, Phoenix Phantasies, and Copper Cloisters. I'm sure that Tim will be glad to help you strategize fleet sales to these and other hot prospects—companies that would benefit by upgrading from P-17s, or better yet, by switching from Involuted to us!

Speaking of sales, Hal, my commitment to the Chairman is a 10 percent increase over last year. That means, of course, that each sales engineer is expected to increase his or her personal production by 10 percent. But you and I know that it won't turn out that way; not everyone will have what it takes to "make it happen."

That's why I'm looking to you, Hal, and a few other very special SEs—people I know I can count on to give it that extra effort. Your production last year was very good, and I was especially impressed with the new accounts you brought in, such as Scottsdale Synergistics. And I'm confident that in this new year you will do even better, now that all the bugs are out of the P-19.

Your official target is $322,000 for the coming year. But I would appreciate it very much if you, O'Neill, and I could agree that your unofficial target will be $358,000, or about 22 percent over last year.

Tell you what, Hal: You make that $358,000 goal and I'll see that your wife gets the best darned turquoise necklace in Phoenix! Is it a deal?

Cordially,

Samuel A. Salamander
cc: T. O'Neil

Now here's Sam's letter to a female sales engineer in Cincinnati. She joined the company only 18 months ago and has not met the vice president of marketing. (Note: The portions of the letter personalized for her are in italic type.)

*Ms. Evelyn E. Curtis*
*4099 Amsterdam Avenue*
*Cincinnati, OH 45107*

*Dear Evelyn*:

I have just returned from Convoluted's annual executive meeting meeting in Honolulu. A detailed account of that jam-packed business session will be in the quarterly newsletter, but I wanted to make sure you and district manager *Joe Sampson* had the important highlights as soon as possible.

Briefly, our business picture looks brighter than ever, and all the officers were enthusiastic about the new P-19 model. As our Chairman phrased it, "The P-19 will knock the socks off the competition, especially in the upper price range!"

He's right, of course, and that started me thinking about you and the *Queen City* territory. The P-19 should be a "natural" for big sales to companies such as *Cincinnati Cybernetics, Florence Foodamation,* and *Sharonville Sureties*. I'm sure that *Joe* will be glad to help you strategize fleet sales to these and other hot prospects—companies that would benefit by upgrading from P-17s, or better yet, by switching from Involuted to us!

Speaking of sales, *Evelyn,* my commitment to the Chairman is a 10 percent increase over last year. That means, of course, that each sales engineer is expected to increase his or her personal production by 10 percent. *I realize that 10 percent may seem like a big increase to you, but I'm certain that Sampson will be helpful as you begin expanding your prospect list.*

*So* I'm looking to you, *Evelyn,* and a few other very special *young* SEs—people I know I can count on *for new ideas and high levels of enthusiasm.* Your production last year was very good, and I was especially impressed with the new accounts you brought in, such as *Millcreek Mailgrams.* And I'm confident that in this new year you will do even better, now that all the bugs are out of the P-19.

Your official target is *$198,000* for the coming year. But I would appreciate it very much if you, *Sampson,* and I could agree that your unofficial target will be *$207,000,* or about *15 percent* over last year.

*Sampson tells me that you and your husband are weekend sailors at Cowan Lake.* Tell you what, *Evelyn:* You make that *$207,000* goal and I'll see that *you and he have exclusive use of the corporate Galaxy 38 for a long weekend of your choice on Lake Michigan!*

Cordially,

Samuel A. Salamander
cc: *J. Sampson*

The conventional method uses a high-quality, self-correcting electric typewriter. Susan, a typist of average proficiency, would require about 1500 minutes to type, correct, and proof the 150 one-page letters and their envelopes. (That translates into three hectic days, two split fingernails,

one lost lunch hour, and the gnawing suspicion that somewhere, somehow, life should be better than this!)

Let's suppose that the office equipment is semimodern;
here Susan uses a magnetic card or memory tape typewriter. This equipment enables her to reduce the total time
considerably, from 1500 minutes to about 600 minutes. She
types each envelope individually; the typewriter then re-
peats that address at the top of the letter, after which the
secretary types in the personalized salutation. The typewriter reproduces from its memory the first string of common words, then pauses while she types the first personalized word or words. Then the machine resumes its
chattering until its memory commands it to pause while the
next personalized entry is made. And so on for about ten
hours (which, in many vice-presidential offices, means
staying until about 7:30 P.M., then rushing to the airport
before the evening's final mail pickup). During this action-
packed period, Susan appreciates her many brief time-offs
from typing while the machine speeds through the letters'
common content. But she doesn't always like the way her
insertions appear on the page. Her critical eye sometimes
detects slight misalignments, imperfections which she
hopes won't be noticed in Wichita, Orlando, or wherever.

Many offices today utilize word processors—typewriter
keyboards tied to display screens and letter-quality, high-
speed printers. In addition to permitting undetectable insertions, these devices have the ability to manipulate text at
will. The secretary can move sentences and paragraphs
around, *rearranging their sequence as if she were cheating
at solitaire.* (But in our simple example, no such block
moves were required.) With a word (or text) processor,
Susan would spend about thirty minutes setting up the common portions of the letters and the file which will cause the
addresses to be printed. She would then key in each set of
variables for each of the 150 letters, confident that the software program will see to it that a young woman in Denver
doesn't receive a personalization meant for a grizzled veteran in Milwaukee. And she can forget about carbon

smudges and erasure marks; those just don't exist in the world of word processing. After keying in, Susan can relax a bit and perhaps begin to move along several unrelated projects. The entire job is complete in about 360 minutes by word processor, and the finished product is, in each case, letter perfect. And even better is the mail service. The vice president, leaving early for racquetball and cocktails at his club, can become personally involved in the process. He can deposit his 150 letters in any mailbox along the way.

But the new office won't stop evolving with word processors, anymore than the factory stopped with NC machines or individual "dumb" robots. Already with us (or soon to appear) in the office are several forms of electronic mail, local area networks, dedicated satellite channels, and videoconferencing. (Marriott, for example, provides this intercity capability in twenty or so hotels strategically situated throughout the nation.) Our vice president, had he wanted to do so, could have "assembled" his field sales force in ten or fifteen such centers. He could then have utilized this new technology to give them more of the flavor of that "all work, no play" meeting in Honolulu.

In the three scenarios of the 150-letter project, no mention was made of how Sam conveyed his thoughts to Susan. Did he use a dictation device or pace his office while she jotted an occasional mumble and planned her vacation? Did he scrawl his immortal words on the back of the Honolulu recreation agenda? How many times did she redraft, retype, and regret his inability to compose his thoughts and stick with them? Perhaps he wrote the first draft directly on his own keyboard, for her to correct and shape into final form. Such executive hands-on practices could be the wave of the future.

Further, scientists and engineers are striving to develop a practical and cost-effective voice recognition system that will permit an executive's spoken words to go directly and correctly to print, without the requirement for keyboard entries. Should such systems become popular, there might be fewer jobs for typists, most of whom are at present, female. But that wouldn't necessarily mean fewer women in the work force. It could mean more female sales engineers and more female executives. After all, the business world is becoming increasingly competitive, and the more enlightened organizations are increasingly alert for both men and women with potential for career growth. They realize that talent and ambition can be found in a female secretary or typist just as it can in a male management trainee. These companies also recognize that the "new Sams" of corporate life must be more adept at understanding and motivating employees than our Sam appears to be. So who knows? Susan's talents, desires, and preparations may find her moving through assignments in market research and advertising, then as field sales engineer, district manager, and right on up. One day, she may say to her secretary: "George, I'd like to send a special message to each of our 200 sales engineers."

# FINDERS, KEEPERS— LOSERS, WEEPERS

Some people will become substantially better off as a result of the new factory and office systems. Other people will experience financial and psychological problems, in some cases prolonged and severe. These unfortunate men and women will be the "losers, weepers" of the new era, disconnected from the economy and unable to exchange work for pay. The nature and extent of society's obligation to this group is beyond the scope of this book. Rather, its purpose is to help you gain, and retain, membership in the successful group.

Age, health, and geography may influence whether a person will flourish or wither, but these factors are not as important as *preparation* and *flexibility*.

The successful men and women will be the "finders." They will have found the way, for *them,* to become prepared—prepared to cope with the new requirements. Most of these "finders" will also be "keepers." They will be flexible enough to stay prepared, to change, and keep changing, as the requirements take on new forms and dimensions.

Not all of these requirements will be technical. To be sure, many people may have to learn how to design, operate, program, repair, sell, or service those new devices, whatever they may be. And that technical learning will be important in the new careers. But at least as important will be learning about a nontechnical aspect of tomorrow: *people*.

The new order, the new economy, is *information* oriented, and that naturally starts us thinking about the technical side of such things as bytes and RAMs and thin-film lams. But the information, no matter how it is generated, stored, retrieved, distributed, and displayed, will end up being used *by and for people*.

That's why many of the biggest problems and opportunities will not be in the technical zone. The eternal "people questions", those teeming with social, psychological, and economic considerations, will be there to demand our best attention and effort.

So, as we shall see, one requirement for success in almost all the new careers is **people proficiency**—the ability (and desire) to understand other people and to communicate with them effectively.

# Chapter 5

# CAREERS IN LIMBO

The following nine people have never met, nor are they even aware of each other's existence. But they have several things in common.

Bradley Monson, 38, is assistant controller of a Pittsburgh producer of industrial chemicals.

Phillip Larghretti, 53, is vice president of sales for a frozen-foods processor in Boston.

Margot Lansky, 29, is patent attorney for a San Jose company that makes machines that make chips for computers.

Peter Haagen, 48, is president of the Home Products Division of a Chicago health care corporation.

Harold Nakahara, 52, is director of quality assurance for a Los Angeles defense electronics/aerospace corporation.

Billy Joe Woodson, 36, is Atlanta district manager for a North American distributor of Japanese duplicating machines.

Malcolm MacLean, 40, is vice president of information systems for an insurance company in Hartford.

Katherine Steiner, 40, is vice president of advertising and sales promotion for a consumer goods company in Chicago.

Joseph Newman, 58, is vice president of human resources for a Manhattan-based retail chain.

Despite the marked disparity in their ages, occupations,
industries, and locations, several career-centered statements apply to all nine. Specifically, each of them has been
with the same company for eight years and on the same job
for the last three of those years; received a salary increase
within the past year; feels stymied, blocked from foreseeable career progress where he or she is; and has no vested
retirement benefits with any employer. Each has met recently with several executive search firms, including mine.

These men and women do not believe that they will be
fired for reasons of poor performance. Nor do they believe
that they will be laid off because of business conditions.
Their main concern is that they are *not moving ahead*.
They feel frustrated because something or someone is im-
peding their upward movement. In short, their careers are
in limbo, and these poor souls are unhappy in their halfway
houses.

True, they have a job, and they were given a pay raise
during a tight budget year. But the thrill is gone. These nine
men and women have begun to think the unthinkable; they
have decided to explore outside possibilities for restarting
their career engines. None of these career-minded persons
has anything against his or her employer of the past eight
years. But all of them feel the need for more personal progress, a need that they believe will be satisfied only in a new
setting.

Well, what about these nine people? Are they to be
consoled or chided? Should they be complimented or casti-
gated? We shall explore each case in some depth later in
this chapter. But first, let's take another brief look at the
new economy, the new era we have already begun to penetrate. Strange events have been occurring during the past
several years, and more unusual turns and twists are on the
way.

We saw in Chapter 1 that America's 1981–1982 recession was the eighth since World War II, and that it and each of the earlier seven had been followed by an economic recovery.

I noted carefully, however, that the course of that eighth recession had been considerably different from the course of those earlier declines. More important, I said that the eighth recovery, already underway, was going to be distinctly different from the seven earlier recoveries.

In earlier years, each dip had been followed by a recovery that saw things returned to just about where they had been before the fall from plenty. Certainly, there were a few changes here and there, but in the main, each recovery was a general recovery and we Americans were soon back to business as usual.

This eighth recovery, although still in the early stages, is already showing signs of being a different sort. As it gathers strength and momentum it promises (to some people it *threatens*) to have at least three unusual and important characteristics:

1. *It will be a selective recovery.* This means that some of our nation's industries, companies, and divisions will not share in the joys of economic resurgence. Some will continue to dwindle and eventually will disappear entirely from the scene. Others will become partially submerged. These semibuoyant businesses will bob precariously along, enjoying about the same level of security as do those companies that supply glass milk bottles, Franklin stoves, and adult tricycles. Still others, such as housing, autos, and major appliances (and the basic industries that supply them), will probably muddle through, experiencing short-cycle surges and slides. At times their quarterly profits may look very good compared to the losses incurred during the depths of 1982, and executives' bonuses may

soar. But these businesses will probably never regain the sustained, robust health they once took for granted. This will be especially true with respect to the number of career opportunities they offer. And with good reason. These industries have suffered for decades under the twin yokes of oppressive union constraints and management's own superstructure: top heavy, rigid, and aft-facing. They have finally realized that they must streamline and automate management as well as the factory.

2. *It will be a spectacular recovery.* This means that some sectors of the new economy will enjoy an upsurge in broad array of exciting new services and products. *This will be the boom—the ideal* time for you to launch your new career as a cluster specialist!

3. *It will be a career-changing recovery.* This will be true for both positive and negative reasons. New career opportunities will emerge; some, of course, are already with us. But the birth of the new often induces the death of the old, and that will certainly typify this eighth recovery. In fact, we are already beginning to witness the decline of some forms of the *traditional generalist*: certain middle managers, surgeons, attorneys, administrators, and shop proprietors are not as busy as they were before. This also applies to some forms of the *traditional specialist*: certain bank tellers, labor negotiators, inventory controllers, financial analysts, nuclear reactor designers, flight engineers, riveters, welders, and reservation clerks are no longer in short supply.

---

# THEN WAS THEN, BUT . . .

In each of the earlier recessions, certain categories of workers were, to no one's surprise, affected most adversely.

Hourly employees bore the brunt of most layoffs. Also, because of union contract requirements, the last workers to be hired were the first to be fired (except when minorities or other protected classes were retained). Generally, these short-service men and women were in the lower wage brackets and in the lower skill groups. Skilled industrial workers seldom felt threatened during a retrenchment. True, there were fewer chances of their being promoted into management, and periodically some of them would have to "bump down" a level or two. But employment security for the high-seniority, highly skilled, blue-collar employee was almost never in doubt.

This was also generally true of most longer-service, highly trained, white-collar men and women. Accountants were kept but junior accounting clerks were laid off. Secretaries were reassigned and kept on the payroll while typists and file clerks were given their pink slips. Engineers (except in aerospace) were generally a protected species, but technicians and lab assistants were often in jeopardy.

Looking backward, we can see that such restructuring (by length of service, by skill level, and by wage level) was not necessarily in the best interests of any of those involved:

*Junior employees.* For both white- and blue-collar workers, it meant the prospect of periodic unemployment. Further, the system had a built-in barrier, a "catch-22" for most of them, especially minorities. If they were to be victims, time after time, of inadequate seniority, how could they ever gain enough of it, or enough basic job skills, to escape the *next* cutback?

*Senior employees.* For them it meant they had a safety net that kept them from falling too far during slack periods. They cherished their seniority rights and would strike to keep them. This is understandable because, if nothing else, some form of seniority recognition protects a person from the whims and vagaries of a management that is often confused and constantly harrassed.

But that protective device can also stifle. It tends to tie a person to one organization and thus to one location. It also serves as a brake on career movement, both within the hourly ranks and above them. The latter is especially regrettable, for some hourly employees are considerably more talented than their supervisors. These underutilized men and women are capable of handling broader responsibilities, perhaps in methods planning, estimating, quality procedures, production control, and line supervision. They often feel the urge to move out of the ranks and into such management positions.

But many of them decide not to take the chance; they know what happened to several of their buddies who, for one reason or another, did not succeed. (Lacking their former seniority protection, some of those ex-hourly workers were fired when things did not work out well for them in management. Others had an option—to leave or to learn the intricacies of operating a forklift truck on the midnight shift.)

*Employers.* For them it meant lower efficiency and higher cost per unit. These undesirable conditions resulted from the "familiarization time" required by senior employees as they bumped semisenior people who then displaced other, more junior workers. The irony of large layoffs is that the company's efforts to cut payroll costs often lead to some unexpected splotches of red ink. Let's examine a typical situation.

Sales have fallen, so management has decided that fewer sales must be matched by fewer workers in the factory, including those at the top of the hourly pyramid. So hourly employees begin cascading down the job ladders, with some of them coming to rest on unfamiliar rungs, jobs they have never held. Some higher-rated employees take over almost immediately for the people they bump; others cannot or will not. Several days, perhaps a week, may pass before Bob, an expert bench toolmaker, meets his production quota after bumping Vic from a vertical turret lathe, even if Bob's attitude is positive. (Lost time will probably be greater when Tom, a tool and gage inspector, bumps Paulette, a plate layout inspector!)

Sales remain low, so management soon decides that it has erred—that it did not cut deep enough. So a month or two later (now that most of the newly positioned employees are performing their new tasks efficiently) along comes a second wave, displacing them again. (This "chain bumping" makes everyone nervous, including the customers, who have the quaint notion that they should receive a reliable product.)

But wait, the worst is yet to come. When orders regain their normal level, workers return to their former classifications *but not necessarily to their former jobs.* The rigors of seniority could even jostle some employees into a different building and to a different supervisor. There they hastily begin applying unfamiliar methods and processes, using unfamiliar equipment, to unfamiliar products. (Let us not even try to estimate these additional losses due to scrap and rework. As for the customers . . .)

# BUT NOW IS NOW

Fortunately or unfortunately, depending on one's point of view, conditions are beginning to change, both in the factory and in the office. In the factory of today and tomorrow, the requirements (skill, knowledge, and attitude) of many new jobs argue strongly against chain bumping, upgrading by strict seniority, and similar practices rooted in the 1950s, those hurly-burly days of militant industrial unionism.

These new requirements coincide with three other important trends:

1. The cost/price pressures of worldwide competition
2. The declining influence of unions in the private sector of the American economy
3. Management's growing awareness of its responsibility to *manage* the utilization of the company's human resources

This economic handwriting is now visible on the walls of many of America's collective bargaining conference rooms. Some of the best minds (often the younger minds) on both sides of the table are trying to deal, imaginatively, with the fundamental problem. Simply stated, it is: How can a union-management contract continue to provide some form of employment security to older, long-service employees, and to minorities and other protected classes, yet not hobble management's struggles to produce and compete *effectively* in this dynamic, intense, worldwide marketplace?

This problem is, in itself, knotty enough. But it also has complications that go beyond the creative zone. Let's suppose that the negotiators construct, after much give and take, concepts and general procedures that are acceptable to both the company and the union and in line with the 1984 Supreme Court decision regarding seniority and minorities. How can they sell these changes to the hard-core membership of the union—senior men and women who grew up *shouting, defending, and sometimes enjoying* the dogma of strict seniority? Or, suppose that the union leaders have concocted an approach that they believe the membership will accept. The situation may then become one of more horse trading. How much is management willing to exchange for such ratification? Everyone agrees that a strike over "seniority take-aways" would certainly be prolonged, bitter, and costly. Is the company willing to grant special wage increases to these senior people? If not, is it willing to recognize the union as the exclusive bargaining agent for all employees in all new plants that the company may open? And so on.

Troublesome as these problems and questions are, both sides appear to recognize that changes must be made. Some unions and some companies are already writing contracts that address the basic problem in various ways. Such agreements are important for the future of all concerned. Unless a management obtains more flexibility, chances are that it may not survive the new multidirectional pressures. If the company fails or a plant closes, the local union loses; it cannot collect dues and assessments from a nonexistent work force. As for the employees involved, it is anyone's guess how they should attempt to restructure their careers, indeed, their lives, after their sole support for so many years can no longer provide them work.

The foregoing may sound rather gloomy, and perhaps it does reflect some of the general pessimism that surrounds much of America's "blackstack" economy. But those same causes for pessimism may induce optimism when one views the socioeconomic culture generally projected for our nation. Here we envision a multitude of new technologies creating almost unlimited new services, systems, and products. We can anticipate more offices, more home/office work, more leisure, more nonunionized employees, and a more enlightened, more concerned, more participative management—all in all, a treasure trove of benign conditions, especially when compared to America's long history of belligerent labor relations.

Most American offices today are union-free except those, of course, of the federal, state, and local governments. (Those public servant organizations often harbor at least as many disgruntled union activists as they do bureaucrats.)

As we saw earlier, our private-sector offices of yesteryear responded to business downturns mainly by squeezing the bottom of the salaried pyramid. But not so today, and probably not in the foreseeable future.

The 1981–1983 crunch was addressed in a radically different, yet more rational fashion by most organizations. For the first time since the Great Depression corporations began learning to live with a leaner, lighter superstructure. There are today, and probably will be tomorrow, fewer *layers* of management. There are also fewer administrative staff specialists and staff generalists.

Since early 1981 several hundred thousand salaried employees have been dismissed. Most of these were men in the age bracket 40 to 60 and earning from $40,000 to $140,000 a year in base salary and bonus. Many of them were, at time of departure, given some sort of salary continuation or severance allowance because of their years of good service. Some of these, veterans of earlier recessions, were surprised at their not being placed in "parking orbit," drawing paychecks for busywork until business picked up again. Others were disappointed when they were not downgraded to lower-paying positions.

Instead, these middle- and upper-bracket people were separated from their companies *at the same time that the base of the pyramid was left largely untouched*. This brave new world of reducing the salaried superstructure sprang from one or more of these considerations:

1. Competitive pricing pressures
2. The "need" to mimic the Japanese management system
3. The widened availability of computerized data that are not only accurate and reliable but also *pertinent and understandable*
4. The need for fresh thinking and fresh attitudes from fresh minds

Generally, this approach seems to be working well so far, except, of course, for most of those dismissed. Today, in almost any large office organization, we can see many examples of junior people busily performing critical work and contributing to the well-being of the organization. Unless some unexpected and powerful factor forces its way into the office work equation, this more rational approach to staffing (and de-staffing) will probably set the standard for several decades, at least.

# CASE HISTORIES

Now that we have reviewed the economic background a bit, we can direct our attention to the nine cases of career limbo. It is important that you have a reasonably sturdy grasp of that background, for two distinct reasons:

1.  You are going to determine what each of those nine men and women should do, if anything, to rekindle the rocket's flame.

2.  You, or someone you know, may be in a situation akin to that of one of the nine. (Could the title of this chapter apply to you today? Tomorrow?)

Here is the way we shall delve into these cases:

*   First, I will furnish you with the pertinent data—enough information about each situation for you to come up with one or more recommendations for the stymied person.

*   Second, you will accept the fact that the names of the persons and their companies are fictitious, maybe even a bit humorous at times. I have, however, preserved the real names of the colleges and universities (why mangle those old school ties?).

*   Third, as you think through each case, you will try to glean a valuable idea or two for yourself, for your boss, or for your friendly IRS auditor.

- Finally, my comments and recommendations on each case will appear later, on pages 243–261. (Actually, they are there right now, but you may wish to work first on the cases by yourself, free from such contamination.)

So, here we go!

## CASE 1:   BRADLEY MONSON
Does This Assistant Need Assistance?

Bradley Monson, 38, is the assistant controller for Imaginative Industrial Chemicals (IIC). This 90-year-old Pittsburgh company has about 1200 employees in seven plants nationwide. Its annual sales total $215 million and its stock is traded on the American Exchange. Monson's base salary is $46,300 and his bonus last year was $3,000.

### Education

Monson has a B.S. in accounting from Villanova, where he lettered in track and basketball and was in ROTC all four years. His grade-point average was 2.9 of a possible 4, but in accounting it was 3.9. (He will receive the M.S. in accounting, at age 39, after fifteen more months of evening classes at Duquesne.)

### Military Service

Two years active duty as inventory officer, Army Quartermaster Corps; six years reserve duty as auditor.

### Professional Progress

At age 24 Monson joined the Pittsburgh office of Young & Sells, a large public accounting firm, as a junior accountant. Progress during his six years there was above average. He frequently uncovered complex problems and suggested sound remedies; also, he passed all parts of the CPA examination at first sitting. But he (and about three-fourths of his peers) were told that they would not be promoted into the partnership. (Translation: They were deemed unlikely developers of new business—new clients—for Young & Sells.) At age 30 he joined IIC, whose books and systems he had audited three times with Young & Sells. He progressed rapidly through several one- and two-year assignments in the accounting department and was named assistant controller three years ago.

## Recent Development

Until three months ago he and a peer, Randy Reedy, had been competitors to replace their boss, the vice president and controller. Reedy, who won that close race, is *not* an accountant. Age 34, he is a former chemical engineer who transferred into financial planning after earning an evening M.B.A. (finance option) five years ago at Drexel.

## Current Situation

Monson and Reedy are still on reasonably good terms, but Monson now views Reedy as heir apparent to the chief financial officer, age 62. Monson believes that Reedy neither understands nor appreciates the importance of accounting disciplines to IIC. He fears, therefore, that he will be passed over again for promotion if Reedy becomes CFO in three years.

## The U Factor

After our interview, Bradley Monson and I were in general agreement on his personal and professional **U factor**:

> *Likes:* a structured environment; problem solving; responsibility, recognition, and reward; coaching junior people; accuracy and reliability; family-centered recreation
>
> *Dislikes:* risk taking; hip shooting; borderline ethics; flamboyant behavior
>
> *Highs:* all aspects of accounting; leadership; knowl-

edge of the industrial chemical industry; communication skills

*Lows:* financial and strategic planning; international operations; lender relationships (lines of credit, debt restructuring, and stock offerings)

## My Questions

Should Monson consider leaving IIC? Why? Why not? If yes, to which industries and which cultures should he move? Should he discuss his concerns with Reedy? With the chief financial officer?

## Your Queries

## Your Suggestions

## Additional Information

(I delayed telling you this for a reason: to remind you to suspend judgment until you see the entire picture, whether in a case study or in real life—especially *your* life.)

You should also know the following about Bradley Monson:

- He will not relocate from Greater Pittsburgh because his elderly parents are chronically infirm.
- He has been invited by a former colleague at Young & Sells to become his cofounder and partner in a small CPA firm. This venture would supply very per-

sonalized auditing and accounting services to small
Pittsburgh businesses.

- He harbors no grudge against Randy Reedy, nor does
  he feel any bitterness toward IIC.
- In his professional life, he hardly ever thinks of himself as a black.

(I promise not to withhold information in the other eight
cases.)

## CASE 2:   PHILLIP LARGHRETTI
A Warm Body for Cold Storage?

Phil Larghretti, 53, is vice president of sales for Fathomless, an old-line Boston processor of frozen seafood. This
$85 million business (three plants, 650 employees) was pur-
chased two years ago by Titanic Brands, Inc., of Indianap-
olis. (Titanic, with annual sales of $355 million, is the na-
tion's largest producer and distributor of canned vegetables
and fruits.) Larghretti's base salary is $55,000, and his sales
incentive earnings last year amounted to about $22,000.
Fathomless provides him with an automobile and a country
club membership.

### Education

Larghretti dropped out of New York University in his junior year. He has since completed several evening courses
and has attended numerous seminars conducted by the
American Management Associations, but he has no degree.
This deficiency concerns Larghretti from time to time,
mainly because it is *hidden*; since age 27 he has always
represented himself as an NYU graduate, and none of his
employers has checked that claim.

### Military Service

Four years' active duty as an Air Force radio operator;
decorated for bravery in combat over Korea.

## Professional Progress

After returning to civilian life at age 24, Larghretti became a driver for a Brooklyn jobber who supplied specialty meats to Long Island restaurants. Two years later he moved to Syracuse, where he supervised the warehouse of his uncle's wholesale food business. He left after nine months to become the Albany territory sales representative for Personal Palate, a leading distributor of sauces and condiments. There he began sharpening his sales skills, and soon Larghretti was rated one of the top producers in Personal Palate. The company then moved him to Buffalo, long a troubled territory for the company's products. Larghretti's performance there earned him a promotion into management as Hartford district manager. After two more sales management promotions within Personal Palate, he joined Fathomless eight years ago as eastern region sales manager and became vice president of sales five years later.

## Recent Development

Larghretti was not disturbed when Titanic Brands purchased Fathomless two years ago. He believed what all Fathomless employees were told—that things would continue much as they had been before. That promise held until seven months ago, when Titanic's chief executive officer, concerned about declining profitability, hired a nationally known consulting firm to recommend improvements. After three months' study, the consultants devised a new method for analyzing Titanic's markets and forecasting sales volume, division by division and product by product. This complex approach to market analysis and planning is one in which Larghretti has neither experience nor faith. He expressed his reservations throughout Fathomless, and his long-time boss, the president of Fathomless, generally agreed with him. Titanic, however, remained adamant: All divisions must comply. (It is especially interested in Fathomless; Titanic's CEO believes that Titanic's future may depend on Fathomless's ability to grow into nationwide leadership of the exploding seafood marketplace.)

## Current Situation

Larghretti's plan, duly approved by the president of Fathomless, has just been returned by Titanic's consultants with comments such as "incomplete," "inconsistent," "inaccurate," and "not meeting the basic intent of the strategic planning process." Larghretti gloomily voices several negatives: He and his boss will never mesh with Titanic's new methodologies, he will never replace his boss, and he will never become Titanic's vice president of marketing and sales.

## The U Factor

After our interview, Phillip Larghretti and I were in general agreement on his personal and professional U factor:

*Likes:* a warm, people-centered environment; informal procedures; socializing with customers; helping new sales reps; personally closing big accounts

*Dislikes:* budgeting and other accounting matters; staff meetings; statistical and analytical studies

*Highs:* "people skills"; sales techniques; training and motivating; knowledge of food distribution

*Lows:* lacks broad marketing skills and interests; narrow business awareness; somewhat rigid

## My Questions

How should he respond to the comments of Titanic's consultants? Can he adjust sufficiently to the new methodologies—enough for him to be considered as a potential replacement for his boss? Enough to stay where he is? Should he even try to adjust?

## Your Queries

*Your Suggestions*

## CASE 3:   MARGOT LANSKY
### Who Holds the Patent on This Attorney?

Margot Lansky, 29, is the patent attorney for SIL-MOS, a San Jose producer of specialized equipment that makes chips and related microminiature devices for computers. This company is fifteen years old, has about 550 employees, and its sales (now about $125 million) have been growing rapidly each year. The stock of this very profitable corporation is traded OTC (Over-The-Counter), but its major owners are the large San Francisco bank and the Boston venture capitalist who supplied most of the seed money years ago. Margot's base salary is $41,000.

### Education

Margot graduated *cum laude* from Berkeley at age 21 with a B.S. in electronics and computer sciences. Five years later she obtained her L.L.B. from Armstrong College (evenings) and passed the California bar at first sitting.

### Professional Progress

Margot joined SIL-MOS as a design engineer upon graduation from Berkeley. Her creative bent and analytical skills soon led to a series of rapid promotions in the engineering department. She was named manager of technical evaluation at age 25, responsible for making sure that SIL-MOS products were technically superior to those of its American and Japanese competitors. She was elated when, one year later, she became the firm's first patent attorney. This job, although not among those eight in the closely guarded management bonus plan, does draw heavily on both of her disciplines.

Margot reports to Leonard Loshin, the firm's general counsel and vice president of administration, but she still works closely with her former boss, Virgil Homer, vice president of research and engineering. She is active in several professional societies, the National Organization of Women, and MENSA (the high-IQ group).

## Recent Development

Six months ago Margot decided to tackle a problem for which an outside law firm had been retained, a year ago, by Loshin. This problem was a crucial patent infringement case, complex and rooted in the dim past. Working nights and weekends, she marshaled obscure engineering details and legal nuances into an unusual pattern of defense. Her defense enabled SIL-MOS to reduce its liability by $750,000. Everyone was pleased, especially Margot; she enjoyed applying her analytical and creative talents to this difficult and critical problem.

Three months ago she was surprised to receive a special one-time award of $2000. She tried to refuse it, telling Loshin that her efforts had merely been part of her responsibility to the company. He insisted that her efforts had been "above and beyond."

## Current Situation

Margot has several dilemmas. She still thinks that she should not have taken the money. But, she reasons, if the company considered her efforts to have been beyond her regular responsibility, the measure of appreciation should have been considerably more than $2000—a mere ¼ of 1 percent of the money she had saved SIL-MOS!

Her second dilemma is more serious; it concerns her future with the company. On the one hand, Margot is reluctant to leave SIL-MOS. She relishes her work, and she is grateful for the company's having paid most of her tuition during four years of night law classes. All in all, she feels that she has been treated fairly and expects to receive periodic salary increases in the years ahead. But Margot is more interested in career growth than she is in salary progression, and she suspects that she has learned about as much as she will at SIL-MOS. She also feels that future progress with the company is unlikely because neither Loshin nor Homer will retire for fifteen years. Worse yet, she believes that her relationship with Loshin is gradually deteriorating: she suspects that he feels threatened by her, and she knows that her respect for him as an attorney is waning.

## Additional Information

Paul, her husband, is 32 and a former programmer for MIB and MacroLimp. He now works at home as an independent contractor, writing personal computer programs for several large software firms. His earnings last year were $32,000, and he expects to earn about $45,000 next year. Paul, too, believes that Margot's upward movement at SIL-MOS has plateaued, and he has suggested that she investigate opportunities elsewhere. The Lanskys would prefer to remain in the Bay area, but if the career opportunity were ideal for Margot, they would consider relocating to another high-technology metropolitan center. (His work can be done almost anywhere.)

## The U Factor

After our interview, Margot and I were in general agreement on her personal and professional U factor:

*Likes:* responsibility; freedom of action; a dynamic, fast-paced environment; working alone or in small teams; solving difficult problems

*Dislikes:* routine tasks; the status quo; low standards; inefficient methods; borderline ethics

*Highs:* intelligence (curious, creative, and analytical); vitality; unusual blend of engineering and legal skills; knowledge of her industry

*Lows:* has few friends; has below-average listening

skills; is reluctant to delegate most tasks; often displays impatience and annoyance with peers, subordinates, and superiors

## My Questions

How should she handle her relationship with Loshin? How much, if anything, does she "owe" SIL-MOS for the fast career track and partial tuition it has provided her? Where will Margot be happiest and most productive?

## Your Queries

## Your Suggestions

## My Recommendation

*You have now read, thought about, and perhaps "solved" these first three cases. You may now wish to compare your thoughts and suggestions for Bradley Monson, Phillip Larghretti, and Margot Lansky with my suggestions for them on pages 243–250.*

*After making those comparisons, you should be better prepared to detect the parallels between the cases and situations closer to home.*

## CASE 4:   PETER HAAGEN
Should He Move On?

Peter Haagen, 48, is president of the Home Products Division of Immaculate Perception, Inc., a Chicago-based health care company with 3500 employees and annual sales of $600 million. The Home Products Division employs 1200 in three midwestern locations; its products are sold by Immaculate's general sales staff, the same people who sell all the corporation's products. This division has annual sales of $150 million, or 25 percent of total corporate sales, yet it is such an efficient organization that it generates almost 40 percent of Immaculate's profits. Haagen earns a base salary of $115,000 and his cash bonus last year was $35,000. He also has several forms of deferred compensation plus a company car and other executive perquisites.

## Education

Haagen, a native of Denmark, graduated from Copenhagen Technical Institute with a degree in industrial and process engineering. He then became an exchange student at the University of Michigan, where he earned the M.S.I.E. degree at age 23.

## Professional Progress

Haagen worked for 18 months in Denmark as a process engineer for a company with ties to LePont. He then obtained a permit which enabled him to work in the United States as a specialist in process cost analysis for LePont. Haagen was later given rotational assignments in several production plants and at age 31 became an assistant plant manager and a U.S. citizen. Two years later he left LePont; he believed that his future upward movement was limited, his avenues to the top blocked by too many older people. Haagen joined the corporate staff of Priest Laboratories as manager of production processes, and two years later was named plant manager of a new facility producing disposable hospital products. His performance there earned him a large bonus and promotion to manager of a larger and more troubled plant. At age 40 he was recruited to Immaculate Perception as corporate vice president of manufacturing, and he was promoted to his present job three years ago.

## Recent Development

Haagen was stunned four months ago when Immaculate's secret attempt to acquire Godiva Cosmetics was bared and foiled. He would have been responsible for this $350 million business—a position promised him nine months ago by Immaculate's CEO when another man, also age 48, was named as Immaculate's executive vice president—and its "Mr. Outside."

## Current Situation

Despite the "golden handcuffs" of his deferred compensation, Haagen is inclined to leave Immaculate. Once again, he feels blocked. Also, he is irritated because he cannot persuade the new executive vice president to allow the Home Products Division to have its own sales staff. Haagen believes that the CEO will try, in two or three years, to provide a promotion for him, perhaps by reorganizing and creating a new group vice president position. But Haagen wants to run his own show, and he has concluded that this opportunity will be long coming, if ever, for him at Immaculate.

## Additional Information

Mrs. Haagen, a Swiss citizen, has not particularly enjoyed her eight years in Chicago. Trilingual and cosmopolitan, she would prefer living in Europe but Washington, D.C., or San Francisco would be acceptable to her. Haagen has no strong geographical preferences, but he doubts that he will find his next career opportunity in an area favored by his wife.

## The U Factor

After our interview, Peter Haagen and I were in general agreement on his personal and professional U factor:

*Likes:* responsibility and accountability; efficiency

and productivity; unlimited horizons; change and variety

*Dislikes:* tight control from above; static situations; being runner-up; sluggish subordinates; restraints of government health agencies

*Highs:* automated production processes; record of profitability; leadership skills; "gut feeling" for consumers and their needs; intelligence

*Lows:* impatient with the world, including himself; self-centered; no leisure interests; overtly critical of rivals; hypertensive

## My Questions

In this and the remaining five cases, all the questions will come from you.

## Your Queries

## Your Suggestions

## CASE 5:　HAROLD NAKAHARA
### Which Direction for This Director?

Harold Nakahara, 52, is corporate director of quality assurance for Iris Interdiction, a defense electronics/aerospace firm in Los Angeles. This government contractor has annual sales of about $1.1 billion and 14,000 employees in eight plants and in some forty U.S. government installations throughout the world. His base salary is $90,000 and his bonus last year was $15,000. He has a company car and participates in Iris Interdiction's stock option plan.

## Education

Nakahara, a nisei, did not attend college. His parents and relatives had lost almost all their possessions during World War II. At age 19 he graduated second in his high school class and went to work as a trainee in radio repair. Subsequently, he has attended evening classes, taken correspondence courses, and participated in technical and management seminars. Nakahara is a voracious reader and knows how to find the best books and articles pertaining to his work and to the technical disciplines underlying it. His counterparts among vendors, customers, and competitors are surprised when he explains that he is largely self-taught.

## Professional Progress

Capitalizing on his hobby of building and repairing radios, Nakahara moved rapidly through early television receivers to TV transmitters and microwave relay systems. At age 25 he joined WEL as a laboratory technician and, after much delay, obtained an Air Force secret clearance. Soon his work habits, innovative ideas, and his knack for solving tough problems caught the eye of "Slim" Halliard, the legendary but eccentric inventor and troubleshooter in those early days of electronics weapons systems. Halliard arranged for Nakahara's transfer into WEL's super-secret research lab; there the two dabbled in a variety of research and development projects. Halliard did most of the conceptual work while Nakahara concentrated on devising ways to make the product reliable and "customer-proof." This penchant for product simplicity and dependability earned him several promotions within reliability engineering, manufacturing engineering, and quality control. Nakahara, although still the protegé of Halliard, was making a name for himself and at age 35 became supervisor of quality control in WEL's Stratotronics Systems Division. Five years later he and Halliard left the company to form an ill-fated and undercapitalized venture having to do with a special navigation device for positioning satellites. After four frustrating and financially debilitating years, Halliard joined Iris

Interdiction as chief engineer, and Nakahara soon followed as manager of reliability standards and processes. When Halliard became vice president of engineering and standards three years ago he promoted his trusted associate to corporate director of quality assurance. The two men understood that at some point in time Nakahara's job would be upgraded to a vice presidency.

## Recent Development

When Halliard died suddenly seven months ago Iris's CEO decided to reorganize. He narrowed the job by removing all quality aspects; the chief engineer then became the vice president of engineering. The CEO also established a new position—vice president of reliability, quality, and customer relations—and recruited a young Ph.D. from Pantheon for the job.

## Current Situation

Nakahara and his new boss have substantially different approaches to the control of product quality and to satisfying the customer, yet they get along surprisingly well. The CEO is pleased that their relationship is good because he believes that each has a lot to contribute to Iris. But Nakahara feels that he has lost credibility, within and beyond Iris, and that he should explore external opportunities.

## The U Factor

After our interview Harold Nakahara and I were in general agreement on his personal and professional U factor:

> *Likes:* large, complex, dynamic environments; precision products; critical projects; continual learning and development; encouraging other minorities
>
> *Dislikes:* intellectual snobbery; far-out theorists; brash, immature M.B.A.s; marketers who oversell the product to the customer
>
> *Highs:* reputation for integrity and professionalism;

knowledge of the industry; determination to excel;
coaching skills; fluent in Japanese

*Lows:* sponsored too long by one person; no degree;
experience mostly in defense work; easily hurt

## Additional Information

For personal and family reasons the Nakaharas will not
move from California, nor will he consider another entrepreneurial venture. He would like to remain with Iris, but
he would also like to move into new and larger responsibilities. Further, his ego requires that his next job, whether
with Iris or another firm, reaffirm his value and importance
to that organization. It must also enable him to continue his
life-long program of self-development.

## Your Queries

## Your Suggestions

## CASE 6: BILLY JOE WOODSON
### A Case of Too Much Southern Comfort?

Billy Joe Woodson, 38, is the Atlanta district manager for
Tokishubi, N.A., the distribution arm for Japanese copiers
and supplies in North America. The Atlanta district's sales
last year were $8.5 million, about 6 percent of Tokishubi's
total in Canada and the United States. Woodson reports to
Tom Hendricks, eastern regional manager. Tom is based in
New York, as is his superior, Pat O'Myhe, the national
sales manager. Woodson's base salary is $39,000 and his

commission and override earnings last year were $18,000. He has a company car and standard employee benefits but no other perquisites.

## Education

Woodson bumbled his way through two years of college (a hodge-podge of business and liberal arts classes) at the University of Georgia. He has since excelled in twenty-four hours of evening business courses at Georgia State University and expects to receive his degree in three years.

## Professional Progress

Woodson entered the family rug-cleaning business at age 20. He disliked the record-keeping and related chores of the office but enjoyed selling the firm's services, especially to businesses. He also liked to create new sales and service "packages"—imaginative new ways of describing, marketing, and pricing the same old product. These approaches enabled him to attract new customers while retaining the established clientele.

But Billy Joe did not like the family entanglements, so he went to work for OKRA INK, an office supplies store, selling the entire line of hardware items, business forms, and custom stationery. He was particularly successful at selling typewriters, and at age 26 left the security of OKRA to become a sales representative for Glovetti in downtown Atlanta. Woodson did well with Glovetti, but detecting the new wave of Japanese copying machines approaching America, he joined Tokishubi eight years ago as their first salesperson in the southeast. He built the business steadily in Atlanta and was promoted to Atlanta district manager three years ago. He now supervises 12 sales and service reps throughout Georgia.

## Recent Development

Woodson had been expecting to be named southeastern regional manager, based in Atlanta and responsible for seven districts in five states. But Tokishubi has just opted to eliminate regional managers throughout its U.S. distributorship. The rationale is that sales training, budget analysis, inventories, revenue reporting, and customer service matters can be handled more effectively by computer networking than by the regional layer of management.

## Current Situation

Woodson does not believe that the projected computerization will be good for the business; he also thinks that it will limit his potential growth with the company. He has been told that he will probably be invited to transfer to New York as national sales training manager. There he would be responsible for planning, preparing, and updating a lengthy series of interactive videodiscs—the new method of training Tokishubi's sales and service personnel.

## Additional Information

Woodson does not like New York; in fact, he is uncomfortable almost anywhere other than Atlanta. Further, his wife is a successful attorney and would not wish to leave her established domestic relations and probate practice.

## The U Factor

After our interview, Billy Joe Woodson and I were in general agreement on his personal and professional U factor:

> *Likes:* personal selling; satisfying the customer; devising new sales techniques; training personnel; exceeding tough quotas; working long hours; established routines
>
> *Dislikes:* autocratic bosses; sophisticated systems; corporate penny-pinching; people who think they understand the south but do not
>
> *Highs:* sales skills; selecting and motivating subordinates; customer orientation; knowledge of office needs and equipment; the will to win
>
> *Lows:* provincialism; no degree; inadequate view of

the total business perspective; resistance to change;
no knowledge of computers

*Your Queries*

*Your Suggestions*

## CASE 7:   MALCOLM MACLEAN
## Too Broad for the Job?

Malcolm MacLean, 40, is vice president of information systems for Constitutional Assurance, a nationwide life and casualty insurance company headquartered in Hartford. This forty-year-old company is growing rapidly and profitably. But it does not rank among the top thirty carriers in any category except growth, where it gleefully outpaces the old-line carriers, and in earnings, where it ranks surprisingly high. The company maintains a small corporate staff and relies on insurance brokers and general agents, rather than a company sales staff, to sell and service its policies. MacLean's base salary is $72,000 and his bonus last year was $11,000. He also received a special award last year, the President's Prize, for his innovative system of preparing and issuing policies. (This grant of 500 shares of Constitutional common stock is now valued at about $15,000 on the American Stock Exchange.)

*Education*

MacLean garnered three degrees from three universities by age 25: an A.B. in mathematics from Yale, an M.S. in operations research and computer sciences from Johns Hopkins, and an M.B.A. from Harvard.

## Professional Progress

MacLean was hired at age 25 in the New York office of Gotham and McKetchum, a prestigious management consulting firm. He did very well as a research associate and as associate consultant to major corporations in matters such as systems analysis, computer architecture, financial analysis, and office engineering. In his fifth year with G and McK he was told, unofficially, that he would probably be made a partner in another eighteen months. MacLean, however, was not all that keen on consulting as a career; he resented the fact that many of his recommendations to his corporate clients were only partly implemented, and months after they could have been. His desire to have his plans carried out caused him to join, at age 30, a major brokerage firm as assistant vice president of data processing. For Sherrel, Binch he managed the very successful design and installation of a state-of-the-art system for the firm's 325 offices. In doing so he also managed to irritate and alienate several senior executives, including his boss and the vice president of finance. Fortunately for MacLean, his multioffice system had come to the attention of the executive recruiter conducting a search for Constitutional Assurance, and he was hired as the assistant vice president of data processing. His boss there was kind enough to let the younger man have his head, and MacLean was his automatic choice to replace him when he retired three years ago.

## Current Situation

Six months ago Constitutional's vice president of marketing left the firm, and MacLean made a strong bid to replace him. He pointed out to the CEO that most of the marketing problems were, in essence, *systems* problems, and that the firm's future growth depended a great deal on the independent brokers and agents becoming more efficient, and thus more productive for Constitutional. The CEO was partly convinced but decided to consider external candidates, as well. Two months ago the same executive search firm that had identified and recruited MacLean presented a slate of four candidates for the marketing job—three external and MacLean. The search firm and the CEO then constructed a matrix to compare and evaluate the four, and it depicted a dead heat between one external candidate and MacLean. The agonized CEO finally decided in favor of the outsider, explaining to MacLean that the decision had turned on the other man's superb track record of dealing with independent agents and brokers. He also said that he felt MacLean was ideally suited for systems work, and he promised that office automation, satellite communications, and a hefty salary increase would soon be coming his way. Bitterly disappointed, MacLean resolved to leave the company. He began at once a surreptitious search for broader responsibilities and has just refused to interview for a much larger information systems position with a huge mutual insurance company in Philadelphia.

## Additional Information

He is divorced and will move to any city for the right opportunity. Recently, he completed a six-hour battery of psychological tests at a local university. There was no interview and the test results were mailed to his home. The results, at least as he interprets them, seem to indicate that he has high potential for general management and that he should pursue a top position, even if it were in a very small organization. His résumé, accordingly, is slanted in that direction, playing down his functional and technical skills and dwelling on his experiences as a manager and as chairman of numerous corporate task forces.

## The U Factor

After our interview, it was clear that Malcolm MacLean and I were *not* in general agreement on his personal and professional U factor. I will delay revealing my assessment of him, but here is how he saw himself:

*Likes:* bright associates; complex problems; managing people; total reponsibility; freedom of action

*Dislikes:* repetitive tasks; mediocre subordinates; detailed and bureaucratic procedures; the status quo; training unmotivated people

*Highs:* managerial skills; creative mind; analytical skills; team player; communication skills; developer of subordinates; builder of strong peer relationships; inspirational leader; educational preparation

*Lows:* experience mostly in financial services; no field sales experience; no exposure to the international scene; no *formal* assignments in finance, marketing, legal, or operations

*Your Queries*

*Your Suggestions*

## CASE 8: KATHERINE STEINER
### Would Her Next Promotion Be a Gambol?

Katherine Steiner, 40, is vice president of advertising and sales promotion for Gramble and Machter in Chicago. This diversified, $2+ billion consumer foods corporation is consistently profitable. Its sales volume has increased, through internal growth and by acquisition, about 15 percent per year since 1974. Katherine's base salary is $68,000 and her bonus last year was $9000. In addition, she earns about $8000 each year teaching evening classes at a local university and conducting special seminars for professional associations.

## Education

Her A.B. at Goucher College was based on an unusual double major: English and mathematics. Her M.B.A. program at Northwestern University exercised those academic strengths and motivated her toward a career in marketing.

## Professional Progress

At age 24, and one week after graduation, she managed to penetrate Marsh & Marchant, the prestigious Michigan Avenue advertising agency, as a typist. (She had declined three offers from smaller agencies—offers of more money and with such titles as research assistant, copywriter, and test market interviewer. This decision shocked her friends, who could not understand the rationale of wanting to "learn the business as it really is, not just the way it is supposed to be.")

While she was learning from the various projects she was typing and proofreading, the account executives were observing that her language skills and proficiency with numbers exceeded her clerical abilities. Two years after joining the firm she had progressed rapidly through three departments and had been named senior research analyst on the Maize Margarine account. One year later she was placed in charge of all copywriting on that account, a two-year assignment. She was about to be named as the Maize account executive when she accepted an offer from her client—Maize Products, Inc., a $200 million corn processor in St. Louis.

Katherine, then 29, joined Maize as manager of advertising, and moved two years later to director of market research. Here she was responsible for investigating and assessing current trends in consumer preferences, competitors' strengths, product developments, governmental constraints, and new techniques in the packaging, pricing, marketing, and distribution of food products.

She was recruited at age 32 by Gramble and Machter as director of market research and analysis, and two years later she became product manager for the bakery products group. She was promoted to her present position three years ago, reporting to the senior vice president of marketing and sales.

## Current Situation

Her boss has announced that he will leave the company in four months for an important post in the Department of Commerce. He told Katherine privately that despite his recommendation, she will probably not be his replacement. He predicted that the CEO will "go for experience" and will select either Tom Brandeis, 55, the vice president of sales, or Jim Farr, 56, the vice president of new products marketing.

## Additional Information

She likes and respects both these men and could work well with either. But she believes that she has the vision and vigor that Gramble and Machter will expect from this job in the years ahead. She likes the company and enjoys her work. She also wonders when and where she will be given the responsibility for managing *all* facets of a marketing department. Her husband, Charles, is a physician with a flourishing family practice in Evanston, and their adopted child is seven years old.

## The U Factor

After our interview, Katherine Steiner and I were in general agreement on her personal and professional U factor:

   *Likes:*   the dynamics of consumer foods; a competitive environment; teaching; predicting and influencing consumer trends; alternative courses of action

   *Dislikes:*   office politics; autocratic management; mediocre performance; stereotyped thinking; ultrafeminists; the status quo

*Highs:* creative bent; analytical skills; vitality; communication skills; ad agency perspective; people skills; self-reliance; intelligence

*Lows:* little experience in field sales and brand management; no consumer products experience except foods; has not managed a large unit

*Your queries*

*Your Suggestions*

## CASE 9:   JOSEPH NEWMAN
## Can He Atone for a Cardinal Error?

Joseph Newman, 58, is vice president of human resources for Baronett, a $1.5 billion retail chain headquartered in Manhattan. This aggressive merchandising company takes pride in its ability to offer high-quality products and superior service at prices that are close to those of the discount houses. Newman's base salary is $80,000, his bonus last year was $15,000, and he participates in Baronett's executive stock option plan. He also has two sources of outside income. He earns about $15,000 a year as an occasional weekend arbitrator of labor-management disputes in the steel and auto industries. He also teaches evening classes and one-day seminars in labor economics and collective bargaining, thus adding about $7000 to his annual earnings.

### Education

Newman attended Notre Dame on an athletic scholarship but discovered in his junior year that his interest in social problems was greater than his love for football. In his final three semesters he concentrated on his studies and surprised himself by graduating with an overall B+ average. He obtained an M.S. in industrial and labor relations from Cornell University at age 25. By age 32 Newman had earned the J.D. degree from the evening division of Fordham University's School of Law, and he passed the New York bar the following year.

## Professional Progress

Newman, who had worked three college summers in the Gary, Indiana, steel mills, joined the United Auto Workers in Detroit as an assistant labor economist upon graduation from Cornell. In addition to his analytical work at Solidarity House, he trained local union officials in grievance handling, labor law, and contract negotiations. He then joined another international union, but resigned abruptly when he discovered that the workers' retirement funds were being siphoned. Newman next taught collective bargaining at New York University for one year, after which he "changed costumes" by joining the corporate staff of National Fabricators as a labor relations specialist. His rise on the "other side of the table" was rapid, and at age 42 he became corporate director of industrial relations for Choquer Chemicals in Newark, New Jersey. Eight years later he was recruited by Baronett as the assistant vice president of labor relations. He succeeded his boss three years ago and became a corporate officer, reporting to Scott Dread, general counsel and senior vice president of administration (whose position Newman has coveted since joining Baronett).

## Recent Development

One year ago the senior vice president and the CEO attended an executive retreat in Colorado; they came away with the realization that Baronett's human resources programs were almost exclusively *labor relations* programs. The emphasis was on dealing with the unions and on complying with the many federal and state administrative agencies. Very little was being done for management and professional employees, nor were their developmental needs being related to the future needs of the business. Newman agreed, in part, with these observations. He stated, however, that budget and time limitations had prevented him from doing some of the things they were now suggesting. They recommended that he hire a recognized professional as his assistant in these matters, expressing their conviction that Baronett must rearrange priorities and devote more attention to these long-neglected, nonlabor programs. Several months later Newman promoted Baronett's veteran training supervisor to a new position: corporate director of professional relations.

Newman's response to his bosses' concerns has not been well received. He has just been informed of their decision to recruit for a new executive position—vice president of management and professional programs—a position roughly equal to his, and also reporting to Scott Dread.

## Current Situation

Newman has been told that his performance in the traditional activities has been superb and that his future with Baronett is secure. He believes this, and he does not view the proposed new executive as a threat—he knows that the new man will not have his depth or breadth in the intricate maze of dealing with dozens of assertive, demanding unions. But his pride is wounded and he suspects that his scope of responsibility will, in the future, be reduced far more than his bosses now foresee. Further, he now doubts that he will replace Dread—the CEO would not be inclined to have Newman direct the activities of the new person. Finally, Newman does not agree with this new bifurcated approach to employee relations. He thinks that it is not in the company's best long-range interests, and he doubts that it will be a workable arrangement.

## Additional Information

Newman enjoys the reputation, on both sides of the bargaining table, of being extremely competent, fair, and totally honest. He makes his arbitration decisions as he sees the facts and issues in each case, and his impartiality is never questioned. The same is true of his posture when teaching—he presents all sides of the complex case studies and philosophical issues. The Newmans' six children have scattered and the Newmans have no strong ties to New York.

## The U Factor

After our interview, Joseph Newman and I were in general agreement on his personal and professional U factor:

*Likes:* the dynamics of collective bargaining; resolving knotty problems; protecting both company interests and employees' rights; being open and forthright

*Dislikes:* borderline ethics; social science fads; academic theorists; emotional behavior

*Highs:* track record in all matters related to collective bargaining; knowledge of four industries; education; vitality

*Lows:* little knowledge of, or interest in, the newer, forward-looking aspects of human resources; at times overly stubborn, outspoken, and ritualistic

## Your Queries

## Your Suggestions

# CHAPTER 6

# TO SPECIALIZE OR NOT TO SPECIALIZE?

Many of us are aware, sometimes painfully so, of the degree of specialization in America today—not only in industry and commerce, but in sports, the arts, and the professions, as well.

Like most facets of life in the 1980s, specialization has its pluses and its minuses. On the positive side, when the specialist actually does what he or she is supposed to do, the job really gets done. Whether it be in performing microsurgery, appearing as the designated hitter, or representing you in court, the successful specialist commands respect and a more-than-respectable fee for the skill, care, and effort expended—for a while, at least.

The term **half-life** is used by scientists and engineers to describe the time required for one-half of a substance to decay or degenerate, in other words, for 50 percent of it to be used up. The time required depends on the particular substance and process and can vary from a fraction of a second to a billion years. A typical example is the half-life of radioactive atoms in a Consolidated Edison spent-fuel storage tank. Another is the half-life of a drug, such as alcohol or aspirin, in your system. The half-lives of substances and processes such as these can be determined precisely by complex formulas.

Measured with less precision are other important half-lives:

- The "knowledge bank" of an industrial engineer, labor attorney, or purchasing supervisor
- The productive years of a ballerina, air traffic controller, or FBI informant
- The "popularity quotient" of a child actor, rock star, or Washington politician

An interesting characteristic of a half-life is that it is followed by a *second* half-life, after which only *one-fourth* of the original material remains undecayed. Then comes a *third* half-life, after which only *one-eighth* of the original is still there, and so on. It's a bit like the old paradox of the frog trying to leap from the well, when in each upward bound, he can move only one-half the remaining distance to the top. He never gets all the way there, at least in theory.

But the problems of half-life are practical problems. Not only are we concerned about the rate of decay in radioactive waste, but also with the rate of decay of useful *knowledge*—yours and mine. True, the theoretical frog will never get out of the well, and equally true, you and I will always retain *something* of value. That's the theory. But, to repeat, the problems of half-life are *practical* problems.

When I began recruiting for General Electric Company's jet engine division in 1952, half-life for mechanical engineers was gauged, roughly, at somewhere between twelve and fifteen years. After that, they needed refresher courses to help them understand at least some of the new theories, concepts, and technologies. In the years since graduation they had become deeply involved in specific mechanical engineering subspecialties of their work. As a result, in many aspects of mechanical engineering they were less knowledgeable than recent graduates of their own engineering schools.

For electrical engineers the half-life was a somewhat shorter period, between ten and twelve years, primarily because of the important advances in electronics, electricity's precocious offspring. For ceramic engineers it was briefer still because of the introduction of radically different materials and the startling new applications for them, such as in turbine buckets, rocket engines, and reentry heat shields.

Today, all such "knowledge bank" half-lives are shorter than ever before; each discipline has experienced (and continues to experience) thousands of breakthroughs, departures, and new beginnings within its own technologies. Further accelerating the pace are developments in related fields. For example, Specialist Q, whose field is cryogenics, devises a new technique for adjusting superconductive control mechanisms. That breakthrough will have obvious implications for her fellow cryogenic engineers. But it may also impinge on men and women specializing in circuit design, magnetic fields, structures, molecular flow, computer architecture, laser optics, and so on.

But Specialist X (a circuit designer) may not even hear about Specialist Q's new idea for superconductive control mechanisms. So at the same time that X's half-life is decreasing because he can't keep current in his own specialty, the clock begins ticking even faster for him because the useful data from Q does not enter X's knowledge bank. Thus widens the gap between what one knows and what he or she *should know*.

So a major reason for not becoming overly specialized is to avoid *technical obsolescence*—to reduce the chances of your being victimized by the ever-shortening half-life of your marketable knowledge. (Ironically, the physical substances with which a person works have predictable and steady half-lives. But the alert person, whether dental hygienist or welder, physician, or professor, knows only that his or her half-life is predictable: faster and faster it will become shorter and shorter.)

A second disadvantage of becoming *too* specialized is the danger of your bank of knowledge being devalued, perhaps to zero, by the introduction of a toally different way of doing the thing you do:

- Many designers and drafters will be replaced by light pens and similar computer-related tools.

- Many production schedulers and expediters will be jostled toward the sidelines by shop-floor tracking systems.

- Some surgeons will spend more time on the golf course and purchase fewer Mercedes because certain surgical procedures are being replaced by other forms of therapy.

- Airline flight engineers are being "bumped" from the cockpits of newer aircraft by sophisticated planning and control systems.

A third reason to resist the siren song of super-specialization is that many specialties, although appreciated when business is good, become *unaffordable* when hard times squeezes the economy, an industry, a company, or a division. Earlier recessions idled many acquisition and merger analysts, strategic planners, and research and engineering professionals, plus a potpourri of marginal performers. In the 1981–1983 recession, companies laid off specialists and specialist-managers in *every* function. Many of these men and women had very good performance records, but the corporate belt-tightening simply squeezed their jobs (and them) into the "not needed" pile.

What happens to your specialized job when your work is affected by foreign competition? By a merger? By your company's decision to discontinue your product line? By your company's decision to move to another state? By whatever the next business adversity might be?

More important: What happens to you?

# WHEN THE PACE WAS SLOWER

Once upon a work-time, a teacher was a broad-gauge teacher. The schoolmaster or schoolmarm taught a number of subjects and did so with authority of knowledge. Also, that teacher had a good grasp of how those subjects related to each other:

- Grammar to rhetoric and composition
- Language to history and geography
- Algebra to physics and chemistry, and so on

Similarly, a lawyer was a versatile lawyer. Problems of licenses and inheritance were handled side by side with questions of domestic relations, contract, and real property.

A doctor was a doctor who functioned at all levels, from applying poultices and delivering babies in the home to setting broken bones and removing tonsils in the office.

The firm's accountant handled all aspects of the company's financial transactions. The local banker was just as capable of appraising the worth of a cattle ranch as of calculating compound interest. Or of deciding whether or not to finance the blacksmith and liveryman in their proposed venture into the brave new world of horseless carriages.

In that age of golden gaslights, meticulous manners, and slow-to-change standards, most professionals provided a full, or nearly full, range of services to their clients.

As for nineteenth century craftsmen, most were graduates of an apprenticeship, having served for years under a recognized master craftsman. These members of the blue-collar elite were *journeymen*—by definition skilled in all facets of their craft and confident that, wherever they traveled or settled, they could exchange their high-quality workmanship for the top prevailing wage.

Does this mean that the age of specialization began sometime around the turn of the century?

Well, yes and no.

*No* in the sense that a few specialists existed thousands of years ago. The Old Testament, Egyptian hieroglyphics, Sumerian tablets, and American Indian petroglyphs speak of certain artificers who wrought in bronze, of seers who predicted celestial occurrences, and of artisans who fashioned quartz chips into spear points for the hunters and warriors of the group.

*Yes* in the context that the forces of change have been gaining momentum and power during each decade of the twentieth century. As conditions changed, more and more professionals and skilled workers began to specialize, to devote their time to one selected portion of their expertise and to ignore developments in the other portions. Later, many of them began to concentrate on only a *subportion* of their chosen portion. Thus began the evolutionary movement toward the career role that has become today's *traditional specialist*.

Today it seems almost obligatory for one to be perched far out on a twiglet. It's almost as if you have failed in life unless you have speared a specific sliver of elegant, esoteric expertise for your very own. Once you have done so, you have expertise to troll past potential employers; as a rule, employers have appreciated extreme specialists. How often in my work have I heard something like this: "What we need is an engineering manager who has 'paid his dues,' one who really understands counterclockwise, submersible reverse-polarity motors. That kind of engineer can hit the deck running and be up to speed around here by Wednesday!"

Also, your narrow niche of know-how can be used to advantage at class reunions:

"And what do *you* do in real life, Amanda?"

"I'm a senior inhalation therapist at the zoo, specializing in rhesus monkeys."

"Fascinating! Imagine, helping rhesus monkeys!"

"But not all rhesus monkeys; only mature males with disenfranchised collaterals."

It can also provide a forum at cocktail parties:

"Yes, Louise, I am a nuclear engineer, but . . ."

"That's disgusting! Positively revolting! You and your kind caused that terrible tragedy in Texas, the one that . . ."

"No, my dear. You see, I am a specialist, designing only the *medium*-size shields for *small* cores of *large*-scale reactors. What happened in Texas was that the *large*-size shields for the *medium* cores gave way unexpectedly in the *small*-scale reactor, and that, unfortunately, caused the main valve . . ."

"Oh, I *am* sorry, John, dreadfully sorry. I should have known that *your* work would have integrity. Now I would like for you to meet MaryAnn. She investigates dirigible disasters. MaryAnn, this is John. He is . . ."

"But not *all* derigible disasters, John; only those that . . ."

In certain circumstances, extremes of specialization are good; good for society, the economy, and for the men and women who practice them.

But many are *not* good, or they are sliding from moderately good toward undesirable. This trend is accelerating as technologies change more rapidly and as our economy hiccups and staggers before setting off on its new course.

Unfortunately, the sins of specialization often result in punishment of the innocent. Who among us has not experienced a situation similar to this?

Your fuel-efficient Serendipity Six has become fuel-extravagant; it also has begun to make strange respiratory-type noises. You, in your own Mittyesque way, know that it should purr along, "zippity, zippity, zippity," mile after mile. But it now sounds something like "bucketa-cheeze; bucketa-wheeze; bucketa, bucketa, bucketa-sneeze."

Even you, engrossed as you are in other equally complex problems (the latest Middle East crisis and the newest tax reform proposal) know what to do. You realize that your pride and joy needs expert clinical diagnosis and repair. You return the car to the Serendipity agency where you purchased it thirteen months and 15,000 miles ago. There you describe the strange sounds and systems to an unimpressive man with an impressive clipboard. Three days later you receive a puzzling phone call:

"Mr. Hutchens? This is Jimmy, at the agency."

(Thus begins your span of confusion; your name is Hodges, and the clipboard said "property of Bill something-or-other.")

"About that blue '84 Serendipity sedan you left here on the ninth—the one you said had a 'cheeze-wheeze-sneeze' problem."

(Now you feel slightly better; Jimmy, whoever he is, has described your car's asthmatic condition. But you left it there on the eighth and it's an '83 model. But anyway . . .)

"Well, you were wrong, Mr. Hutchinson; it ain't the tappets. I checked 'em myself, but just to make sure, I had Felipe look at them. As far as I'm concerned, he's the best tappet man in town! Naturally, he replaced 'em once he was in there, 'cause they were worn down some, but he wasn't sure what the real problem was. So . . ."

"But I didn't mention the *tappets*. I don't know a tappet from . . ."

"I had Smitty pull the headers and footers; he really understands the highs and lows of a six-cylinder engine. They were worn and pitted some, which is to be expected after all those miles you've put on that old car, Mr. Hudson, but . . ."

"You must have me confused with . . ."

"That's exactly what we thought, Mr. . . . uh, mind if I call you Fred?" (By this time you are sufficiently numb to persuade yourself that, relatively speaking, Fred isn't all that different from Frank.)

"We thought maybe you confused that 'cheese, wheeze, sneeze' thing with what we call 'condition X.' That's a real nasty problem we run into every now and then in a Serendipity Six. It's always in the number 3 cylinder and I think it's got something to do with the way the piston rubs against the frammis. So I call in Don, the district expert, the guy who tackles all the 'condition X' problems for every Serendipity agency in this state. Well, sir, Don personally ran a digitalized diagnosis on that number 3 cylinder. But after 2½ hours on the computer and our reg'lar three-minute road test, he still didn't . . ."

Of course, the Serendipity situation smacks of several things that are grievously wrong with the way some businesses do business today, including an obvious lack of customer orientation and a horrifying inattention to detail. But it also says a few things about the *traditional specialist* and the extent to which technical knowledge has been split, scattered, and stuffed into separate compartments—in this case, labeled Felipe, Smitty, and Don. The tendency today is for each specialist to know quite a bit about his own small sphere and almost nothing about that of the next specialist. *The interrelationships are missing!* Missing just as they are missing when:

> Your children are expected to learn English composition from a teacher who doesn't understand the elementary rules of grammar, spelling, and punctuation.

> or

> Your father is treated for a suspected heart condition by a complacent physician who is unaware of recent developments in nutrition and exercise medicine.

> or

> Your personal life insurance policies are written without certain desirable retirement options because the agent is really a specialist in providing buy-sell and "key partner" coverage for small businesses.

I believe the Serendipity story also tells us something about the current condition of the oldest of career roles: the *traditional generalist.* Jimmy and, presumably, Bill something-or-other are supposed to have sufficient breadth and depth to know how to assign the needed work to the appropriate specialists—and then to build *bridges of understanding* between those specialists when impasses occur. Perhaps they were capable of doing so—years ago when autos were less complicated and standards of workmanship for mechanics were higher.

But most of the hundreds of thousands of Jimmys who cling to the "I can do anything" facade actually accomplish very little in the formal structure of today's fast-paced business world. So much has happened in so many sectors of a Jimmy's generalized world that he has become both an endangered species and a dangerous specimen!

# THE WAVE OF THE FUTURE

So what does the future hold for these two traditional career roles? My answer is: "Something, but not nearly as much as in years past."

Once we have doffed our blinders and stored them carefully between our class yearbook and those 1979 W-2 forms, the signals should be detected with reasonable clarity.

On the positive side, there will always be a need for some *traditional specialists,* especially at the breakthrough points of the newer technologies. And not all of this need will be in the new tech/high tech industries. Rather, some of these specialists will help infuse high-tech *processes* into old tech/low tech companies and products. But outweighing these positive signals for specialists are the danger signs mentioned earlier in this chapter.

The future appears even more bleak for *traditional generalists.* There may be a few places for them in those few businesses which, somehow or other, remain relatively stable, slow-paced, and immune to change. Others may survive by practicing nepotism and chicanery in large corporations or by becoming important administrators in state or federal governments. Perhaps the kindest thing that may be said for these unfortunate souls is that, as they understand less and less about more and more, they will never be accused of outstanding performance.

So, with relatively few exceptions, the best long-range career role for you and me is that of the *cluster specialist*. And that's what the rest of this book is about—how to veer your career, from wherever you are, to the career role of the future.

# CHAPTER 7

# THE CLUSTER SPECIALIST

Let's get several things straight right now!

First, there is absolutely nothing illegal, immoral, or inhibiting about clusters. In fact, society seems to accept, even relish, them. (It is true that some clusters are considered more attractive than others, but that is opinion and, like beauty, is in the eye of the beholder. People will argue for their cluster preferences over yours, just as they will tout the merits of their favorite football team, personal computer, or favorite candidate for coroner.)

Second, we should understand that clusters, whether natural or of human origin, are all around us, almost everywhere. You should have no difficulty finding clusters of:

*Stars,* in the constellation Orion (or at the Polo Lounge)

*Gears,* on the power shaft of a multiaxis boring mill

*Nougats,* in candy bars and bonbons

*Flowers,* such as lilacs and bougainvillea

*Personal traits,* such as "he was mean, ornery, vicious, and wicked" (or, to observe the rules of equality, "she was wicked, vicious, ornery, and mean")

*Tents,* in base camp at 18,000 feet and with a wind chill factor of minus 90°F

*Fruits,* such as grapes or elderberries

*Bachelors,* around a millionaire's debutante daughter

These examples illustrate the dictionary's primary definition of **cluster,** which is "a number of similar things considered as a group because of their relation to each other, or grouped together in association or physical proximity."

Although some of us may be interested covertly in nougats or gears, most of us are overtly and primarily concerned about our careers. More specifically, we are deeply concerned about our career *roles* and career *paths*. So let's repeat the definition of cluster specialist:

The **cluster specialist** is the man or woman, white- or blue-collar, who works effectively, at reasonable technical depth, in a small number of technologies, crafts, or markets *having one or more unifying relationships*.

Today the chances are that your career role is either that of the *traditional specialist* or the *traditional generalist*. And by now you realize that your new career role, the cluster specialist, lies somewhere between those two more familiar roles.

The precise somewhere will be different for you than it will be for your friends; in fact, it will differ even from that of a fellow worker. This is because your cluster will be located at a very personal somewhere, determined for the most part by all those personal ingredients that make you *you*: your talents, skills, interests, desires, education, training, age, health, and geographical location. (Later, as technologies evolve and markets shift, the location and design of your cluster will also be influenced by your levels of alertness and flexibility.)

All of which is positive, because this new "you-centered" role will help display your total effectiveness and will help separate you from the crowd. To a large extent it will free you from the whims and vagaries of company policy, from the straitjacket of a union contract, and from dependency on the spurts and stops of governmental "help."

Another positive aspect of moving toward this new career role is that *you* are in charge; you decide where you want to go and how you want to get there. Although you and I will be exploring in these chapters many of your personal ingredients, you have the final responsibility for analyzing them, assessing their relative weights, assigning priorities, and staking out that "personal somewhere" that is best for you.

## FATTEN UP OR SKINNY DOWN

To begin your movement toward your ideal cluster, you must first decide where and what you are—whether your present role is too specialized or too generalized. If you believe that you are (or fear you may soon become) a traditional specialist, your need is to expand yourself, to add a few carefully selected tools to your kit. If, on the other hand, you believe that you are (or fear you may soon become) a traditional generalist, your need is to restrict yourself, to discard, selectively, most of those rusty and seldom-used items in your kit.

In your remedial actions, whether you are fattening up or skinnying down, you will be searching for and building on those *unifying relationships* that will shape and help bind the elements within your optimum cluster.

## BROAD AND DEEP,
## BUT ALSO NIMBLE

But this bond is not forever. In fact, one of the nicest characteristics of career clusters is their *plasticity*. Conditions change, and so can your cluster. You can form and reform your cluster just about any way you wish. Another way to look at this desirable characteristic is to realize that the "same you" can establish clusters in several different directions or planes. That is, you can elect to cluster by product, market, industry, geography, craft, profession, job family, discipline, and so on.

There is still another advantage in constructing a personalized career cluster. In many cases, you will be drawing more on your basic aptitudes, attitudes, and broad skills than on your accumulated (and decaying) detailed knowledge.

Now let's have some fun! Let's begin to build two *hypothetical* clusters, clusters that are not intended to be "right" for you. (You may, however, know someone for whom one of our imaginary clusters might be reasonably appropriate.)

## AUDITING PHIL

### Background

Phil, 28, is one of five supervisors of internal audit for a major oil and gas company. He earns $32,000 a year leading small teams of internal auditors in the conduct of financial audits for this nationwide corporation. He travels about 50 percent of the time and, despite the many absences from his young family, generally enjoys his work and likes his employer. He reports to the manager of financial auditing, who, in turn, reports to the chief auditor.

Phil has a bachelor's degree in accounting from a midwestern university from which he was hired by a Big Eight public accounting firm. After several weeks of indoctrination, Phil (and scores of young men and women with similar interests and educational backgrounds) were assigned as "go-fers" on relatively simple financial audits. Working under the direction of an audit supervisor, Phil would check and test the books, inventories, and accounting systems of client companies.

Three years after graduation he had progressed through senior auditor to audit supervisor, after which his career suddenly plateaued. The senior partners decided not to promote him to audit manager because they had already decided he did not have what it takes to eventually become a partner in the firm. (Translation: Nothing was wrong with Phil's work as an auditor, but he didn't appear to be good enough at sales to bring new business into the firm.)

Like most such organizations, Phil's firm had an "up or out" policy; when Phil was passed over for promotion to audit manager, he was counseled to "begin looking." The firm gave him more than adequate notice and, in typical fashion, helped place him as an internal auditor with one of its clients, Amalgamated Oil and Gas.

Phil has now been with Amalgamated for almost three years and is beginning to worry that he may become too specialized. In the seven years since his graduation, he has done almost no accounting work other than financial audits. He has not pursued an M.B.A. and has yet to pass two parts of the CPA examination. (He reasons that he has been so busy travelling and helping raise two small children that he has not paid sufficient after-hours attention to wrestling with the complex problems of taxation, business law, and general accounting.) He believes that he will be one of two candidates to replace his boss, who will retire in five years, but he isn't sure he should remain that much longer in his specialty.

## Discussion

At the moment, Phil is not very mobile because:

1. He has yet to acquire his "ticket" as a certified public accountant. This professional designation has, of course, substantive value. It also has great "face validity," serving as a door opener into many situations which would otherwise be closed.

2. He is already "tagged" as an *auditor*. Although most corporations appreciate their auditors, they aren't about to promote them to corporate controllers or treasurers.

3. His industry, oil and gas, has been depressed for several years and there are not many opportunities in competitor companies.

## Recommendation

Phil should begin to cluster by broadening his professional or job family experience, rather than by industry, market, or other type of cluster. To do this he should:

1. Accelerate his pursuit of the CPA certificate, and in that 12- to 18-month process, begin deciding which of the several major zones (clusters) of the accounting profession mesh best with his abilities and interests.

2. In the meantime, obtain a lateral transfer into Amalgamated's other branch of auditing, called *operational* or *management* audit. (Here the emphasis is not on cash, inventory, receivables, and the like. Rather, the main thrust is verifying that appropriate business policies and procedures are in place, and that management is, indeed, operating in compliance with those guidelines.)

3. Then rapidly become as proficient in operational audits as he is in financial audits.

4. Then obtain his CPA, after which he should decide whether to:

   (a) Seek promotion to a division controller position in Amalgamated

   or

   (b) Obtain another lateral transfer in Amalgamated, this time out of the finance function and into that portion of corporate administration that *writes* and *issues* the business policies and procedures that managers are to follow

   or

(c) Leave Amalgamated to become general auditor of a small oil and gas firm

or

(d) Leave Amalgamated for a broader and higher-level finance position with a company which is either a customer of or supplier to Amalgamated

or

(e) Return to public accounting, to a small, local firm as the partner in charge of operational auditing (a field largely neglected by most public accounting firms).

## MARKETING SUSAN

*Background*

Susan, 26, earns $22,500 as secretary to Sam Salamander, the vice president of marketing for Convoluted Corporation. We met Susan in Chapter 4 as she was preparing Sam's "motivational" letters; a closer look at this young woman is now in order.

Susan, after completing high school and a six-month secretarial training course, joined Convoluted in Chicago as a junior typist in the headquarters typing pool. After a year of performing the thankless, faceless, overflow work of every department, she was promoted, routinely, to junior secretary in marketing. There she progressed rapidly because her secretarial skills were good, she displayed eagerness to learn, and she did her best on every assignment. Her habit of performing "completed staff work" was noted by several Convoluted executives, including the vice president of marketing.

When Sam's secretary, Clarice, retired to the ancestral home in Crevice, Connecticut, Sam "asked the system" for Susan as the replacement. The personnel director advanced mild objections, pointing out that several longer-service secretaries should be considered. But Susan's qualifications prevailed, and she has now worked closely with Sam for about three years.

Two years ago she was selected to be the first Convoluted secretary to be trained on a word processor. She was an apt pupil, completing the vendor's poorly constructed training program several weeks ahead of schedule. (In doing so Susan detected and corrected numerous grammatical errors and several improper operational sequences in the hastily prepared user's manual.)

Susan, although moderately interested in this new technology, had been an eager student for a totally different reason. She recognized the Protean Plus for what it was, a timesaving tool. She saw it as a tool that once understood and properly applied, would free her for other, more important duties within Sam's sphere.

Gradually she became more involved, more knowledgeable in various marketing activities. She began to understand transactions which in earlier days had been mere numbers and phrases in documents she prepared for Sam. Sales engineers, shipping schedules, and customer complaints became real people and real problems. When, unexpectedly, the first shipment of P-19s developed serious vibration problems, Susan identified with the problems of the sales engineers and service reps in the field. She voluntarily canceled a long weekend skiing at Aspen to help Sam and the engineering department as they scrambled to solve the problem and soothe the irate customers.

Susan likes her work and enjoys helping (and learning from) Sam. She has now decided that despite her lack of a college degree, she wants a career—a *professional* career—in marketing.

## Discussion

At the moment, Susan appears to be relatively mobile because:

1. Her "track record" is excellent and is composed of an attractive blend of high performance, positive

attitude, and reasonably wide aptitude. This record has earned her a shot at a larger, faster-moving target.

2. She has, for the most part, gained the respect and acceptance of the district managers and headquarters marketing professionals.

3. She is part of a growing industry, and Convoluted is already challenging Involuted for market leadership (just wait until the P-21 models are introduced!).

## Recommendation

Susan, much like Phil, should also begin to cluster by broadening her experience base in relatively familiar settings. She, too, will benefit from continuing education. To do this she should:

1. Apply for a lateral transfer to a junior professional position in the headquarters marketing staff. There she will be working (alongside recent college graduates) in market research, advertising, customer service, or wherever her interests are high.

2. While there, work as enthusiastically and energetically for the director of that unit as she had worked for Sam (whose name she will wisely refrain from using in her new job).

3. Solicit the director's suggestions for courses, seminars, books, and professional societies which will help her sharpen professional skills.

4. Apply herself diligently to these after-hours investments.

5. Seek promotion to a higher-level position, working directly for another headquarters marketing director.

6. Intensify her after-hours learning efforts and investigate the pros and cons of earning a bachelor's de-

gree from an accredited university which gives some college credit for *related work experience.*

7. Discuss with her director and Sam the pros and cons of her gaining field experience—of leaving the "ivory tower" and getting into "the trenches" as:

    (a) A postinstallation service rep
    (b) A sales engineer, or
    (c) A district sales support supervisor

By this time, Phil, Susan, you, and I understand a general concept of clustering, *as it applies to Phil and Susan.* We can, therefore, extract only bits and pieces of their models for application to your real clusters (and yours are the only ones that count).

---

# BEFORE YOU CLUSTER

We have more exploring and thinking to do before we tackle that first real cluster. Let's pause for a moment while I remind you that the cluster specialist career role is not for everyone. Some men and women, perhaps you, should not make the career veer. In certain cases, it could be disadvantageous. Let's look at a few such real-life cases that I have encountered as a personnel director and as an executive recruiter.

Sheila was a specialist in executive compensation who worked for one of my subordinate managers in a large aerospace organization. She was more than competent technically, and when her detailed analysis revealed that the weighted average salary grade in engineering was 14.28, you knew it could not be 14.27 or 14.29! Sheila was *precise,* almost to the point of agony. Her need for detail was enormous, and each day her greatest fear was that she would be asked to render an approximation of something.

"Sheila, roughly how many executives, level 16 and above, received stock options last year?"

"Let me get the actual number tomorrow for you, Bill. This could be important, so . . ."

"Not really; all I want is a ballpark number. What would you estimate? Somewhere between twenty-five and thirty-five?"

"Well, if you can't wait until I can get the *right* answer tomorrow, I suppose I must pull a number out of the air: twenty-two." (The next day she would deliver, unasked, the precise number, and it would never be more than one digit above or below her grudgingly yielded "estimate.")

Sheila was a super-specialist—driven, perhaps almost compulsively, in a quest for extremes of detail and accuracy. Her narrow niche satisfied those needs, and she was so happy in her work that she declined such developmental opportunities as rotational training assignments in employee benefits, incentive compensation, and hourly wage administration. Generally speaking, the Sheilas of the business world should remain traditional specialists, satisfying their psychological needs and taking the chance that they will not be replaced by a robot named APINAC (AProximations INstantly, ACcurately).

I suspect that John, the nuclear engineer of Chapter IV, is also well suited as a traditional specialist. He seems to enjoy displaying his sub-subspecialty at cocktail parties: "I design only the *medium*-size shields for the *small* cores of . . ."

Tom is manager of advanced development for a company that produces microprocessors. (These are the tiny electronic chips that make possible the miniaturization and reliability required for satellite communications. They also are the heart of those low-cost home computers that allow elderly aunts and preschool grandchildren to extract cube roots and repel alien spaceships on the TV screen.)

Tom is a brilliant engineer with numerous patents to his credit. He is an avid reader of technical papers and seldom misses a technical symposium sponsored by one of the several professional societies in which he holds membership. Tom thus minimizes his half-life problem and enjoys being referred to as "the engineer's engineer." When he leads a small technical team on a tough problem, that problem gets solved!

But Tom himself has a problem: He does not communicate effectively with other people. Not everyone in the company speaks his jargon and fewer still grasp his scrawled equations. To complicate his communication problems, Tom speaks rapidly and tersely; he then assumes that because he has explained things, the other person should understand. Finally, he is rated a poor listener by his peers and subordinates. Some attribute this to his fast mind, always racing ahead. Others believe that he is less than interested in the opinions and questions of those people who lack his technical prowess.

Tom's communication deficiencies are tolerated (although grudgingly) in his company because of his brilliance and his expertise in technical matters. I decided, however, not to refer him to my client, and my suggestion to him was that he remain in his technical shell, becoming perhaps *even more* of a traditional specialist.

My explanation to Tom was that, as I perceive where things are headed, some outstanding traditional specialists such as he will survive in the role, *at the proper level,* despite certain personal deficiencies. I cited his poor communication skills, brought about his many years of bad listening, speaking, and writing habits, as a major barrier to success in most other types of work. I also explained that I did not believe that he would change enough—and fast enough—to succeed in the broad-gauged vice president of engineering position for which I was evaluating candidates.

Louise is market research supervisor for a major division of a pharmaceutical firm. She has many positive personal and professional attributes, but she lacks one key ingredient: *She doesn't understand people.* In fact, she doesn't even try to understand why Joe acts this way and Charles that way, or why Lucille performs as she does. Rather, Louise expects subordinates and peers to work as their job descriptions say they *should* work, and if they don't . . . !

Louise is obviously inadequate as a supervisor of workers and shows little aptitude for becoming a cluster specialist. She is better equipped to function as a traditional specialist, perhaps at a rather high level, in a major corporation. Needless to say, I could not consider this bright young woman for an executive marketing position where the primary requirement was the ability to integrate individual effort into team effort.

As for traditional generalists who should remain such, there is Bob, the only attorney in a $75 million corporation that processes and distributes frozen snack foods. His father had been successful as a small-town, general-practice lawyer, and Bob finds it repugnant to think of himself as less of an all-around attorney than Dad had been.

Bob is reasonably bright, industrious, and generally speaking, adequate as a lawyer *in his setting*. His company is very stable, its legal problems are few and relatively straightforward, and he knows how to use the internal support systems available to him. Above all, Bob is a realist; he understands himself and his situation very well. As a result, he has backed away from several invitations to move into higher-paying legal positions with larger corporations. He realizes that in those faster-paced, higher-pressure situations he would probably fail unless he narrowed his professional scope, an adjustment that he knows he cannot bring himself to attempt.

Assuming that you are not *too* much like a Sheila, John, Tom, Louise, or Bob, you are probably a good prospect to become a cluster specialist. And there are persuasive reasons why you should move toward this career role of the future:

- You have already seen how this new role minimizes the obsolescence and half-life problems of the traditional specialist. True, as a cluster specialist you may have to scurry at times to keep up, and you must always be alert for the signals of impending change. But you will not be living in fear of the consequences of knowing more and more about less and less.

- Conversely, you will not be saddled with the survival problems of the traditional generalist. (Imagine Bob's predicament if a new CEO should decide to reduce costs by eliminating Bob's job and using outside counsel when needed.) By concentrating on fewer zones of expertise, you will not be living in fear of the consequences of knowing less and less about more and more.

But these are negative or "security" reasons; they tell only why you should be glad to leave behind the dangers of the old roles. More important are the positive reasons for becoming a cluster specialist. As I see this role, there are several:

- The new role provides the opportunity to satisfy a basic need that most of us feel: for variety in the work we do. The chairman of ITT would quit in a huff if he were required to do the *same* things day after day after day. ITT's newest junior secretary might not quit precipitously if she found her duties to be equally repetitious, but we can be reasonably certain that she would be interviewing other companies on her lunch hour.

- A related need for most of us is to apply our brainpower, aptitudes, and attitudes, rather than repetitive know-how, to our work. Many of our nation's thorniest management/labor relations problems stem, directly and indirectly, from the way shop work has been chopped up and compartmentalized by industrial engineers and union negotiators. And the same might happen in the "new office" if management fails to read its own history books and take preventive steps. But even assuming such mismanagement in the future office, the cluster specialist will be best equipped to tackle those portions of the work requiring broad skills, imaginative approaches, and sound decisions.

• The cluster specialist, being alert for the early signals of change, will be in the best position to decide when and how to modify his or her cluster—in other words, to change, and thus take advantage of brand-new career opportunities.

• The cluster specialist will be highly regarded and handsomely rewarded in the new order, mainly because he or she can be applied to a variety of related situations. (The value of this "utility factor" was demonstrated in numerous industries during the recent recession. Cluster specialists were kept on the payroll at the same time that thousands of traditional specialists and traditional generalists were being laid off.)

Finally, from management's perspective, there is an additional reason for favoring the cluster specialist: *cost reduction*. In the years ahead, worldwide competition will intensify as more and more nations become efficient suppliers of goods and services. Management will, of necessity, become increasingly conscious of *total* payroll costs and will try to apply tighter cost controls to employee benefit plans. (On the average, these official and unofficial plans account for about *40 percent* of a corporation's total payroll costs.) But the benefits are prized by employees, especially when they have some say in the "mix and match" of their individual benefit packages. Employers, realizing that they have little hope of withdrawing benefit plans and only an outside chance of putting a permanent cap on their costs, will opt for *hiring fewer employees*.

This decision will, in turn, cause management to hire

those employees who are broad enough and deep enough to handle several sets of responsibilities—cluster specialists.

For example, let's say that *two* cluster specialists can effectively take the place of *three* traditional specialists or traditional generalists—a reasonable assumption. The arithmetic is quite revealing.

Assume that each of the three "traditionals" earns a salary of $40,000 and costs the employer an additional $16,000 per year in benefit plans. Each then represents a total payroll cost of $56,000, and the sum total payroll cost for all three amounts to $168,000 a year.

Other considerations being relatively equal, the employer is substantially better off by acquiring *two* cluster specialists and paying each of them a higher salary, say $50,000. To this salary would be added $20,000 in benefit plan costs, making each cluster specialist represent a total annual payroll cost of $70,000. By hiring two cluster specialists at a total annual payroll cost of $140,000, management will spend $28,000 (or about 16 percent) *less* than it would spend for the three "traditionals." This 16 percent savings *could* provide the competitive edge and make the difference in whether or not this company can underbid a competitor. Further, if it wins the bid, the presence of the two cluster specialists *could* enhance the caliber of the work performed on that contract. An additional advantage to the employer is that the two cluster specialists will, over time, prove to be more flexible, more adaptable than the three other employees. They will be more capable of anticipating (and adapting to) the firm's changing requirements and thus be more valuable to the firm.

# TODAY'S CLUSTERS

The career role of the future is, in part, already with us and on each of the five basic career paths. A surprising number of men and women are (whether they know it or not) playing the role or are at least playing at it. Let's look at a few examples on each career path.

## Worker

In the factory we can identify the master mechanic (or master maintenance technician). This person is capable of troubleshooting and performing all *mechanical* work required in the installation and adjustment of factory equipment. An emerging counterpart is the master electronic technician, responsible for all electrical, electronic, and instrumentation work on that same equipment.

In the office we find the lead (or utility) word processing operator. This person is proficient in the operation of all the different keyboards and terminals. He or she also understands enough of the software and data links to make sure that they "talk" to each other (almost as promised in the brochures!). In many cases this person also serves as the firm's main contact with hardware and software vendors and maintenance technicians.

In the field sales force we have the senior sales engineer. This person began clustering as the territory began to shrink. He or she has broadened the product base considerably, now representing the company effectively on all three of its hydraulic product lines.

## Supervisor of Workers

In the shop is the maintenance supervisor, who directs skilled workers such as millwrights, pipe fitters, welders, plumbers, and air conditioning mechanics. This person has usually worked in two or three of these crafts and unlike Jimmy at the Serendipity agency, knows how to detect the real problem quickly. This supervisor knows how to assign the needed work to the right workers and how to bridge the gaps between them to make sure that the total job is done properly.

Near the shop is the purchasing supervisor, who is responsible, through eight purchasing agents and clerks, for buying all products for a division that produces computers.

This supervisor still makes purchases, but only in three related product clusters: power supplies, line noise regulators, and inverters/converters.

In the office is the marketing supervisor, who is the working leader of staff professionals and workers in such interrelated activities as market research, market analysis, and market planning, or of advertising, trade shows, and sales promotion.

In the field (or on the department store floor) is the sales supervisor, an accomplished selector and trainer of sales personnel. This man or woman also knows enough about a given cluster of related products (electric motors or ladies' sport clothing) to take over and make the critical sale when that is the thing to do.

## Staff Professional

The project engineer is, in many instances, a cluster specialist. This person is responsible for all aspects of the development of a critical product or system, marshaling ideas and resources and guiding the product from conception through prototype and into production. In so doing, he or she interacts with employees in all functions and at all levels in the organization.

In the personnel function is the person who, although effective as a labor attorney, is also active and adept in a cluster of quasi-legal activities: union contract negotiations planning and conduct, arbitration proceedings, compliance matters, and union representation campaigns.

In the health care field are the doctor and nurse in the hospital emergency room. These front-line practitioners are broad enough to apply effective first and "second" aid in life-threatening situations and to patients in pain. They are also deep enough in their clusters to understand the potential interrelationships of the various injuries, ailments, and symptoms. They are committed to staying on top of the latest emergency care techniques and refer only special cases to be treated immediately by a super-specialist physician.

## Manager of Resources

Clustering here is the general manager of a division or company whose same products (personal computers, for example) are sold in radically different markets, such as in company-owned stores, to competitor discount houses, and to a foreign government. Another clustering general manager could be producing and selling diverse products (oscilloscopes, infrared cameras, and telephone scramblers), but to a single customer—the Department of Defense.

Another cluster specialist is the managing partner of a medium-sized law firm. In addition to maintaining a partial personal practice in two related clusters (personal liability and criminal), this person also directs and blends the firm's total resources, including the administrative systems that support all attorneys in the firm.

## Entrepreneur

One entrepreneurial cluster specialist is the woman who provides three related cleaning services (rugs, drapes, and windows) for two distinct markets: small businesses and elegant residences.

Another is the manufacturer's representative who, as an agent of five companies, calls on purchasing agents and chief engineers in 100 California electronics firms. Although his five companies produce some 250 products in fifteen product lines, he restricts himself to twenty-four products in four related clusters: wiring harnesses and cables, connectors, potting compounds, and circuit test instruments.

Still another is the former factory worker whose welding, brazing, assembly, and repair skills are now applied to his own small business. This entrepreneur began by expanding the hobby corner of his garage. One year later he had converted his recreational van into a mobile workshop and had deserted his garage for a small shop across town. He avoids all electrical/electronic work but provides a broad base of mechanical "fix it" services to households and small businesses. He also works as a subcontractor to his former employer and to several machine shops, responding rapidly to their "rush" needs for custom welding or brazing on small production lots. This ex-union steward is now negotiating to become the local authorized repair shop for a new brand of lawn mowers and snow blowers.

# MORE CLUSTERS—
## AND *DIFFERENT* CLUSTERS—
## WILL BE NEEDED
## IN THE FUTURE

Each of these activities probably contains several near-future clusters:

- Designing machine-controlled machines
- Helping interpersonal communication
- Understanding and explaining human behavior
- Teaching language skills
- Counseling and training/retraining
- Caring for patients, medically and psychologically
- Gathering and processing self-help information
- Performing in the arts
- Family consulting in financial matters
- Family consulting in legal matters
- Providing integrated services to homes and small businesses
- Planning for the aging
- Caring for the aged, the dying
- Engineering, processing, and marketing genetic improvements
- Introducing and facilitating change

Perhaps the most exciting thought about this list of future activities suitable for clustering is that it is only the beginning. No one knows for sure when (or even if) a particular activity will emerge and begin to flourish. But even a superficial scan of the forces of change—technological, social, political, and economic—assures us that you and I will have more than enough attractive clusters from which to choose. And we must make those choices, or other people will make them for us.

I cannot tell you what to do, but I can tell you what tomorrow's successful career builders will do *today*:

These men and women will welcome these choices, viewing them not as problems to avoid, but as *opportunities to grasp*.

# Chapter 8

# ORGANIZATIONAL CULTURE: FIT THE MODE OR HIT THE ROAD

Most Americans shy away from the term **culture**. For them it is a highfalutin' word that smacks of high society, pink tutus, and statues with fig leaves and no arms. It suggests to them the enjoyment (genuine or pretended) of things not in the mainstream of American values.

This Everyman stance may have ancient roots, embedded in colonial pride, Yankee ingenuity, and our young republic's aversion to foreign tastes and entanglements. Or there may be merit in the theory that cultural values stem entirely from our environment—that we obtain (or do not obtain) an appreciation of high culture in our formative years at home, in school, and through associations with influential peers. (This theory leaves one with the distressing thought that most of us have chosen the wrong parents, schools, and companions.)

Still another argument has it that heredity is the real agent at work—that different mentalities and intellectual capacities account for these differences in cultural values. (This theory is disturbing also; it says that there aren't very many of us bright people!)

For whatever reason or reasons, most Americans have yet to display much enthusiasm for Italian opera, Chi-

131

nese pottery, Russian ballet, Japanese poetry, English drama, French painting, or Greek sculpture. Instead, the general attraction seems to be toward rock and country/ western sounds, space-war films, spectator sports, situation comedies, and TV commercials which instill an appreciation of the pleasures to be derived from the use of certain beverages, vehicles, and detergents. Wagnerian opera ranks a distant third to our domestic varieties (horse and soap), and ballet slippers and arabesques are not about to supplant the cleats and downfield patterns of Monday night football.

The point here is not that in the United States high culture is good and pop culture bad, or vice versa. Rather, the purpose is to accent the obvious—that different people choose different ways to express themselves in their pursuit of leisure.

And so do corporations in their pursuit of earnings and other critical goals. Each corporation, just as each nation, has (or claims to have) its own distinct set of basic beliefs, values, and ongoing missions. These ways of thinking about things—these shared beliefs, these ways of doing things— form a *pattern of culture* in each corporation. In fact, my dictionary defines culture as "the integrated pattern of human behavior that includes thoughts, speech, action and artifacts and depends on man's capacity for learning and transmitting knowledge to succeeding generations."

The established pattern at Procter & Gamble, for example, includes intense internal competition (especially among brand managers), aggressive marketing (based on the importance of the consumer), and a strong pro-employee orientation in its personnel practices and benefits plans. And the P & G culture is both strong and pervasive. Alumni meet periodically to renew contact with each other—men and women who, no matter for whom they now work, still adhere to many of the beliefs they shared while at "Ivorydale."

At Caterpillar Tractor the emphasis, year after year, has been on product reliability, customer service, and fair-and-square dealings with its dealers and distributors. In each of these "zones of emphasis," Caterpillar has generally taken the long-range view. It has resisted the temptation to cut corners, squeeze research and development, or otherwise mortgage the future just to look better on today's quarterly or annual report.

How do other corporations describe and explain themselves to their various publics? The following statements were pulled at random from my file of annual reports, proxy statements, and other corporate literature:

*Abbott Laboratories:* "The factors to be considered in assessing the strengths of a company are many: return on investment . . . skilled and prudent management . . . corporate integrity . . . diversity of markets . . . productivity of its people . . . high technology . . . aggressive development of promising new products, and innovative new uses for older ones . . . and many others. If we were to name the one outstanding strength of Abbott, it would be the 96-year-old organization itself, proud of its past and poised to pursue a vigorous future."

*The Pillsbury Company:* "The Pillsbury Company of today has been built with care and dedication over 112 years. We take pride in our heritage and commitment to being the 'BEST' in all that we do. Pillsbury has always been equated with quality . . . since the days of baking from scratch to the frozen convenience foods of today. . . . Pillsbury has grown over the years by meeting genuine consumer needs for new, convenient and high-quality food products. Our advertising and basic business philosophy will continue to be guided by these same attributes. . . . After all, the appeal of quality products which represent fair value, quality and convenience never becomes old-fashioned."

*Avco Corporation:* "For half a century, Avco has been a company on the frontier. . . . Today, Avco's operations span four continents. Its products and services are available worldwide. It is a diversified company whose structure promotes adaptability and strength in a world of change. . . . It is a company that welcomes challenge and change, a company whose diverse skills and financial strength create a corporate climate where customers are served well because people are stimulated to perform well. Avco, today a 50-year-old company, is still probing the frontier.''

*L. L. Bean:* ''We believe in the quality and value of our products and we won't sell anything we wouldn't use ourselves. We also believe, as 'L. L.' did, that each customer is a real person to be treated with the same respect and personal consideration as we ourselves would like to be treated.''

*Sperry Corporation:* ''Our investment decisions always need to balance long-term interests against short-term gains. I know that if circumstances arise, you'll understand just how important investment is to high technology and to Sperry's growth and position in the markets that we serve. We must take the long view because it's essential to prepare properly for the future.''

*National Education Corporation:* ''More important, National Education brings to its programs a dedication to quality which is the key reason why more than 90 percent of its graduates are ultimately employed using the skills in which they were trained.''

*INA Health Care Group, Inc.:* ''Change is everywhere. And it is on the skilled management of that change, particularly in the areas of applying business diagnostics to the quality of the world's health care, that the INA Health Care Group is focused.''

*Hilton Hotels Corporation:* ''The success of a large corporation depends on the skillful application of several distinct business disciplines. Marketing is among the more important of these disciplines.''

*Shaklee Corporation:* "Shaklee is recognized not only as one of the world's leading nutritional products companies, but also as the provider of an outstanding business opportunity for enterprise-minded individuals as well. America is today in the process of reinvigorating the spirit of hard work and free enterprise. We at Shaklee are proud to participate in this renewal by combining products meeting today's needs with business opportunities in the entrepreneurial tradition that is the cornerstone of the American economy."

*Minnesota Mining & Manufacturing Corporation:* "Hearing you is our business at 3M. We listen to people like you in a wide variety of fields and industries. We understand people's problems, their needs, their questions, their ideas and their challenges. By listening and understanding, 3M can respond to your needs and sound out new ideas, new products. That's how we were able to develop all the products you see in this brochure. Each one was designed to solve problems, fill needs, and save time and money."

*Tymshare, Inc.:* "As we redirect the efforts of this company—both in R&D and in marketing—this means a fair amount of retraining, reorientation of people—in new marketing approaches, certainly in new sales strategies and techniques. Tymshare management, all down the line, will be expected to show increasing flexibility, expand their ability to adjust and to cope with a new set of circumstances, a new set of parameters." (Note: Tymshare has subsequently been acquired by McDonnell Douglas.)

*Consolidated Foods Corporation:* "Consolidated Foods is guided by a set of principles that defines the corporation's view of itself and describes the values it embraces. Together with our financial goals, these principles characterize us a corporation.

1. To build our business on demonstrably better products or services than those offered by our competition.

2. To achieve leadership positions in each principal product or geographic area in which we compete

3. To ensure that our corporation and each of its operating companies has in place a management group superior to our competition

4. To manage ourselves as a decentralized operating company

5. To dedicate ourselves to consistent improvement in the productivity and efficiency of our business

6. To search always for better ways to manage our company

7. To deal with integrity, fairness and responsibility toward all our constituencies. . . .

The seven operating principles stated above are an expression of our commitment to excellence. Success in meeting these standards enables Consolidated Foods to strengthen its position as a welcome and productive member of the many communities in which it operates."

*Merrill Lynch & Co., Inc.:* "Our leadership has been and will be based on creatively and efficiently meeting the needs of our customers—individuals, corporations, institutional investors and governments—with professional excellence and integrity. . . . Whatever direction the financial services industry may take, Merrill Lynch will be in front. We will anticipate and guide this change, not just react to it. We will shape our own destiny."

Each statement is (or purports to be) a key element in that company's **corporate culture**. Of course, no company applies its basic beliefs and values day in and day out with total consistency, but the better and more successful ones generally practice what they preach. Although that practice may not make for perfection, it does form the groove for subsequent corporate decisions and actions, and thus reinforces that culture.

Even a company which usually shouts one thing as it does another has its own culture. That company becomes known, within and beyond its four walls, for what it *does* rather than for what it says it does.

Organizations other than nations and business entities also have their own cultures, of course. Each church, school, professional society, trade association, labor union, lodge, sorority, and family unit has at least several of its own characteristics. Each organization takes some degree of pride in those ingrained value structures which set it apart from other, perhaps competitive, organizations. It draws satisfaction from these peculiarities and flaunts one or two to bolster its claim of being unique—that it is different from the Holy Rollers, Yale, Illinois Nurses Association, Communication Workers, Loyal Order of Moose, Junior League, or the MacQueen clan.

And we understand those distinctions. We don't expect the Elks to mirror the Shriners, or Purdue to resemble Slippery Rock. We seem to realize that the basic values inculcated over the years in the Kaplan family will not be the same as those of the Lombardi family.

Yet all too many of us take a surprisingly simplistic view of business organizations, even when we are considering one of them as a potential employer! We tend to reject or embrace it, in debonair manner, for such reasons as:

- "But it's such a long commute, and . . ."
- "They have a super vacation plan . . ."
- "But they make you wear those silly badges, and . . ."
- "They sponsor a lot of athletic activities, and . . ."

- "But they don't want a union there, so . . ."
- "Their offices are near that new shopping mall, and . . ."

At a slightly higher level of thought are those many generalizations often applied to the business world. For example, we may consider all big businesses to be either

*Good,* because they are well established, have vast resources, and provide security

or

*Bad,* because they are bureaucratic, impersonal, and greedy for sales and profits

Conversely, we may view all small businesses as either

*Good,* because the climate is informal and friendly, and team spirit prevails

or

*Bad,* because the benefit plans are thin, the systems and equipment inadequate, and promotional opportunities limited

In similar manner we often grade companies by level of technology. It is common to regard high-technology firms as either

*Good,* because that's where the action is and will be, the work is exciting, and the industry is recession-proof

or

*Bad,* because everything changes every day, the competition is fierce, and there are so many weird scientists and engineers

On the other hand, we may think of low-technology firms as either

*Good,* because most things are predictable, and there is a lot of interaction among employees

or

*Bad,* because the work is boring, the company is always pleading poverty, and the aging work force lacks modern skills

At a still higher level of thought process we become aware of corporate **culture clashes**. These occur in several different forms. The first form is noisy; it consists of internal dissonances—the grindings and clashings that indicate that one division of a major corporation is thinking and acting differently from other divisions. It may even be straying beyond the corporate landmarks. This type of culture clash occurs most often when a mature corporation such as Exxon, a world leader in the petroleum industry, diversifies into a totally new market, such as sophisticated office products.

Others occur as a result of mergers and acquisitions. Consider the cultural implications when:

- ITT, an aggressive, "manage-by-the-numbers" conglomerate, acquires Howard K. Sams, a well-established but relatively docile publishing firm.
- Quaker Oats obtains Fisher-Price Toys.
- Sears, Roebuck broadens its financial services by purchasing Coldwell Banker, H&R Block, and Dean Witter Reynolds Inc.
- Twentieth Century–Fox takes over a Colorado ski resort.
- One giant, diversified corporation (Esmark, with large divisions such as Playtex and Swift Foods) merges with an even larger conglomerate (Norton Simon, best known for its Avis and Max Factor operations). Then Beatrice Foods buys all!

- Kennecott Copper acquires Carborundum Corporation (a leading abrasives producer) only to be acquired, in turn, by Standard Oil of Ohio (in which the British Petroleum Company holds a 53 percent interest).

The history of American business is chock-full of such situations, each with its own potential for culture clash. Let's look in detail at another type of danger-laden venture—when a conservative major corporation decides to diversify internally. It then relies on its research and development prowess, its financial strengths, and its management talent to ensure the successful entry into totally new technologies and markets. The case in point is GE's thirteen-year effort to become a force in the computer industry.

General Electric Company's computer business, struggling since its inception in 1957, was finally sold to Honeywell in 1970. GE was, and is, one of the world's best managed and most respected corporations. It had, and has, an enviable record of developing new products and gaining a strong position in those markets it serves. Yet it took this planning-oriented, blue-chip corporation some thirteen years and several hundred million diverted dollars to realize that it shouldn't be in the computer business, at least at that time.

That frantic Soaring Sixties computer market (mostly large, general-purpose mainframes and peripherals) was dominated by International Business Machines. IBM was *the* industry leader in pricing, terms, new product introduction, field service, and other critical factors. Its market penetration was awesome, generally estimated at about 80 percent of total industry revenues. GE, Univac, Honeywell, Burroughs, Control Data, RCA, and NCR scrambled, gouged, and clamored for about 15 percent of this market. This frenzied fandango was dubbed "Snow White and the Seven Dwarfs"—very funny unless you happened to be working for one of those dwarfs! The term was even more gruesome for those people struggling in the eleven "midgets"—small companies that pummeled each other as they squabbled over the remaining 5 percent.

As personnel director for GE's computer business between 1963 and 1967, I observed managers at all levels chafing under corporate constraints, real and imagined. They argued that their catch-up efforts were being hampered at every turn by corporate policies and procedures designed years ago for GE's old-line businesses. Their complaints, often justified, were many and diverse:

- "How can I hire good sales personnel (or engineers, or product repair supervisors, or district managers) when I can't pay a competitive salary and bonus? When I was at Univac . . ."
- "NRC makes decisions rapidly, but it takes us forever to get approval for . . ."
- "But he's already a vice president where he is, and we can't even give him a director's title for the same job at GE!"
- "He wants to join the GE team, but he will have trouble selling his house in Dallas. IBM would buy that house instantly, and move him and his family *now*."
- "RCA has a highly sophisticated training center at Cherry Hill, New Jersey, where . . ."
- "But he heads up our entire software development effort. Why can't he have a company-paid club membership? For that matter, why can't I?"
- "His position at Burroughs entitled him to a company car, but here . . ."
- "We can't keep our best designers because the incentive compensation plan excludes them. It also excludes their managers, and often *their* managers."

One of my responsibilities was to investigate these contentions and evaluate them within the context of GE's total

compensation and benefits package (or training opportunities, or relocation policy) and compare that total package
with that of our competition. Often I found the complaints
to be exaggerations or to be based on inaccurate data. But
sometimes the protesters were correct. They *were* being
burdened by plans and procedures not in keeping with the
computer industry. So in some of the cases, decisions were
made and remedies applied right within the computer division.

But other changes involved bigger issues, *policy issues,*
and these usually required a two-pronged approach to corporate headquarters. My boss, the division president,
would try to obtain the approval of his superiors, the group
and sector vice presidents. At the same time, I would be
explaining the peculiarities of our problem to GE's corporate vice president of employee relations and beseeching
his assistance. Sometimes corporate policy was bent a bit
to accommodate the division's needs. Sometimes it was
not.

GE's abandonment of its computer businesses embar-
rassed and demoralized most of the division's 4000 hardworking managers and professionals. This is not to say that
the sole cause of the costly failure was that corporate executives, reared in the appliance, turbine, lamp, or motor
businesses, were not willing to consider the unusual characteristics of the exciting new world of computers. Five or
six equally strong reasons could be cited, none of which is
important to our line of exploration.

But "culture clash" *was* there, and all over the place.
Many highly motivated people (including this writer) did
not detect it before joining the division. Talented people
deserted competitive computer companies because they believed GE's innovative concepts, image, and vast resources
would eventually prevail in that marketplace. So did those
talented men and women who transferred from other GE
divisions. None of us seriously believed that GE would
overtake IBM in the twentieth century. But most of us
believed that if we worked hard enough and smart enough,

the computer industry could soon become "Snow White, Prince Charming, and the Six Dwarfs."

By now you may be wary of casting your career lot with a new tech/high tech arm of a major corporation. Perhaps you should, perhaps not. But before deciding that issue, there are other forms of culture clash of which you should be aware. These, too, must be detected, assessed and dealt with.

One form, fortunately rare, occurs when the fundamental beliefs of a corporation (or small partnership, for that matter) run counter to the tenets of an employee's professional society and thus his or her ethical code. The company may believe that it is perfectly acceptable to confuse the customer, ignore the public, conspire with competitors, mislead the union, doctor the books, hide the facts, turn out unreliable products, strew toxic waste, and otherwise bend the law—as long as it doesn't get caught. The attorney, the accountant, the professional engineer, the physician employed by this company are each confronted, day after day, with ethical problems to resolve. Many of these puzzlers are in a "gray zone" where the most ethical of experts could differ as to the legality or morality of a certain act. Other issues are clearly beyond the letter and intent of the law, or are in violation of the profession's ethical code. And there's the rub! These professional employees, as well as the company's outside counsel and external auditors, must decide whether to cling to their professional obligations or to their continuity of service.

Other forms of culture clash are more personal in dimension; few, if any, professional overtones may contribute to the discord. Generally, men and women are able to avoid the necessity of earning their livelihood from an employer whose products, services, or practices conflict with their religion, moral code, or self-image. These conflicts, very personal in nature, could involve contraceptives, liquor, tobacco, gambling, pornography, nuclear weapons, garbage collection, or used cars.

There are still other forms and examples. These are not

so obvious, but once detected, they deserve your careful assessment, and this will not be easy. You will be assessing not only the organization that you may join, but also *you* and how *you and the organization* will react to each other.

Which leads us to the first cardinal rule of cultural cognizance: **Do the best you can to understand yourself**.

This is probably important in every aspect of your life. It certainly is critical for two reasons which concern us in this book:

1. You will be with yourself for the rest of your career, your life. The organization may disintegrate, may excommunicate you, or may move to Morristown. Or you may leave it as you proceed on your career.

2. The better you understand yourself, the better the decisions you will make about your career role and career path.

But how does one get to really know oneself? Is it possible to bypass all those internal filters that nature and society have inserted, those filters that caused Robert Burns to observe that the greatest gift of all is to be able to see ourselves as others see us?

But even the poet may have oversimplified things a bit. Different "others", a proud parent, an exasperated teacher, a jealous spouse, a petulant offspring, might see the same person quite differently. Indeed, the eye of each beholder has its own set of filters and prisms!

This business of getting inside yourself, of learning how to learn the *real* you, is one of life's most engrossing puzzles. Thousands of books and technical papers have been churned out on the subject of the **U factor**. Supermarkets display magazines which often contain ten-minute, do-it-yourself tests that purport to do the job for you. These magazines may be identified by their dignified headlines—

Flatten That Tummy by Next Tuesday!

TV Execs Nabbed in Malibu Raid!
Researchers Prove Cat Serum Cleans Toxic Waste!
New Miracle Pill Cures Migraines and Scabies!

Failing (or failing to take) the do-it-yourself test, you may wish to seek other sources. Experts abound: psychiatrists, psychologists, marriage counselors, social workers, and encounter-group facilitators. These people have one primary professional objective: to help you in your search for the basic you. How well they do this seems to vary from one practitioner to another and from one seeker to another.

I can't show you the real you, nor can I point out the path that will lead you to knowledge of self. But I have caused you to think about it for several pages, and I may have stimulated you to continue doing so. You now recognize that if you're serious about planning your career, *you* are responsible for the U factor in the planning process.

But there's no need to become morbid about this! As important as the U factor is, there is also the **O²P factor,** and I can help you quite a bit with that. It consists of the "organizations and other people," business entities that you may join and the people that populate and flavor them. So let's think about them, and their cultures, for a while.

Earlier in this chapter we talked about corporate cultures: how they differ from one corporation to another and from one division to another in the same corporation. Those differences are important to those organizations; they are even more important to you. Not everyone can work successfully in the IBM corporate culture, and not every successful IBM-er could work well within the "Mom and Pop" confines of the Colorado Computer Clinic, even if they were selling IBM Personal Computers.

Which leads us to the second cardinal rule of cultural cognizance: **Some cultures are for you, others are not**.

For many years, General Electric Company believed that "a manager is a manager is a manager"—that a person skilled in the techniques of professional management could manage well in any setting. Such people could move with little difficulty from one division to another, from a mature business to one just beginning to flex its entrepreneurial muscles, or from a high-production consumer goods group of businesses to one whose low-volume capital goods were sold to public utilities. Of course, such transferring managers were expected to become genuinely interested in their new associates and to begin learning the new business. Beyond that they needed only to apply the principals of *professional management.* In particular they would plan, organize, integrate, and measure the efforts of subordinate managers. Leading by persuasion, they would manage the work to be done.

These concepts were not only encouraged by executive management but were drilled into us daily at GE's ten-week Advanced Management Course at Crotonville, New York. Generally, these principles were and are sound. The techniques of applying them have been refined by GE and other organizations that consider the practice of management to be somewhat of a profession rather than black magic, blind obedience to "the book," or dominance based on technical superiority.

The problem with the theory in the case of GE was that the company underestimated the difficulty of transporting practices effectively from one subculture to another. In their zeal to promote the idea of the *professional manager,* people at the corporate office, especially, assumed that what worked well in the television receiver business would meet with similar success in the eerie world of nuclear reactors. Not many decision makers were persuaded that the kinds of managerial traits and skills essential to success in a mature, steady-state, profitable business differ substantively from those in a brash, entrepreneurial, negative-cash-flow venture—or from those critical to the successful winding down and divestiture of an effete business entity whose glory days are but dim memories unlikely to return.

General Electric still transfers high-potential managers from one part of that immense corporation to another, of course. But the level of this internal traffic is much lower these days, and those men and women in transit approach their destinations with a more realistic view of the potholes and pitfalls that may lie ahead. Today one seldom hears the buzz of the old GE saw:

"Plan your move, move your plan, and keep your clothes in a moving van!"

During my seven years as corporate director of salaried personnel and communications for Rockwell International (and an antecedent company, North American Aviation), there were relatively few interdivisional managerial moves. Generally, if you started in an airplane division (or rocket engine, truck axle, printing press, or electronics division), you stayed there.

The guiding principle was that your effectiveness was linked closely with a particular discipline, technology, product line, or customer:

- "Rogers could be very effective, technically, as program manager on the QT-3. But that's a NASA program, and all his strong customer contacts are Navy."
- "Jones did a great job of reducing costs on the web press line, and he probably deserves a shot at running his own plant. But Thompson is also promotable, and he understands the axle business."
- "But this entire division consists of very complex electronics systems. Smith may be a talented manager, but he's a chemical engineer, accustomed to directing rocket engine projects."

In recent years, however, Rockwell has improved and intensified its program of identifying high-potential managers. Developmental assignments for these men and women are meshed, at the corporate level, with the needs of Rockwell's various businesses, a program that necessitates a reasonable number of cross-company moves.

So over the years, and coming from almost diametri-
cally opposite positions, these two large corporations have
moved toward the middle zone of managerial mobility.
Each works diligently in its efforts to link strategic business
planning with human resources planning. Each recognizes
the importance of the cultural peculiarities that exist in the
various divisions, and that recognition causes them to evaluate each proposed transfer carefully. As a result, they
transfer only those managers whom they consider attuned,
or readily attunable, to the culture of the organization involved. Should *you* be less concerned with cultural compat-
ibility?

The reason for pondering that question may best be explained by the third cardinal rule of cultural cognizance:
**You won't change the organization, but it may change you**.

One of my firm's clients is the chief executive officer of
a thriving organization that is largely his own creation. On
each executive search assignment he goes out of his way to
specify requirements in the candidate profile, such as "cre-
ativity, imagination, innovative processes, and a knack for
off-beat solutions." Only after serving up several men and
women with these characteristics on several assignments
did I realize that my client was merely verbalizing textbook
platitudes. I think he believes, at the casual conversation
level, that he really wants those traits in the additions to his
management team. But deep down, he does *not* want
change, other than superficial departures from the culture
he has nourished so carefully.

We may well take issue with his split images and mis-
leading specifications. But he is probably correct, at least
most of the time, in hiring only those executives who will
mesh with the beliefs, values, and policies—the culture of
that successful company. The culture there is strong, and
its strength has, over the years, sustained and enhanced the
company's overall performance. *Substantive* change (not
to be confused with ongoing, incremental improvements in
product, process, distribution, and service) is probably not
called for at this stage of the company's life cycle.

Nor is it likely to occur, not even if this CEO were to hire a competent executive whose value system differed markedly from that of the organization. Even then, the odds would be against fundamental change because the establishment's way of looking at things—its cultural pattern—is shared widely and deeply throughout the organization. The CEO established the pattern and nurtured it during the organization's critical and formative years. The key players understand that despite what the CEO *says,* he prefers the status quo. Further, all employees are aware that the culture helped make their company successful. They *like* their culture, and may continue to do so long after they should have implemented a change here and there.

When change comes knocking at the door in the form of a competent "outside" executive, a group may well decide to pay lip service to the rash of new ideas, new approaches, new ways of doing things. It might even bend, with mock resistance, on a few matters of little import to its real workings. But once its ganglia detect the threat of basic change, the immune system begins planning the counterattack. In a number of ways, the invader will be harassed: first deceived, then outflanked, then deflected. Finally, surrounded and immobilized, the foreign body will be expelled.

This resistance movement often produces an unexpected side effect. The organization's informal leaders put aside any petty differences they may have and display selfless loyalty for "the common good," thus reinforcing the culture.

The recently hired, recently de-hired executive then begins his reentry into the job market. Although severance pay of several months' salary may partially cushion his tumble from that executive suite, he complains bitterly to long-time friends and other members of his network:

- "You won't believe this, Charlie, but they are still using the old Strudel system for inventory assumption. I tried to convert them to Brudel, but . . ."

- "One of the first things I called to their attention, Peggy, was their antiquated distribution system. They agreed to my suggestions on warehousing and inventory control, but they never *did* anything about them!"
- "Their bonus plan was all out of whack, Bob, so I wanted to bring in a compensation consultant, but . . ."

The problem here is not just that bad ideas might have been thrust upon a good organization or that a bad organization might have been blindly resisting good ideas. There are at least three identifiable tragedies in this example:

*The executive* left a company in which he was successful and well regarded for a new environment which, for one reason or another, was antithetical to his culture. His hasty departure from the second company will be something of a smudge on his track record, although not necessarily dark enough to prevent his regaining career direction and momentum. Eyebrows will be raised, jokes and rumors circulated, and questions asked. The most important of these will be: "What have you learned from that experience?"

*The organization* squandered many precious dollars—"hard" and "soft" dollars—in this ill-fated mating dance. The hard dollars include the executive's salary, his family relocation expenses, the press parties that trumpeted his arrival, and the severance settlement that quietly lubricated his departure. Even greater is the organization's loss in soft dollars. This includes the hidden costs of all those meetings and memos, the clandestine conversations and conspiracies—in short, all the time and effort diverted from productive work while the organization was watching, appraising, scheming, and rejecting. The presi-

dent and the board of directors may ask the important question: "What have we learned from this
experience?"

*The executive search firm* also suffered in this three-ring
circus of blunders. Its reputation has been damaged
(probably rightly so), and it was obligated to replace
that executive at no new expense to the company.
The recruiter and his partners may ask the important
question: "What have we learned from this experience?"

Beyond these three identifiable losses, I believe, lurk
other potential losses—future losses for each of the three
parties—because they may have learned nothing of substance from the experience.

*The executive* may join another company with all five of
his senses still slumbering. Should he be turned out again,
his judgment will be criticized by friend and foe. His career
options will be few, and those few will be relatively unpalat-
able to him.

*The organization,* its culture made even stronger by the
elimination of the "change agent," may resist with greater
ferocity the next outsider who extols foreign views—and
the next, and the next. This resistance can readily harden
into rigidity, and some of those rejected ideas might have
contained nuggets essential to the long-range health of the
haughty organization.

*The executive search firm,* nerve-attenuated by its errors in the initial process, may do a better job in the replacement work. It now realizes that the client wants to preserve
the status quo, so the terrain is scoured for candidates quite
unlike the recently departed. The new prospects will have
attained success by not "making waves" in their present
organizations, and those organizations will have cultural
characteristics somewhat similar to that of the status quo
client. But beyond this immediate (and fee-less) replacement activity, the chances are that the recruiter may have
learned surprisingly little for broad application in the fu-

ture. Unless he or she has an unusually keen understanding of human nature, I suspect that the next search for a different client will also be launched incorrectly. The recruiter could easily fall into the same old trap of becoming too excited about the technical aspects of the new assignment: "ten years' advanced design and test of underwater welding fixtures"; or, "M.S. in electronic engineering, followed by an M.B.A. (finance concentration) and five years' strategic planning in laser defense weapons systems for condominiums and apartments"; and so on.

Let's see what *you* might have learned, directly and by inference, from our little horror tale of cultures in conflict. You might have surmised that attention to the three cardinal rules of cultural cognizance would have minimized the extent of the tragedies. You might have also decided that these were not sufficient to preclude disaster; perhaps you felt the need for another guideline. Well, there is such a maxim. It is the fourth cardinal rule of cultural cognizance: **Understand your present organization before you leave it.** I am amazed when, representing a corporation in, say, Parsippany, I interview and evaluate candidates who know little about their present employer in Minneapolis, Maclean, or Miami. These men and women usually know almost everything about their particular department and many have a good working knowledge of how their part of the company relates to the whole. But most have only a hazy view of what their peer departments are trying to do and how their efforts relate to their departments and to the whole. Even more disturbing is the fact that many do not really understand the corporate culture within which they are toiling. Sometimes this ignorance exists because the culture is vague, vacillating, and therefore weak. More often, however, it is because these people are so busy flailing away at their own little demons and worshipping their own little angels that they fail to perceive the satanic or saintlike characteristics of the company itself. All of which is rather unfortunate because when preparing to leap, one should know the composition of the springboard!

And that leads us to the fifth and final rule of cultural cognizance: **Assess the new organization, and project yourself into it,** *before* **you are in it.**

One might argue that this rule (or perhaps its partner-in-pattern, rule 4) is the ultimate, or payoff, rule. Rule 5 *is* important, and I suggest you become proficient in its use, whether or not you are now thinking of changing organizations. But all five rules are interrelated, and you must think about those relationships if you are to learn how to assess a culture, whether that of a new organization or the one in which you are now a member.

Because rule 5 is critical to your career choices (and so devilishly tricky to plan and execute), the next chapter is devoted to learning how to master it. In fact, you might say that it is the only topic discussed in Chapter 9.

# CHAPTER 9

# THE ASSESSMENT PROCESS

Well, rule 5 will be *almost* the only topic in this chapter. That's because the best way to get at that fifth rule is through the other four, due to all their interrelationships. Let's look at the rules again. As we do, you will begin to detect interrelationships—those ties that connect any one rule with the others.

## CARDINAL RULES OF CULTURAL COGNIZANCE

1. **Do your best to understand yourself.**
2. **Some cultures are for you, others are not.**
3. **You won't change the organization, but it may change you.**
4. **Understand your present organization before you leave it.**
5. **Assess the new organization, and project yourself into it, *before* you are in it.**

Your objective in this chapter should be to understand rule 5. More precisely, it should be to learn how to assess a new organization without becoming engaged, entangled, or entrapped in it. To do the assessment properly is difficult but far from impossible; people accomplish it every day. It requires, however, a fair amount of dedicated thought and action, more than many men and women are willing to devote. But as I have often observed, those are by and large the same people whose careers are most problem-prone.

Some of the rules' interrelationships are rather apparent, and you have already identified several, perhaps including these:

- If you don't understand yourself, how can you tell if a particular culture is or is not for you?

- If you believe that a certain new culture is for you, in which critical elements does it differ from your present organization? In which critical elements is it similar?

- If an organization tries to change you, which elements of the U factor are most apt to be changed? Which are most important for you to preserve?

Many of the other interrule connectors are discoverable only after some digging. As an interesting and pertinent exercise, see how many additional ties you can find in the next twenty-five minutes. This suggests that you allocate a mere five minutes to each rule, less time than you may devote, day in and day out, to practicing midwifery, sharpening your skittles skills, or writing the Great American Novel.

Surprisingly, the more interrelationships you discover, the more you begin to appreciate the importance of each individual rule. Each has its stand-alone value, yet each supports the others. By now you may have noticed there are two different types of rules: *acceptance* rules and *action* rules.

# CAN YOU BELIEVE?

The acceptance rules are:

2.  **Some cultures are for you, some are not.**
                          and
3.  **You won't change the organization, but it may change you.**

These are acceptance rules because, after thinking about them, you merely recognize and accept them for what they are: maxims that apply to the most important person you will ever encounter in your career—*you!* This act of acceptance is a bit like embracing a religion, entering partisan politics, showing up for a blind date, or ordering Yorkshire pudding in a Mexican restaurant; it requires faith!

I recommend, therefore, that you simply accept and believe these two time-tested truisms, which may be paraphrased something like this:

**Rule 2.**   Let's face it: You *cannot* be successful in all cultures. Your lack of universality places you alongside a motley array of famous men and women, winners in some of their environments but losers in others. It is extremely difficult to prevail in all situations. Lincoln, Einstein, Churchill, and Marie Antoinette couldn't do it; nor have John McKay, Frank Borman, Lore Harp, Archie McCardle, Billy Martin, and Anne Burford.

All these men and women found certain cultures more to their liking than others. So have you; and so it will be throughout your life. Some cultures are better for you, more compatible with the total you, *and those are the ones on which you should concentrate.*

A competent culture-chooser suppresses that "I can do anything" ego and shucks that "the world is my oyster" attitude. To retain those simplistic beliefs is to set unrealistic goals and baited traps for yourself. Only a chamelion can blend in anywhere, and you know what happens to chamelions!

**Rule 3.** Now turn the other cheek, friend, and absorb this second blow to your ego: Do not join an established organization expecting (or being expected) to bring about substantial change.

There are two exceptions to this otherwise across-the-board prohibition: the professional **business doctor** and the **compleat competitor** (a key officer of a rival corporation). Probably you are neither of these rare species, but because you may think you are, we shall examine them in some detail.

Victor Palmieri and Frank Grisanti are among a handful of free-lance business doctors renowned for their skills in what are called "turnaround" situations. These situations come in different sizes and shapes, but a typical scenario might go something like this:

An entrepreneur has a brilliant idea, something to do with a method for transmitting vitamins from the processing plant by telephone directly into the home. She is an engineer, the type of person to whom scores of these innovative and technical breakthroughs seem to come rather easily. Money is raised to finance this brave new venture (VITA-TEL), the idea catches on, and production levels mount. Soon more money is needed for a new plant and more employees. Three years later there is a modest profit, soon offset by overseas expansion, legal fees, and the move into fancy offices. Suddenly, more capital is required for national advertising and a broader dealer network, because competitors now challenge VITA-TEL.

VITA-TEL's sales climb, but profits evaporate overnight as the company runs into serious problems in the factory. It no longer turns out a reliable product, and critical shipments to key dealers are delayed. Per-unit cost escalates. Cash flow turns negative, employees grumble under the increased pressures, and a union begins passing out its literature and sign-up cards.

The founder now has no time for what she does best— new product development. Instead, she is immersed in all those portions of the business where she is most apt to make damaging decisions: finance, manufacturing, dealer contracts, and employee relations. Enormous sums of new money are now needed, but the bankers balk. They realize that despite the attractiveness of VITA-TEL's products and the dedication of its founder, the company has a critical *business* problem, one that will not be solved by the founder. At this point they may elect to swallow their losses and write off the venture as "a good idea that just didn't work out."

Or they may decide to try to recoup—to invest even more money, attempting to regain their earlier investments, but with a new approach to the business problem.

---

# THE DOCTOR MAKES HOUSE CALLS, BUT KEEPS HIS ENGINE RUNNING

The bankers, together with the company's board of directors, may decide that the time has come for a change in top management and that they will invite a business doctor to become CEO. Perhaps entreat is the proper term; to attract the person of their choice they approach him with a "fat package." They will grant him absolute control of the troubled business, as well as a highly leveraged compensation plan. This means that his equity or "piece of the action" will make him very wealthy if he succeeds in the turnaround and, later, lassos lenders' long-lost lucre. He is motivated. (Besides, he relishes the *power* of the role.)

So the savior storms in, rapidly and decisively. While still studying the problem and its alternative solutions, he acts, *now*, to stem the flow of red ink. He pares expenses, reduces inventories, eliminates frills, fires complacent managers, streamlines the organization, and reduces VITA-TEL's product offerings from twelve to four.

He works a seventy-hour week and expects all members of management to do likewise. He romances dealers as he hears their complaints. He meets with employees and promises that things will improve but "only if we all work together on these problems."

The entrepreneur-founder, if retained at all, is relegated to an out-of-the-way "tinker room," where she is permitted to play with paper models for product enhancement. She may remain on the company's board of directors, but everyone understands that she is no longer involved in the mainstream of VITA-TEL's business.

The bankers, the board, and the doctor have made the organization aware of several conclusions:

1. The business is in grave danger—*now*.
2. Its only chance for survival lies in everyone working with the new CEO.
3. His ideas, actions, and managerial style will be different from those of the founder.
4. The doctor's stay with the company will be temporary. As soon as the company is profitable and all trend lines are moving in the right direction, he will help select his replacement (internal or external) before moving on to his next corporate patient.
5. VITA-TEL, if it survives, will emerge as a *changed* organization.

These business doctors are sometimes successful, sometimes not. They may arrive on the scene so late that their only contribution is to minimize losses before the business fails or before it seeks protection from its creditors under Chapter XI of the Federal Bankruptcy Act. At other times they can reach deep into their personal travel kits and extract potions and lotions that help bring about the cure. In either event, these doctors display dazzling diagnostic, surgical, and repair skills. And they exercise these skills with great authority, working rapidly (and often ruthlessly) to resuscitate the dying patient.

---

# THE SHADOW WALTZ (OR, WHEN WILL I EVER GET TO LEAD?)

The compleat competitor play is called for under circumstances that are both similar to and different from those of VITA-TEL. The biggest difference is in the background of the key player. He or she is not a traveling technician, a peripatetic physician who has treated a variety of sick corporate patients. Rather, the person is a successful general manager, thoroughly grounded in a given industry, perhaps the chief executive officer of a small but highly regarded firm. The chances are, however, that the person is an officer, probably the second in command, of an industry leader. Further, the person is ambitious and beginning to chafe within the shadow of his or her boss, an all-too-vital CEO.

In this scenario, the company in trouble (let's call it SUDSCO) is larger and older than VITA-TEL. It is listed on the New York Stock Exchange and its products have been familiar names for decades. SUDSCO's CEO was its former vice president of finance; he has now held the top job for twelve years. For the past four years SUDSCO's profits have declined steadily, and last year the company barely broke even. *Large losses loom!* The primary reason for SUDSCO's poor financial performance has been its outmoded product lines (Scottydog Shampoo, Raccoon Rinse, Dingo Detergent, Ocelot Ointment, and such). But the CEO has misread, repeatedly, the signals from the marketplace. His recovery plans reflect his early days as a junior cost accountant: Each year he drives costs down, down,

down! And each year the already inadequate research, development, and marketing budgets lead to further decreased earnings.

SUDSCO's problems have been building for a long time and unless resolved will soon approach the critical zone. The board of directors, having a legal responsibility to protect the stockholders' interests, meets with the bankers and discusses remedial action plans. Because the directors (and the stockholders) tend to the think in terms of the marketplace and the competition, the decision is rather straightforward: to recruit from within the industry, perhaps even the person responsible for the marketing (and thus financial) success of FRESCHCO, the dreaded competitor.

So in comes a Lee Iacocca, a Fred Silverman, a Bob Wilson, a Sandy Sigoloff, or some other "number 2" who, for one reason or another, despairs of ever becoming the number 1 executive in the firm for which he has worked so effectively. He is well regarded there and handsomely paid, but his main goal is to run his own show. Because of that goal he is attentive to the call he receives from a SUDSCO director, a banker, or from an executive search firm such as mine.

The compensation package offered him may be similar to that which VITA-TEL extended to the "here today but gone tomorrow" professional doctor, but some provisions will be different. (The objective in this situation is to have the FRESHCO emigrant *stay*, perhaps until retirement.)

Another important difference is in the amount of power he is given. SUDSCO is, of course, in financial difficulty, but the specter of bankruptcy is still relatively remote. His authority, although extensive, will not be unlimited.

He may introduce some of the same corrective measures that the doctor prescribed for VITA-TEL. He will also concoct and apply other remedies and balms not appropriate for VITA-TEL. In either action, however, he will do so (if he is wise) in a manner that is neither autocratic nor crisis-oriented. Where the doctor moves briskly and brusquely, making sure that everyone understands that he is "the word and the light," the career CEO is well advised to use a somewhat softer approach. He too, may work long hours, but his pace will be more deliberate and relaxed than that of his counterpart at VITA-TEL. Although SUDSCO's new CEO will not wield the naked power of the itinerant internist, his prestige, product knowledge, market savvy, and managerial skills may be enough to get the SUDSCO job done, provided, of course, that it is doable at all.

## NOW, ABOUT YOUR "MEDICAL LICENSE" AND OTHER CREDENTIALS . . .

I suspect that if you had the skills, knowledge, and temperament of the business doctor or those of the compleat competitor you would be applying them at this moment. You would be working those seventy-hour weeks in a troubled but potentially lucrative situation, rather than reading this book. You would be meeting with bankers, charming the financial press, being photographed for articles in *Fortune, Business Week, Nourishment News, Detergent Daily,* and the like.

If my suspicion is correct, it is unlikely that you will be asked to *lead* a turnaround effort. Bankers and boards of directors are peculiar: Once they realize they have a top management problem, they search for experience—successful experience.

## SO BACK TO YOU AND REALITY, TOO!

OK, so you are not yet in the position to lead a long-suffering organization out of creditor captivity and into the promised land of financial freedom. Does that exempt you from the temptation of trying to violate rules 2 and 3? Read on.

It is quite possible that as your career progresses you

will enter an established organization, one new to you, as the head of a particular function. Your new job could be the director (perhaps even vice president) of sales, marketing, finance, manufacturing, quality assurance, engineering, or personnel. Your new responsibilities could be at the division, group, or corporate level. Great opportunity, right? *Be careful!*

Except in the rarest of circumstances, you will have neither the mandate nor the power to bring about substantial change, regardless of *who* assures you of *what* when you are being recruited for the job. So if your expected role is to bring about marked and lasting change, hold out for the top job—the CEO.

Few, indeed, will ever have the privileges and problems of entering an established organization at the very top—or in a powerful position near enough to the top that it might offer a fair shot at inducing and sustaining basic change. With that as a given (and such is the heart of rule 3), it behooves you to join only those organizations whose cultures are right for you, compatible with your concepts, philosophies, and ways of doing things.

If a culture you enter is incompatible with the U factor, your frustrations will increase, week after week, faster than you may realize. And those baffles and impediments may lead to ulcers, hypertension, or insomnia—perhaps even to jitters on the putting green or when skydiving.

Several other undesirable reactions may occur. The first (and worst) is that you may surrender something of value— perhaps a bedrock principle—in your desire to be accepted by your new boss, by *her* boss, and by your new peers and colleagues. You may try so hard to "go along" and to avoid "making waves" that you will soon forget about all those wonderful changes you were going to make. So we have a double tragedy: you have sold out to the establishment, and that establishment will never have the benefit of whatever it was you were going to do for it.

Another possibility is not quite that bad, although it may seem to be of gargantuan importance when it occurs. In this scenario, you roll up your sleeves and try, valiantly but stubbornly, to bend a rigid organization. You push, pull, press, ram, jam, cram, and otherwise try to force that poor, misguided entity to move in the right direction.

In the world of material things, rigid physical objects often shatter when sufficient pressure is applied. Not so with organizations. Organizations aren't the lines, boxes, and titles drawn on an organization chart—they are people. And people generally resist change that is not of their own design. If you persist in your pressure, these otherwise charming, hospitable, and kindly people will expel you from their midst. You will be ejected, and probably not as painlessly as was the recently hired–recently fired executive profiled in Chapter 8.

We have taken, deliberately, a lengthy trip through the maze of rules 2 and 3. May the Great Career Counselor in the Sky personally tell you where to go if you knowingly disobey either of those two acceptance rules. (And thanks to this chapter, you now have no right to plead ignorance of career catechism.)

---

# DON'T JUST ACCEPT ACCEPTANCE RULES: DO SOMETHING

Rules 1, 4, and 5 are termed *action rules* because after thinking about them you must *do* something. Thought must be translated into action. In fact, you must do a number of things if you are to: understand yourself (rule 1), understand your present organization (rule 4), and assess other organizations you might join (rule 5).

In the preceding chapter the responsibility for the U factor was placed squarely on you, as it must be. But at that same time I said that I could help you quite a bit with that other critical factor—$O^2P$—organization and other people. This chapter assumes that you have been working on the U factor and that you have (or will have) a reasonably sound working hypothesis of *you*. This hypothesis, on which so many important career thoughts will depend, is based on *your* evaluation of many personal traits and characteristics. These might include, for example and in random order, items such as your:

- Likes and dislikes
- Beliefs and disbeliefs
- Motivators and demotivators
- Comfort corners and anxiety cellars, and so on

This working hypothesis is, of course, subject to change as you learn (and unlearn) more about yourself, and it may be drawn from any number of sources. However it is obtained, it should include answers to a variety of questions, such as these:

On which topics are you generally rigid? Usually flexible?

In which areas are you most tolerant? Least tolerant?

In which bodies of knowledge are you most curious? Least interested?

In which aspects of life are you unusually cautious? In which do you often take risks?

In which types of situations are you most creative? Least creative?

On which kinds of problems are you most analytical? Least analytical?

In which types of situations are you most self-reliant? Most dependent on other people?

On which types of projects are you generally persevering? On which are you most likely to give up?

This brief treatment of the U factor is not intended to do the job for you. As mentioned in Chapter 8, I can't do this for you. It's a very *personal* evaluation and like the housework of a role-reversed husband, the job is never totally done. After all, I am still fine-tuning the work I have done, over the years, on my own U factor.

Even though I placed the responsibility for the job with you in the earlier chapter, I decided to mention rule 1 again here, for two reasons. The first is that you might be motivated now that I have dangled a few examples and "think-abouts" before your eyes. Perhaps they will stimulate you into earlier and more productive action on the U factor—that mysterious, complex, frightening, yet wonderful collection of chemical compounds and psychic syndromes that make you *you*, that set you apart from all other organisms in the universe.

My second reason for mentioning rule 1 again was to reemphasize its interrelationships with all the other rules, now that we are about ready for rules 4 and 5.

If you are still not clear on those ties, it's back to the beginning of this chapter for you! (Fast learners may proceed directly to the following discussion of the final two rules.)

# RULES FOUR AND FIVE: DON'T LEAVE WORK WITHOUT THEM

A good way to begin forging these important tools is to examine some of the different types of cultures—the shared beliefs, objectives, and methodologies—whether in your present organization or the ones you may consider entering. *Caution!* In doing so, please remind yourself that no culture is bad, as such, as long as that organization's actions are within the law, on a par with commonly accepted standards of ethical and professional conduct, and generally consonant with the U factor. Nor, for these purposes, is any one culture better than any one of the others that meets these same tests.

For the most part, then, it is not a matter of good or bad

cultures, except as they pertain to you and your personal value system, all of which says that your main concern should be to identify and interpret that delicate interplay between two powerful factors: U and O²P.

# LABELS, LABELS

There are many different ways we could categorize or label the various cultures; labels are applied every day by consultants, professors, writers, and other students of the business parade. In their excellent book, *Corporate Cultures: The Rites and Rituals of Corporate Life,* professor Terrence Deal and consultant Allan Kennedy discuss four generic cultures they have identified in their thorough study of large, successful American corporations. These environments they have labeled as:

1.  The "tough-guy, macho" culture
2.  The "work hard/play hard" culture
3.  The "bet-your-company" culture
4.  The "process" culture

The authors also describe a cultural environment which they believe will prevail in the future. This they call the *atomized organization.*

Deal and Kennedy are competent researchers. They are close to the heartbeat of American business and have a good grasp of the reasons some companies flourish while competitors founder. Theirs is a book well worth your thoughtful attention.

So are the many articles and books by James O'Toole of the University of Southern California. Among his several activities, O'Toole serves as director of the Twenty-Year Future Forecast at USC's Center for Futures Research. I believe that this futurist shares my belief that tomorrow will offer a wide variety of organizational cultures. Yet he and a colleague, Kenneth Brousseau, have postulated four work-places of the future, alternative scenarios of what the relatively small industrial workplace may be be like in 1995. These are called:

1. The meritocratic workplace
2. The behaviorist workplace
3. The entitlementarian workplace
4. The humanistic workplace

But useful as all these labels may be from these authors' points of view, I have reservations about labels—any labels—being affixed to organizations and to the ingredient that makes them tick, people. I have two main concerns in this regard.

The first concern has to do with a label's ability to magnetize our thinking. The word or phrase that forms the label usually serves as a banner, a distillation, of a collection of subordinate elements that are related to each other in one or more ways. But the eye and the ear (and thus the brain) are all too easily drawn to the label alone. By concentrating on the label, the tag hung on the entire collection, you or I could easily overlook a subordinate element, maybe the very one that is essential to the decision at hand.

My second reason for approaching labels cautiously is that many of them are catchy; they have been carefully crafted to attract our powers of attention and retention. This means that labels, much as surnames, can be quite capable of arousing prejudices that should remain dormant. For example, to tag a particular organization as "bureaucratic" might turn away a person who "knows" that bureaucracy is bad. Yet examination of that person's U factor might reveal that he or she would flourish in a structured environment.

Similarly, the label "high technology" has become the darling of many politicians, educators, labor leaders, and business managers. This is especially true as far as that label can be made to pertain to training/retraining programs, massive efforts aimed at preparing displaced workers for skilled jobs in the information and services area. The idea of retraining is, at least on the surface, appealing to the hearts and minds of all fair-minded people. (But just what *is* "high tech"?) Undoubtedly, many workers displaced from the steel, auto, rubber, chemical, and other dwindling industries will acquire new job skills and thus become employable again. But disturbing questions remain:

- How effectively will most of them *apply* their new skills in their new environment? (How long will the veteran Ford assembly line worker be motivated to operate a computer console at 60 percent of his former pay?)

- How will they mesh in a culture markedly different from what they have known throughout their working lives? (Can the pro-union, former Frigidaire inspector find happiness in an office setting where her associates worry more about software glitches than about antimanagement bitches?)

- What happens when the technology that required those new skills is, in turn, made obsolete by a still newer technology—one that requires totally different skills and attitudes? (How flexible will the welder-turned-technician then be? How willing to start all over again?)

Tough questions! You might wish to ask yourself those same questions about several people whom you know well—perhaps a favorite relative, a former neighbor, or your spouse's best friend. Or you might elect to reflect on the adaptability of those TV characters who often serve as metaphors for real people, characters such as Archie Bunker, Gomer Pyle, Alice, or Shirley.

I suggest that instead of reacting to the labels which other people place on a culture, *you* become proactive by asking questions about that culture, questions that could be applied to any organization, including the one that knows you all too well. These questions about a particular culture might include probes such as these:

What attitudes and actions does it appreciate and reward? Dislike and discourage?

What does it believe in? Not believe in?

What kinds of events spur it on to greater effort and achievement? What kinds demoralize it?

What is its decision-making process? Who makes decisions, and how rapidly?

How rapidly are those decisions carried out? How well?

What is the communications atmosphere, closed or open? Formal or informal? Superficial or substantive?

How much of the total communications are top-down? Bottom-up? Across departments and functions?

What are the ongoing purposes? Who knows about them and is working on them? What is the progress report?

Compared to its competition, what has been the company's overall performance during the past five years? What can be reasonably expected during the next five?

To what extent does the company admit its errors? How soon, and to whom?

What are the stated policies toward customers? Suppliers? Unions? Minorities? Women? The handicapped? The community?

To what extent are those policies actually carried out?

To what extent are employees *really* an important asset?

What are the transfer and promotion practices? Are lateral transfers (one good way to hasten your becom-

ing a cluster specialist) tolerated? Are laterals encouraged? Planned? Related to the strategic
business plan?

The important thing about these questions is that they
are designed not only to delve into critical areas but also to
stimulate you to raise still other questions. These probes
must be directed to several different sources, then cross-
checked against other sources. If the annual report claims
that the company stands for a certain thing that is important
to the U factor, you should verify its reality by checking
with employees at different levels, in several departments
or divisions, and perhaps by talking with customers, suppliers, and competitors. If a disgruntled former employee
complains of her treatment, try to hear what fellow-em-
ployees have to say about the situation. If the stock price
has been behaving strangely, you may be able to gain insight by talking with your broker, a financial analyst, or by
direct query to the chief financial officer of the company.
Problems of labor unrest, layoffs, product recalls, lawsuits,
and the like plague almost all companies. These problems
may be superficial and temporary, or they could be sympto-
matic of deeper, more serious problems. And it is you who
must sort them for size, by whatever means are available to
you.

Probe. Ask. Challenge. Cross-check. Verify. Think.
Then think again. That's the routine, the investigative routine that forms the backbone of the assessment process for
rules 4 and 5.

By now you may be awed by the scope of the inquiry I
have recommended. You may also be depressed by the
number and types of probes I have suggested that you conduct. And you may be wondering if you must explore that
unfamiliar terrain at all, let alone with such thoroughness.

Need you be so diligent and painstaking? Of course not.
You may elect to take at face value those few signs you
chance to see; you may decide to hope for the best in all
those aspects of the new culture that, for one reason or
another, you have not examined.

And who knows? You may be lucky. You may, by pure happenstance, cast your lot with an organization that is ideal for you, one just right for the U factor.

But I doubt it, and if I were you, I would not bet on it. The terms "lucky," "happenstance," and "cast your lot" mean just what they appear to mean. So if you feel lucky, rush in. And be sure to hurry, to get there before the wise men and angels.

My twenty-two years in industry and my eleven years as a consultant to the business world suggest a better way than guessing or trusting to luck. My data base is jammed with cases of men and women whose guesses were preposterous and with cases of people whose luck ran out and suddenly turned sour when they relied on it as the key ingredient in their culture choice.

But I have just as many examples of successful cases of people who made safe and satisfying transitions from one organization to another. Those career moves resulted, primarily, from a structured investigation of the new culture— an exploration similar to the type I have outlined for you.

You could argue (and with some justification) that the assessment process is time consuming, too time demanding because you are in a hurry. You feel pressed to get a job, to change jobs, to get out of town, to do *something*. And under certain circumstances, perhaps you *should* move rapidly. But you should try to do at least these three things first:

1. Complete as much of the preliminary investigation as you can under the circumstances.
2. Recognize that you are making a *job* decision rather than a *career* decision and that the outcome may be far from ideal.
3. Promise yourself that once safely inside the new environment, you will actively pursue rule 4. You will begin preparations for your career decision by investigating thoroughly that which has just become your "present organization."

This is not an irrational approach in certain circumstances, and it does give you some practice in assessment. That practice should be helpful to you later when you begin considering your *next* move, whether internal or external.

But wait, if you can. Take the time and make the effort to be thorough, objective, analytical, and skeptical.

Especially be skeptical, because situations often have a funny way of appearing to be one thing when they are really another. Situations that seem to be good may upon closer inspection display flaws that disqualify them from further consideration. Conversely, every now and then the onion turns out to be a pearl once we have peeled away the outer layers.

In Chapter 8 we saw how a number of companies described themselves. Those statements of credo, policy, and organizational emphasis were extracted from those companies' official publications. Those statements purported to be true and to typify the thing or things which each company considered to be important.

I have no reason to doubt the sincerity of those particular companies. In fact, what knowledge I have of them is favorable: They are successful, well-managed institutions, leaders in their respective fields and highly regarded in the business community. But does each of them *really* believe in what it says it believes in? And if so, are those specific beliefs at the core of the operation of the business?

Frankly, I don't know, at least in some of those companies. Which means that you may not know, either. But those thirteen companies, as well as almost any other entity in which you may become interested, will yield to the process I have outlined. Most reputable and progressive companies welcome and appreciate intelligent inquiries, especially from prospective employees, provided, of course, that the information you seek is not proprietary and thus of great interest to competitors. It is true that privately held companies are also termed "closely held" with good reason: They normally divulge much less data, to anyone, than do those whose stock is publicly traded. But even a closed company will disclose a surprising amount of data pertinent to your assessment if you approach the "right" people properly.

But let's assume that a company, whether privately or publicly held, shows marked reluctance to respond to your nonproprietary inquiries. That is not all bad, either. The company may not realize it, but its reluctance to communicate may have revealed the answers to some of your most critical concerns.

So you move on to the next prospective organization, thankful that you did not become entangled with *those* guys, and begin the routine again. So once more it is: Probe. Ask. Challenge. Cross-check. Verify. Think. Then think again. After all, this is a career decision—your career decision—in the balance.

The recommended investigative routine and assessment process applies to all of us, regardless of how experienced or sophisticated we may be. At times they may apply even more to the veteran than to the rookie. An example may be found in the discipline of airline flight safety procedures, chock-full of routine, standardized checks, and counterchecks. These routines serve several purposes, one of which may surprise you. So we shall peek into the flight deck of an Ajax Airlines 747.

Captain Klear has an unblemished record: no accidents, no crises, no panics. He is known for his habit of "thinking ahead," visualizing all possible contingencies and weighing the alternative courses of action. Today, while still at the gate at JFK and halfway through the computer loading process, his attention drifts, momentarily, to the possibility of severe turbulence over the Rockies. Should he request a different altitude? Divert to the south? Or would it be better to . . .? Fortunately for all concerned, First Officer Tyro is monitoring the standard preflight checklist. He notices that Captain Klear has forgotten to reposition the sidereal status switch on the terrain tuner! Horrified, Tyro coughs diplomatically. The sequence is halted, the switch repositioned, and the cockpit check resumed.

Discipline in a career decision has a number of virtues, the principal one being that it could help protect you from sloganeering, a technique often used by public relations wordsmiths. Sometimes a sloganeer's objective is fairly straightforward; it is merely to distill an idea into a few catchy words, words that will magnetize your attention needle and keep it directed toward the organization or product being represented. At other times, however, the aim is to mislead and deceive, to cover a multitude of corporate sins and ills with a few finely forged phrases.

But even when the purpose is pure, the fact remains that an easily ingested slogan may curb your appetite for more substantive information. That could lead to your becoming addicted to a diet of nonnutritive data!

Another value of the routinized process is that it helps you check the present-day value of phrases created years ago but still on display.

I recently attended an annual conference of the World Future Society in Washington, D.C. Feeling the need for a break from the brain-boggling sessions on technical/socio-economic projections, I skipped a breakfast discussion in favor of a stroll near Capitol Hill. My mind was still grappling with such centuries-old questions of people and machines, capital and labor, and stability and change, when I came upon a huge granite building four stories high and at least one block square. I did not recognize it, and its name was not apparent. Then I glanced near the top of its northwest corner, and that glance delayed considerably my return to thoughts of tomorrow. Up there, carved in letters three feet tall, was the following inscription:

> MESSENGER OF SYMPATHY AND LOVE
> SERVANT OF PARTED FRIENDS
> CONSOLER OF THE LONELY
> BOND OF THE SCATTERED FAMILY
> ENLARGER OF THE COMMON LIFE

I was fascinated! What could this be? Again, I could find

no name, but what an inscription! I stared at it, again and again, as questions flooded my mind:

MESSENGER OF SYMPATHY AND LOVE
(A greeting card company? Flowers by wire?)

SERVANT OF PARTED FRIENDS
(Domestic relations counselling? A mortuary?)

CONSOLER OF THE LONELY
(The Salvation Army? The National Bartenders Union?)

BOND OF THE SCATTERED FAMILY
(A private detective agency? A photographic service?)

ENLARGER OF THE COMMON LIFE
(A public library? The American Civil Liberties Union?)

I pondered these and more as I lazed along to the next block. Still puzzled, I spied another inscription, high above the building's southwest corner. It, too, sparked ideas and questions:

CARRIER OF NEWS AND KNOWLEDGE

INSTRUMENT OF TRADE AND INDUSTRY

PROMOTER OF MUTUAL AQUAINTANCE OF
PEACE AND GOODWILL
AMONG MEN AND NATIONS

I was flush with ideas and confusion. What *was* this place? The Pan-American Union? The Washington branch of the UN? The long-lost U.S. outpost of the League of Nations?

At nine o'clock the massive doors opened and people, rather ordinary-looking people, began entering and leaving. I bounded up the twenty-two steps, confident that I would soon unlock this fascinating puzzle. Then I stopped abruptly as I encountered an armed guard. (The CIA? The FBI? The NSC?)

I decided to use the "interested student" approach: "I have been admiring your credo, and I wondered if you could tell me . . ."

"My what?"

"Your credo—you know, the things your organization stands for—those descriptive phrases near the top of the building, so I would like to know . . ."

His eyes rolled upward and he seemed to be searching the vaulted ceiling.

"No, no—not up there! Outside! Carved in those huge granite blocks on top of the corners, it says . . ." and I rattled off what I could recall of those cryptic phrases. Then I tried again.

"So who *are* you people, anyway? Are you the International Red Cross? The National Council of Churches? The . . ."

"Sir, I don't know what you're trying to do, but I'll be nice and polite, just like it says to be in the manual. Sir, this is the United States Postal Service! Now, if you want to buy some stamps, just get in that line over there."

# Chapter 10

# CAN YOU AFFORD TO BE YOUR OWN BOSS?

No doubt about it; almost every American man (and what may be a surprising number of American women) has considered, perhaps even dreamed, of becoming an entrepreneur. They have thought of heading out on that "lone eagle" career path where brave souls (sometimes single-handedly, sometimes with a partner) start, nurture, and direct their own business venture.

This oft-expressed, oft-repressed urge is the stuff, the *right* stuff, at the core of the American Dream. This "I want to run my very own business" drive has been the foundation of most corporate success stories and the essence of almost every successful sole proprietorship and partnership.

A friend of mine has successfully headed his own small, high-technology think-tank consulting service for more than a decade. Says he, "It's much more fun than working directly for a TRW, a Northrop, or a Lockheed. My findings and recommendations to them carry far more weight than they would if I were one of their own engineering managers. I enjoy the variety of assignments and the types of problems we are called on to solve. Also, being president

179

of a small, private corporation allows me to build substantial tax-deferred funds for retirement.''

But not all "do-it-myself-ers" are so fortunate. Government figures show that only about 35 percent of the hundreds of thousands of new ventures that emerge each year in America will still be around five years later. True, a few of the remaining 65 percent will have been sold as successful businesses and their identities changed by the new owners. *A few*. But most of the nonsurviving businesses will have failed. For one or more compelling reasons, that captivating entrepreneurial dream will, for about three hundred thousand of them, have degenerated into pathetic nightmares—a jumble of bitter bankruptcies, partnership dissolutions, and years of drudgery. Sometimes it is difficult to decide which of these failures has been the less fortunate: those who failed grossly but quickly, and went on to other things, or those who struggled for years, eking out a living while lunging nervously ahead of the fast-approaching foreclosure folks. For almost all it proved to be an embarrassing experiment, a humbling and costly ordeal.

But that may not be the end of these tragedies. Some of those people who failed will try again, although they clearly should not. Equally disturbing, others of them may never try again, although perhaps they should (J.C. Penney finally made it on his *fourth* try).

But about one-third of the new businesses started each year in the United States will survive. Many of them will do spectacularly well, capturing the attention of shrewd investors and "going public" at the opportune moment—with their entrepreneur-owners becoming millionaires overnight!

Some succeed, some fail.

This twin-edged urge has given our nation such rags-to-riches heroes and heroines as Ben Franklin, Colonel Sanders, Mary Wells, Andrew Carnegie, Howard Johnson, George Westinghouse, Ray Kroc, Helena Rubenstein, Steve Jobs, Marie Callender, Thomas Edison, Jeno Palucci, Harvey Firestone, George Pillsbury, Mary Kay

Ash, Walt Disney, Henry Ford, and George Halas—a tiny fraction of those pioneers generally regarded as having made substantial contributions to American society through their successful personal business ventures. My list is, admittedly, a rather peculiar assortment. But I constructed it to illustrate a point: success lurks around many different corners, waiting for alert, positive-thinking men and women who can recognize opportunity, *especially when it is masked as a problem.*

The entrepreneurial urge has also surfaced in business people toward whom, for one reason or another, we may not feel as kindly disposed as we do toward the Franklins and Edisons. These might include such people as:

> *Adam Osborne and John DeLorean:* visionaries and new-product geniuses who, for different reasons, fell from the grace of earlier successes

> or

> *Victor Posner and James Ling:* superb technicians at the high-stakes game of taking over unwilling corporations and then, just as suddenly, discarding others they have reorganized

> or

> *Robert Vesco, Polly Adler, Charles Ponzi, and Al Capone:* hardworking people whose business philosophies and methods clashed with the social value systems of their eras

What a dazzling array of products and services has sprung from the entrepreneurial urges of these and hundreds of thousands of other pioneers. The numbers and types are awesome:

- From bifocal lenses and room heaters to mass-produced autos

- From electrical generators and distribution systems to household appliances and personal computers
- From milled flour and coiled steel to animated cartoons and the National Football League
- From almanacs and air brakes to an infinity of cosmetics, advertisements, hamburgers, pies, and flavors of ice cream
- From vulcanized rubber to frozen pizza to take-home chicken

Earlier chapters explored the various cultures you might encounter in corporate and governmental organizations. They also emphasized the hazards of joining the "wrong" culture and the merits of becoming part of the "right." I suspect that in doing so those chapters may have enticed you to think about the joys of creating *your own* culture by soaring off as a lone eagle.

I hope that is the case, because I believe you should at least think about being your own boss. To many people it is the most appealing of the five career paths, and it certainly deserves your scrutiny. But that means much more that an occasional, wistful thought. It means that you should explore the possibility very carefully, at least as carefully as you should ponder whether or not to sign on with a specific, well-established organization.

So how do you go about measuring the angle of your entrepreneurial bent? Testing the firmness of your "founder's footing"? Plumbing the depth of your desire to be your own boss?

As you may suspect, thousands of books and articles, some excellent and some terrible, have been published on this elusive thing called **entrepreneurship**. To me, the term refers to the total situation that surrounds (and usually dominates) the life of the **entrepreneur**—that combination creator/copycat; visionary/drudge; rugged individualist/government grant grabber; dynamo/resistor; loner/joiner;

master/slave; borrower/investor; risk taker/play-it-safer; reward reaper/loss accumulator.

Most of the books and articles I have read on entrepreneurship contain checklists of detailed things to do and not to do. The reader is bombarded with items such as:

Do engage the services of a reputable accountant.

Do *not* storm away from your job at the extrusion plant and try to open that gift shop next Monday.

Do analyze the market potential for your product or service.

Do *not* rely on the part-time, gratuitous help of friends.

Do expect long hours and short memories, hard work, and soft pay.

Do *not* underestimate your need for those three **critical Cs**—capital, credit, and cash.

Do check zoning laws, postal rates, utility services, recent interpretations of the Mann Act, and on and on.

Such cookbook approaches can be important. They deserve your attention, as do the case histories, startup estimates, and profit forecasts to be found in *Inc., Venture, Entrepreneur, We-Woman Entrepreneur,* and several other magazines oriented toward the entrepreneur/small-business manager. I suggest that you compile, study, and retain those checklists.

However, our purpose here is somewhat different. Rather than looking at a litany of lists, we shall consider a catechism. It will be a sort of reverse catechism in which I respond to those questions I have heard most frequently over the years—questions from men and women at all levels in the business world (as well as from women at the top level of homemaking), people seriously considering this fifth career path.

By this method we shall delve into the basic issues, the

real "go/no go" matters. And we shall do so after we agree on one key assumption: If, after reading this book, you believe that you are destined to be your own manager, you *will* study several checklist-type books and articles before you test those entrepreneurial wings!

With that assumption as a given, I am ready to begin the fascinating process of examining the basic reasons why you are most likely to succeed or fail as an entrepreneur, that rather unusual man or woman who *makes things happen,* that quarterback who both calls and executes the plays while friends lounge in the relative comfort and safety of seats in the stands.

So, if you are ready, let's go!

**QUESTION**  How can I tell if I should even consider this fifth career path, the name of which I can't even spell?

**ANSWER**  Don't worry about your spelling! Poor spellers who became successful entrepreneurs include John D. Rockefeller, Lydia Pinkham, W. F. "Buffalo Bill" Cody, and a surprising smattering of Silicon Valley's young hardware and software tycoons. Far more important than *any* acquired skill or body of knowledge is the U factor, especially those elements having to do with your:

- Need for independence, *even though* you like your boss and generally respect his or her managerial skills
- Level of self-reliance, *especially if* your present employer provides high-quality support systems
- Willingness to assume risks, *especially if* you have few assets
- Desire for accountability (as well as for responsibility)
- Capacity to work long hours (often alone)
- Ability to perceive how a commonplace idea or

item may be reshaped into the unusual and appealing
- Flexibility and adaptability as conditions change
- Perseverance, *especially when* Murphy's Law sets in

High levels of basic elements such as these are in the U factors of most successful entrepreneurs. These fundamentals seem to apply to almost every entrepreneurial venture, regardless of the product or service offered—whether the venture is the world's first underwater-laser-actuated bookkeeping service or merely another franchise operation for Tom's Toasted Turkey.

**QUESTION** Are personal traits and characteristics the only requirements for success?

**ANSWER** Not quite. Although these fundamental elements of the U factor are *necessary* for success as an entrepreneur, they are not *sufficient*. To them must be added the appropriate elements of *experience*.

But let's be careful to distinguish between horses and wagons, and to place them in proper order! The horses are the U factor elements that make the trip possible in the first place. The wagons are the experience elements that can increase the chances of a successful journey. They can also make the trip more comfortable, especially if the load is heavy. But these wagons are not self-propelled, a fact overlooked by many who fail as entrepreneurs.

So a final thought or two (for now) about the U Factor elements: Test and retest! Make *sure* that you have them, and in good supply. Remember, if you don't have them now, you probably won't have them in the months and years ahead—when you will need their support through unexpected crises. And that support will have to come from *within you*; these elements cannot be borrowed from a friend, nor can they be purchased from a consultant.

Either you have them or you don't. And it is essential that you know whether you do or not.

However, it is no disgrace if your test and retest procedure reveals that you do not have enough of these necessary elements. It merely means that you are probably better suited for certain situations on one or more of the other four career paths: worker, supervisor of workers, staff professional, or manager of resources. Our society and economic system need competent men and women on all paths; you need to be on the one that is best for you in your role as a cluster specialist.

But if the U factor does contain those necessary elements, you can move into the second round of considering whether or not the fifth career path is for you. You are now ready to evaluate the appropriateness of your *experience* for the situation you are contemplating.

The list of *sufficient* elements is never complete, of course. The world around you keeps changing, faster and faster, so the list has a nettlesome habit of growing. But you will also find yourself looking backward, and rummaging about in some curious crannies, as these particular elements are *experiential* in every dimension. They include all the skills you have mastered, the bodies of knowledge you have acquired, and all the personal ties you have established, up to this moment. In short, these are the sum total of all your experiences: good and bad, serious and silly, recent and ancient. Once you have launched your venture, you must know which particular experience to retrieve, reshape, and apply when:

- That critical shipment from Joplin is lost, perhaps forever.
- Your banker suddenly asks for a revised pro forma income and expense sheet.
- The city building inspector rejects your remodeling plan.

- A customer complains about the price (or quality, or delivery schedule) of your product or service.
- You discover that your phone number in the Yellow Pages is the same as that of the county morgue.
- A competitor captures your most valued account.
- Your only employee (the young woman who answers the phone, handles all correspondence, keeps the books, and applies the shipping labels) informs you that she wishes to be represented by a union.

**QUESTION** Are some experience bases better than others?

**ANSWER** Yes, but only as they may apply to a particular entrepreneurial venture. Although certain U factor elements are critical to the success of any new venture, the experiential elements are much more specific in application.

Let's say that you are thinking of opening a telephone answering service. Your experience as an inspector at Levi's will not be of much help, nor will those summer months in the microfiche room at city hall. Somewhat more pertinent could be your work as a retail salesclerk for Marshall Field or as an information clerk for TWA. Better yet would be six or seven months at Macy's switchboard, or as the chief directory-assistance operator for Hughes Aircraft's numerous facilities in Greater Los Angeles. Best of all, of course, would be your having held two or three jobs in an already established telephone answering company. Ideally, these jobs would have included work at the board, supervising other operators, handling customer complaints, preparing and tracking the budget, making sales presentations to obtain new customers, and so on. Thus you would have had a good opportunity to see, firsthand, how well (and how poorly) certain things were being done. And that should have lead to your determining how they would be done if you were running that company.

This process of having someone else "pay for your apprenticeship" is highly recommended. It is the route followed by most professionals whose services are proffered to the public, professionals such as architects, accountants, attorneys, business consultants, engineers, executive recruiters, morticians, and the like.

And it can be of great value to you. At best, it can help prepare you for the successful launch of your own telephone answering service: You can profit by avoiding all the business mistakes made by your boss and by amplifying those things that he or she did well. At worst, that experience may cause you to decide *not* to get into telephone answering, after all. And that may not be all bad, either, especially if your goal is to make a name for yourself. Mr. Watson, who answered Alexander Graham Bell's very first phone call, is remembered only by his kin and by the crusty custodians of ancient archives. But Father Bell is renowned for his transformation into Ma Bell, and Ma Bell . . . !

**QUESTION**    Suppose my idea is to open a business that will be the first of its kind anywhere?

**ANSWER**    Good for you! You may have one of those original ideas or unique applications that will break barriers and establish new limits in technology. You may be, as Jack Heckel, president of Aerojet-General expresses it, one of the "modern-day Merlins who hold the promise of tomorrow in their minds today."

If so, you may be eligible to receive federal assistance, courtesy of the Small Business Innovative Research Act of 1982. This act provides, through 1987, sizable awards and grants to selected small engineering and high-tech companies. Its main purpose is to bankroll their building demonstration models of their proposed concepts, thus helping them compete against larger firms. So look out Xerox, General Dynamics, and Honeywell!

On the other hand, your idea is probably not highly technical or overly complex. Most of the new ventures started each year, the enterprises that create far more new jobs than do the large corporations, are low to moderate in technology.

I hope that your new idea represents a new and better way to solve a common human need. That's because, in the long run, the level of technology is not nearly as important to your success as are the freshness of your product or service and its sustained appeal in the marketplace. The very fact that you do not plan to open a gift shop or to operate a Presto Pizza franchise is generally in your favor. You will have the opportunity to exploit all those aspects of your idea that will make it unique. But wait . . .

Unfortunately, being ahead of your time is not totally positive. There are some inherent potential problems:

- A novelty item may catch on quickly, but the sales curve of the business supplying it can plummet just as sharply as it once soared.

- The cash and capital required to educate prospective buyers of the brand-new idea could be enormous, or at least much more than you and your backer had estimated.

- Your idea may be neither patentable nor protectable; Galactic Amalgamated may seize and exploit your brainchild, without even showing the courtesy of offering to buy you out.

- There may be a good reason why no one has opened such a business before; it could be that you have a "great idea in search of a need." In other words, the product or service may have little or no appeal in the marketplace. (The U.S. Patent Office and the Smithsonian Museum are jammed with such examples—brilliant contrivances that aroused great interest among everyone except the buying public.)

On balance, however, being in the forefront has many pluses, even though the *specific* required experiences cannot be drawn intact from a prior business venture. Fortunately, the U factor elements are much more important than specific work experiences. You should, however, explore the possibility of drawing on your earlier experiences in settings that were somewhat related to the new venture. Those relationships are there for you to find, and I suspect that many of them reside in your *managerial methods*. Your new idea, no matter how different from all others, concerns a product or service that must be researched, designed, priced, produced, marketed, serviced, and updated. And your new business will have the age-old requirement for the effective management of money, time, and human effort. The trick here is to build on as many related experiences as you can, benefiting from your earlier mistakes as well as from your *right* decisions and actions.

**QUESTION**  Why do so many small businesses fail?

**ANSWER**  I doubt that there is one predominant reason, although a commonly held view is that most failures are due to an inadequate supply of the critical Cs: cash, credit, and capital. And it is probably true that few, if any, small businesses have ever suffered from having *too much* money on hand or available.

But I have some difficulty in isolating the lack of adequate money from several other related causes of failure: inadequate knowledge of the business world, inadequate financial planning and control systems, inadequate (or erroneous) market research and analysis, poor management practices, and so on.

Another frequent cause for failure is attempting to

convert a hobby into a business *without recognizing the difference between the two*. I realize that this is sometimes done successfully, and that it is the avenue often recommended by slick magazine writers whose flair is for the obvious.

But there is a fundamental difference between *work* and *play*. To paraphrase Mark Twain, work is what our economy and our society *obligate* us to do, while play is what those same forces *allow* us to do. Of course, we all know a person or two who insists (sometimes shrilly): "I really enjoy my work here at Logan's Laundry. My work is my hobby. It's the kind of thing I would do for free, and I feel that I am cheating the company when I cash my check!"

A person or two.

But let us also look in on a somewhat larger number of our acquaintances—men and women such as:

*The insurance executive* who averages about fifty-five hours a week for Prudential. He likes his work about as much or as little as the average $80,000 executive, but what he talks about on the train is his hobby of restoring old MGs.

*The college chemistry professor* whose off-campus activities include Sierra backpacking and racing her Hobie Cat.

*The technical writer* who allocates twenty hours each week to his passion for breeding and racing homing pigeons.

*The registered nurse* who fills her leisure hours with nontechnical pursuits such as refinishing furniture while listening to Mozart.

*The factory supervisor* who collects driftwood and seashells and fashions them into objects of art.

*The executive secretary* who delights in creating personalized, illustrated birthday cards for her friends and relatives.

In each of these cases, the person is devoting generous amounts of his or her spare time to an enjoyable activity—one that has been chosen over all other activities competing for those precious "anti-job" hours. These men and women are engaged in a particular activity because they enjoy it.

But it does not necessarily follow that they would continue to enjoy that particular hobby or leisure-hour interest when they must do it, sixty or seventy hours a week, week after week after week! In fact, there is the very real possibility that the play that once provided them with needed relief from an obligation may soon become a new obligation from which they will require new play, new *zones of relief*.

True, there are exceptions, but most successful entrepreneurs have learned that very subtle, yet crucial, difference between work and play. They enjoy their work and prize their product or service, but their hobbies were and are unrelated to their work.

Still another cause for failure is *improper organization*: The entrepreneur decides to solo when his real need is for a counterbalancing partner. Or he selects the wrong partner, or perhaps there should be no one in the business but himself and a part-time clerk.

Or the venture starts as a family affair. Ah, yes! How nice it sounds! Mother will keep the books and handle correspondence, and son-in-law Stuart will serve as evening sales clerk. Sixteen-year-old Sam will help on weekends—he has a knack for electronic repairs (besides, it will shield him from that bad crowd he runs with). And John, the business administration senior, will make deliveries and begin learning the *real* world of business. And all the while, Father will manage the operation, personally involved with customers, suppliers, and bankers, thoroughly enjoying his seventy-five hour workweeks and never once regretting his early retirement from the executive suite at Exxon.

A healthy scenario? Well, maybe. More likely, *not*.

But it is a very common scenario if you are willing to substitute brothers and uncles, sisters and aunts, for the family characters mentioned in the preceding paragraph. It has been estimated that about 90 percent of all new businesses started in 1983 were family affairs! Shall we peek at a typical example?

Smithson & Sons, Quality Roofers! Now that sounds like a solid, substantial business, one that you could trust to do good work and to be around four years later should the new roof begin to leak worse than the one that Smithson & Sons replaced. Perhaps theirs *is* a totally reliable business, characterized by careful planning, high-quality materials, attention to detail, and a strong sense of dedication to customer satisfaction. Some such family-centered businesses have prospered for well over a century. Such generation-after-generation business health is probably due to those positive characteristics being embedded so firmly that all other considerations became inconsequential.

But Smithson & Sons does not measure up. Unfortunately, the firm will not be around to make good on its guarantee of your new roof—the firm, it seems, teems with internal dissention! It had the three critical Cs, but it lacks internal cohesiveness and management discipline. And no wonder!

Sid Smithson, Sr. is a master roofer; he served his apprenticeship at an early age and worked for several contractors before opening his own business last year. He knows that the world is changing, but he also sees it as changing far too fast and in many undesirable directions. Also, he is disturbed that although both sons "sort of grew up" in the roofing trade, neither had the discipline of a formal trade apprenticeship. Most important, he feels that neither Sid Jr. nor Ralph will be capable of taking over the newly founded family business if something should happen to him.

Sid Jr. has completed two years of college and still takes evening courses in accounting, marketing, and labor relations. He admires his father but believes that he is too set in his ways, blind to the importance of the newer technologies and trends, such as solar-centered buildings. He has little respect for his younger brother's business sense, but he admires his innate ability to detect and solve unexpected mechanical problems at the job site.

Ralph has learned a lot of the tricks of the trade from his father, and he respects his technical know-how. But Ralph thinks the business should branch out, setting up an office in an adjacent city and getting into allied trades such as carpentry and painting. He appreciates Sid Jr.'s ability with the financial parts of the business, but he considers him to be too much of an egghead to understand the day-to-day problems of a small building-contractor business.

So Smithson & Sons is not as it seems from the outside. It is enmeshed in turmoil, with one son and the father arguing about bidding practices, the father and the other son at odds over whether or not to employ nonunion labor, and the two sons in heated contention to assume the presidency of the firm. And there is *no* way that these will remain the only issues dividing the enterprise. Personality differences will sharpen, listening will become a lost art, and new combat zones will be identified each month. Tolerance levels will decline, faultfinding will increase, and soon the three "partners" will become so concerned with their individual perspectives and interests that their customers (you included) skid to the very bottom of the firm's priority list. Shortly, Smithson & Sons will file for protection from its creditors, and the family will never understand why the business failed or why the family is no longer a family.

Launching your new business as a family venture may not be a no-no, but it is certainly a careful-careful. It can be fun *and* profitable, but it carries its own special risks.

(However, you may wish to precipitate a divorce, or perhaps excommunicate that sniveling, ungrateful relative, or steer an errant son toward the Army recruiting office. If so, you may do well by avoiding the classes and seminars offered by the business schools at Harvard, USC, and Wharton/Pennsylvania—academe's efforts toward helping disturbed members of family businesses grasp and grapple with their emotionally charged situations.)

**QUESTION** Why do some small businesses prosper and grow despite the fact that their entrepreneur-founders are no longer in charge?

**ANSWER** The reason lies, all too often, within the realm of the word *because* rather than the word *despite*. In earlier chapters we looked at situations that illustrated the necessity for *being alert for change*—detecting it early and *managing*, rather than *resisting*, its entry into the organization.

Every organization has its own phases or stages—its very own life and death cycle. Some groups develop spasms quickly and die in infancy. Others, such as the Catholic Church, the University of Padua, the Freemasons, and the Cook County political machine, display enormous staying power. Certain consultants, writers, and professors delight in analyzing and labeling the evolutionary developments experienced by different groups. They all agree that various stages exist, but as you may have anticipated, they differ on how many stages there are and how they should be tagged.

Many of these experts are "five-stage" advocates. Some of these "fivers" see the phases as *existence, survival, success, expansion,* and *maturity*. Other students, less scholarly, may hang, on those same five stages, tags such as *startup, scramble, surge, explode,* and *maintain*. Still other "org-oglers," perhaps more realistic, see a sixth chapter in the history book—one titled *dissolution,* or *demise,* or *death.*

Meanwhile, other authorities on this subject, more simplistic than their erudite peers, see fewer phases. These people are successful practitioners of entrepreneurship, men and women who are actually doing it rather than merely philosophizing about it. To these folk, a bankrupt-bound business is simply a matter of *start, stop*! Or, in the case of a prosperous venture, the sequence is *start* and *grow,* then *change, and keep changing*!

The essence here is that all these people, theoreticians and practitioners alike, concur on the requirement for change—the right changes and at the right time.

And those downfield change patterns are the very kinds of movements that most entrepreneurs make so poorly, and with such reluctance and poor timing. Which is why most small businesses that have grown and remained successful have brought in professional managers, men and women with the precise skills needed by the organization at that particular stage of its life cycle. (I still cherish my totally dependable and error-proof Osborne I microprocessor. But I can't help wishing that Adam had stepped aside for his talented successor a year earlier. Perhaps these pages would have been written on an Osborne II or III, on a system that might have had a futuristic program guaranteeing the sale of every manuscript, or at least one that disciplined the author, under threat of magnetic shock or a severe case of the fantods, to write six hours *every* day, or . . . What am I saying?)

**FINAL QUESTION** How specialized, or how generalized, should my entrepreneurial venture be?

**ULTIMATE ANSWER** The bad news here is that your new business is probably heading for a fall if you allow it to lean too far in either direction. The good tidings are that, with appropriate planning and monitoring, you can place it and keep it at or near the optimum position.

Earlier chapters pointed out the hazards awaiting those employees who had allowed themselves to drift into either of those dangerous career roles: traditional specialist or traditional generalist. Owners in "small-businessland" face similar dangers. Some of these threats are difficult to detect. They may lurk within the shadows of an international cartel such as OPEC, or they may be activated by the next cancer scare or by an adverse ruling from the Supreme Court.

Fortunately, however, many of the dangers of either extreme—overspecialization and overgeneralization— are readily apparent. All you need do (after testing and retesting for the U factor and assessing your experience base) is that which your elders did when they approached an unguarded railroad crossing: Stop, look, and listen! For example, you might want to:

1. *Stop*.  Stifle your desire to *sell* a particular item (or a trainload of unrelated items) until you have determined what the market *wants* and will *buy,* now and in the foreseeable future.

2. *Look*.  Examine your options within the context of depth versus breadth of product offering. This means that you will calculate the risk/reward ratio, making trade-off decisions of the pluses of carrying in stock everything a customer could conceivably want against the risks of sitting on a large and costly inventory of many slow-moving items.

   Let's suppose that your interest is, generally, in selling musical instruments—more specifically, guitars. Today's market for expensive classical/acoustic guitars is quite limited. Most youngsters (remember, they are the ones with the buying power) bolt from the idea of owning such a reversion to yesteryear: "I mean, man, where's the amp? You know? I played an acoustic once, and my buddy, who was only two blocks away—you know—I mean, he couldn't even hear it!''

On the other hand, to stock several full lines of brand-name instruments and accessories for all types of guitars—rock, jazz, country/western, and classical—ties up a lot of scarce dollars in inventory. But we've forgotten bass guitars and all *their* accessories! And what about mikes, booms, filters, mixers, amps, power conditioners, and other recording equipment? And have you considered drums, cymbals, gongs, tambourines . . .?

On second thought, you may decide to hold off going into the guitar-shop business. You may conclude that the fad portion of guitar sales has peaked and is declining. But you, a lover of musical instruments, need not despair; perhaps America's next musical craze will be for tubas and sousaphones! Now there's a business for you! All you need is . . .

3. *Listen.* Pay close attention to what the market winds are whispering. They could alert you to new directions, new trends, in marketing your product(s). Suppose, for instance, that instead of opening that downtown tuba shop, you consider a totally different approach to moving those noise pollution devices into the grasp of the end users. One way could be to place a series of low-cost ads in the "right" media and route buyers' money directly to your post office box. Then you would arrange for direct shipments from the factory to the customers, after which your middleman role is ended and you are contemplating your next venture. (I trust that you will pause long enough to send some money to the factory; those people deserve *something* for their part in your business venture.)

The arrangement outlined above may be attractive to you for several reasons. It could minimize your cash flow problems, keep you out of warranty hassles, avoid all lease and insurance obligations, and preclude your worrying about after-hours vandalism. Besides, where would you have stacked all those tubas and sousaphones?

In the next chapter we will look at several models for *clustering* on each of the five career paths. These will be understandable examples that should set you to thinking about other models and other examples. You will then begin to see personal variations, models that will pertain directly to you as you plan your future, whether it is to be in someone else's organization or in your own.

But before we leave entrepreneurland, we should understand that not all small-business ventures need be spectacular successes or frazzled failures. Many of them rock along, year after year, more as a way of life for their owners than as business enterprises. These owner/entrepreneurs seem to be happy doing what they do and how they do it.

And there is absolutely nothing wrong with that for you, either, provided you enjoy that way of life and have the financial and other wherewithal to bridge those occasional chasms. After all, there is much more to life than amassing great wealth or creating a business dynasty. Sometimes we can find those deeper values in the personal relationships that we build with other people in our own organization. In other cases they flow from our appreciation of the attitudes and skills we see in our customers or our suppliers.

Which brings to mind the story of the proprietor of a small store at the junction of two seldom-used rural roads. A big-city motorist, lost and overdue for an appointment, barged into the store. He was greeted warmly by the smiling owner, who began a rather lengthy explanation of how to get from the crossroads to the county seat.

But the stranger wasn't listening. His eyes were roving, and he was fascinated by what he saw no matter where he looked around the store—salt! Salt was everywhere: on the shelves, in the aisles, in the windows, and on the counters. Iodized salt, non-iodized salt, low-sodium salt. Salt in tiny shakers, in 100-pound bags, in two-pound boxes. Salt for deicing roads, for regenerating water softeners, for preserving dressed meat. Even salt licks for animals in the fields. Salt all over the place!

"I've never been in a store like this."

The proprietor smiled and said, "Well, it ain't your usual run-of-the-mill business. But it's all mine, and I like it."

The motorist, still astounded by the variety and amount of salt, mumbled, "I've never seen so much salt in all my life! Or so many different sizes and kinds! You must have, by far, the biggest retail salt business in the whole state."

Still smiling, the owner shook his head. "Nope. Matter of fact, I don't sell very much salt at all. Reckon I ain't no great shakes as a salt salesman. But there's a feller from Morton Salt who comes in here every month. Mister, *he* can really sell salt!"

Which may provide a glimpse into one way of life.

And may say a thing or two about salesmanship. And inventory control.

And may illustrate one method of how *not* to cluster!

# CHAPTER 11

# DECISION TIME

## DECISIONS, DECISIONS

Unless you are still hiding in school, you have already made a career decision or two. The chances are that you have already selected your career path, the one you are now treading: *worker, supervisor of workers, staff professional, manager of resources,* or *entrepreneur.*

Perhaps "selected" is the wrong term. You may feel that you were *forced* into your current job and thus placed, torso twisting and feet dragging, on your present path.

Whether forced or not, you may be thinking of changing career paths. Some of your friends have crossed over; you may have made an earlier change, yourself. Most Americans change career paths once or twice during their working lives, and it is normal for a person on one path to speculate about life on the others.

Like most of us, you probably entered your career path at or near its lower reaches. You have struggled to progress on that same path—job after job, promotion after promotion, perhaps even company after company. But while pressing onward and upward, you catch yourself wondering about the men and women on the other paths. Sometimes you glimpse a few of those other climbers, because the paths tend to wind about the organizational pyramid and sometimes one path runs close to another. And you ask yourself questions about that other lane as you pause for breath on your own:

201

Does that other path stretch higher and farther than
mine?

What are its joys and rewards?

What are the tolls along the way?

Is it more hazardous than mine?

What is *she* doing on that path?

How would she fare on mine? I on hers?

Are the jobs over there more fun? More secure?

You have asked good questions, and you might benefit
from an overview of all five paths. This overview will describe the paths and their usual points of entrance. It will
also look at you on each path, *as if you were following it*:
first as a satisfied traveler, then as one who wants "something more" and is considering other paths.

## CAREER PATH 1:
Worker

This path, familiar to most Americans, is teeming with trav-
elers, men and women of all ages. Most of them entered
fresh out of high school, college, the military, or a foreign
country. They toil in factories, offices, hospitals, department stores, hotels, banks, restaurants, and the nation's
stations: service, train, and police. Whether in the private
or public sector, and whether unionized or not, most of
these hourly and salaried employees are in the lower levels
of what the more cynical refer to as "the grand scheme of
things." It is true that most workers do report to low-level
*supervisors of workers* and that many perform work from
which they would like to escape.

They seldom make headlines, except when charged
with a fascinating felony. Sometimes, however, they are
mentioned in the company newspaper, items of recognition
such as:

- "Johnny Gruellbroth (Commercial Pricing) bowled a
  252 game last week, tops in the Office League! His
  team, the . . ."

- "Helen Hasty is back in the Bldg. C tool crib after an extended bout with . . ."
- "Rumor has it that Bob Burr (Payroll) and Cynthia Scythe (Adv.) will tie the knot as soon as . . ."
- "Turbo assemblers Ralph Gretch (left) and Roderick MacMulch put finishing touches on a model X-6 Sand Scrubber, the new product which . . ."

Most workers are on jobs covered by federal and state legislation pertaining to working conditions, overtime pay, and union representation matters. These people are the arms and legs of the company, the ones who actually do the work and provide the service for which customers pay real money. In a sense, then, most of the employees on other paths perform *peripheral* work, in support of the workers.

You are a worker, a good worker, satisfied on your path. In general, you like your job and your fellow workers and you usually understand and cooperate with the system. You have had two promotions since entering the path as assembly trainee (or filing clerk, or messenger) and you expect continued progress in the years ahead. Your ambitions and needs are relatively modest, and you certainly do not envy the supervisors and professionals whom you notice scurrying from one pressure-laden meeting to another. Your leisure hours are reserved for hobbies, friends, and family. You have little interest in continuing education because you believe the company (or somebody) will provide the training that will qualify you for a better-paying job farther up your career path.

Not you, you say? Then let us examine a different scenario. Again, you are a good worker, but now you are ambitious. You read a lot, take an occasional evening course pertaining to the business world, and are a keen observer of your company and how it operates. Rather than waiting to move farther along as a worker, you are hoping to better your lot by crossing over to another path. You realize that to leap directly from *worker* to *manager of resources* is unlikely, but you are eager to leave the rank and file. You have three options to consider: *supervisor of workers, staff professional,* and *entrepreneur.* Read on.

## CAREER PATH 2:
## Supervisor of Workers

This path represents a "move into management" and has been, for hundreds of years, the common avenue of escape from the ranks for factory and office employees. More recently, it has provided the first "real" jobs for college graduates who have just completed a company's formal training/indoctrination program. Also, it is sometimes entered, at low or midlevel, by talented *staff professionals* who feel the need to manage people rather than ideas or things. Such is the main task along this path, directing the activities of workers (later, of their supervisors), people much closer than you to the *real* work.

This path usually begins in the office with jobs such as mail room supervisor, office manager, supervisor of market research, or supervisor of accounts payable. In the factory its roots are jobs titled assembly supervisor, supervisor of production planning, purchasing manager, or quality control supervisor. In off-site locations this path may have entry-level jobs called supervisor of customer service, district sales manager, regional training manager, or manager of application engineering.

The men and women holding these supervisory jobs have several things in common, in addition to being at the starting point of the path. All of these people:

- Direct the day-to-day activities of a number of workers, from two or three to as many as thirty-three, depending on the product and the work processes
- Still do some actual work, sometimes when helping train a new employee, sometimes during an unexpected emergency
- Know more about the *total* work (and how to do it) than do most of their workers

- Know less about *parts* of the work (and how to do it) than do most of their workers
- Relay *many* messages from higher management to the workers
- Relay *some* messages from the workers to higher management
- Work longer hours than any of the workers
- Are *exempt* employees under the law—excluded from coverage of wage and hour laws and similar protective legislation
- Are prohibited by law from union representation unless their employer specifically grants permission
- Depend on their peers in other functions (engineering, finance, personnel, quality control, advertising, etc.) for support in getting the work done effectively
- Believe that they have a real knack for understanding, selecting, coaching, measuring, and motivating people
- Are viewed as considerably less than the ideal supervisor by most of their subordinates, peers, and superiors

You know all these things, of course, and more. You have been on the supervisory path for several years now, and you like it. You have had several promotions since entering from Notre Dame (or market research, or the toolroom). You now supervise those who supervise workers, and you expect one more promotion along the way. But you have seen many executives tumble from the top floor, so you don't push. You are content to coast, along with most of your peers, to the popular rhythm of your career path.

Or you may be quite eager for a change, to get ahead, to become a key executive in the organization. At the right time, then, you may cross over to the *manager of resources* path.

On the other hand, you may still be in an entry-level supervisory job and thoroughly dissatisfied with the nature of the work and your responsibilities. You may have become burned out, exhausted by the inexhaustible supply of day-to-day problems. You may have decided that yours is the most impossible job in the world: You are caught between the endless demands from top management (for higher production, lower costs, better housekeeping, less scrap) and the incessant pleas from workers for more understanding of their problems and needs. You realize that you are not "one of the gang." You know also that, despite what top management says at the annual supervisors' outing, you are really not part of management, either. You have just about decided that the pay, power, and prestige of this path is not worth its problems and perils.

Disheveled, distraught, and disturbed, you often envy those whom you supervise. They have fewer job worries than you, and the difference in pay is not all that great when their paid overtime is taken into account. But you are reluctant to become "just another worker," whether or not you rose from the ranks. You have two options: *staff professional* and *entrepreneur*.

## CAREER PATH 3:
### Staff Professional

Many people enter this path straight from college. Sometimes a *manager of resources* will move (or be moved) onto this path when he or she fails as a top executive. *Workers* and *supervisors of workers* usually sneak up on it obliquely. They do this, while still on their regular jobs, by devoting innumerable leisure hours (often at night) to the study of a discipline or technical curriculum such as law, accounting, robotics engineering, computer architecture, seismology, economics, and embalming.

This path is thought (by many people on other paths) to be rife with "cushy" jobs: private offices, high pay, and little responsibility. But you know differently.

You have been following this path since your graduation from Vanderbilt Law School (or from an evening engineering or business college). You began applying some of your newly acquired skills as soon as you entered this path, gradually tackling tougher and tougher situations. Trusted, you now attack some of your company's most important problems and opportunities. Most of the time you still work as an individual contributor, responsible only for your own work. Occasionally, you lead a small, "all-pro" team on a critical, short-fuse project. You relish the "authority of knowledge" feeling that comes from such ad hoc assignments, but you also appreciate not having to suffer the frustrations of the full-time *supervisor of workers*. For the most part your boss tells you which tasks to work on. But you have a considerable degree of latitude as to *how* to do them, whether in that nice office or on a week-long, fact-finding trip for the company.

You entered this path with more pay than almost any *worker* received and now, several years later, your salary, benefits, and perquisites are greater than those of most *supervisors of workers*. True, you do not command the stratospheric pay and "perks" of those people in the executive suite, but there are trade-offs: You enjoy practicing your profession, and now and then you represent your company at symposia, clinics, and similar technical/professional gatherings. You have found your niche.

Or maybe you haven't. Maybe you aspire to the "bigger and better," to your boss's jobs, perhaps even the CEO position. If so, your next path is that of *supervisor of workers,* directing the activities of other professionals of your same discipline or function. After a promotion or two on that path, who knows? You might be ready to change over to *manager of resources* in preparation for that top job.

Or maybe you haven't found your niche because you admit, to yourself, that the long hours and pressures are beginning to get to you. You find yourself dreading unpleasant confrontations—those periodic meetings with that unreasonable auditor, or with that flaky product manager, the one with the penchant for slippery statistics, exaggerated claims, and gooey grammar. You don't like the tension you feel each time your boss requires you to predict the outcome of a new situation before you have had time to assess it. And speaking of time, the backlog of work keeps piling up, even though you are working more and more overtime, all unpaid. Worse yet, you are becoming unsure of the scope of your duties: How much of you is the expert internal consultant, suggesting interesting alternatives to line managers, and how much of you is the *corporate conscience,* telling them what they must do? You are between the devils and the deep blue backlog! If you have no real desire to continue practicing your profession in the corporate structure, or if you would feel uncomfortable supervising people, you have an interesting option to explore: becoming an *entrepreneur.*

## CAREER PATH 4:
## Manager of Resources

This lofty, exclusive path is sometimes penetrated by a drifting son-in-law, or by a deposed federal bureaucrat to whom the CEO feels obligated. Occasionally, a heavily sponsored *staff professional* slips in. Such things occur, but not often. Most of the time, entry jobs on this career path are open only to the highly successful *supervisor of workers.* (This is *you,* remember?)

Top executives are always on the lookout for new talent, alert for that special man or woman, such as you, whom they can "sponsor" to manage a troubled (or promising) portion of the corporation. (Note: Your sponsor will expect reciprocal help should *he* or *she* encounter unexpected trouble from the CEO or the board.)

You have caught the eye of one of your company's top executives. She is especially impressed with how you have raced up the supervisory path, leapfrogging scores of your startled contemporaries. You haven't spent much time on any one job, or at any one level, but on each assignment you have worked hard, meshed with the culture of that part of the corporation, and used all the support systems adroitly. Each year you have managed your budget prudently and met all your commitments. Finally, as the division vice president of a major function or key project, you have let it be known that you were ready for profit and loss accountability, that infallible litmus test, the one used for separating potential CEOs from run-of-the-ledger executives.

Your new title could be division president, general manager, program manager, or merely plant manager; title is not nearly as important as the *scope* of your new job. Because of that P&L stewardship you now direct, through several layers of supervisors, the activities of many different functions: marketing and sales, finance, engineering, production, personnel, business planning, and the like. Subordinates, as well as superiors, count on *you*.

You still deal with people, of course, both inside and outside the company. But you are also expected to plan and monitor the most effective utilization of all other scarce corporate resources: money, capital equipment, image, market share, and the goodwill of your customer base. You seldom see the real workers anymore, except at the annual St. Swithin's Day festivities.

Still, you must try to convince them of your understanding and friendship as you orchestrate their efforts through a hierarchy of directors, managers, and supervisors, and a fog-shrouded communication system. Social distances and communication barriers are immense.

All of which is quite unfortunate, because you need those remote workers at least as much as they need you; they are the ones who determine, for the most part, whether or not you achieve your goals. By their collective efforts they help shape your individual performance and thus influence, for better or worse, the sponsor's opinion of you. In the final analysis, they have a strong say in whether or not you succeed as a *manager of resources*.

Or perhaps you begin to wonder about it all and its relative worth. You and your family "need" that big income, of course, and appreciate those executive "perks": the country club, company car, and those "working" vacations in Hawaii. If you should quit (or be fired) you would miss riding to the airport in those chauffeured, shaded limousines and then boarding the firm's corporate jet for the monthly meeting at headquarters. And you realize that you would no longer participate in the armed camaraderie of the executive dining room:

- "I heard this morning that Acme-Ajax is in real trouble with the SEC because Tom Smith—yes, *our* former controller—submitted a document that . . ."
- "Sorry, Bob, I haven't seen your memo on the new advertising campaign and my role in it. I've been on the road since . . ."
- "Of course you haven't seen Fred today—J.B. fired him Monday, and I don't blame J.B.! Fred was the worst . . ."
- "Why *did* we lose that contract, Sue? You seemed so sure . . ."

You may be tired of the complexities, concerned about your health, and no longer certain that you would like the next rung on the ladder, even if you were in a position to grab it. And you didn't like the way J.B. frowned when you tried to explain the reason for the delay in announcing the new schedule. Perhaps, you confess to yourself, you are over your head, on the wrong career path.

Your ego will not allow you to take a lower-level, lower-paying position in your company, or in any other, for that matter. So you are contemplating a new career path, one that could lead you to a prestigious, yet less pressure-prone position. You have an interesting alternative path to consider: *entrepreneur*. Think of it—your own shingle—Sue S. Fortesque, Unlimited Appraisals, Ltd!

## CAREER PATH 5:
### Entrepreneur

This career path, as we have seen, is readily available to just about everyone on all other paths, whether fit for the course or not. And speaking of fits, it is all too easy to become frustrated with the boss, or with the system, and suddenly throw in the factory towel (or the office towelette) and grab for shingle, hammer, and nails. Often it costs surprisingly little to tack up a new shingle; the big costs are in keeping it up there, year after year. The low startup cost is a good thing, of course. It has enabled many an enterprising person to launch a venture that met or exceeded the best expectations for it. Low cost has also snared the unwary, people who were not prepared for the adversities that are prone to pounce on almost any new venture and demand either more money, more effort, more time, or all of the above. The unwary person, suddenly wary, then tries to decide whether to cut losses and return to the old life or to plough more precious personal resources into a troubled business.

But this is not you. You have been out there on your own for quite some time now. Your venture is no longer a squalling brat, but neither is it a husky young adult. You and your organization have passed the tests and resisted the temptations of early entrepreneurship, and you believe that you are beginning to see a few specks of paydirt at the far end of that tricky tunnel you have been digging. The product is coming along very well in the marketplace, and the shop will soon be able to produce it in quantity. You have built a great team, especially those twelve district sales managers you lured from Lurid Lingerie! Further, your attorney and accountant assure you that if all continues well, the firm can soon "go public," thus making you and your team wealthier than the average lingerie tycoon.

But something may be missing; perhaps it is the thrills and uncertainties of the startup phase. It could be that as more and more controls and systems are built into your business venture, you are finding it too much of a business and not enough of a venture. Or as you approach that time when your private corporation, *your personal creation,* becomes property for the vulgar to fondle and fight over, you may secretly wish that you could keep it, simple and small again, all to yourself.

You have begun to think about making a change, perhaps onto a path where jobs have less risk, make fewer demands of you . . . Now, wait just a minute! Are you saying that a dynamic, successful loner such as you would be happy and effective working for Sears? Standard Oil? McDonald's? I don't believe it! You were cut out to be *independent,* to follow the entrepreneurial path, to conceive, develop, and *cash in on* an idea or two—to do it *your* way—until the Big Venture Capitalist in the Sky buys you out!

But I could be wrong; I may even be looking at the wrong person. Perhaps you are the other sort of entrepreneur, one whose great idea didn't pan out, one of the many mavericks who tried hard and failed. That being the case, which career path for you now?

Maybe the recent debacle was your first entrepreneurial fling. Looking backward, you believe that you know what went wrong. You are confident that you will avoid those and similar mistakes, if only given a second chance. Your lone eagle vision is still clear and compelling, and you are reluctant to slink back to the comfort and conformity of Marshall Field's. So you are thinking of selling the second car, mortgaging the house, and . . . *Hold it!*

Perhaps you should take a brief break—a respite from the pulls and panics of the entrepreneurial world. You could benefit by a temporary retreat into a sheltered zone. There, earning steady pay and smothered with benefit plans, you would have time to clear your mind, to test and retest that newest idea, to determine the resources required, and to plan your approach to new financing. More importantly, you would have ample time to reexamine/reassess the U factor. Were you on the wrong career *path,* or was your career *role* at fault?

# THE ROLE'S THE THING

The previous pages, peppered with provocative thoughts about career paths, illustrate the established way of thinking about careers and the world of work. It is the way your elders "got ahead," or tried to, in those simpler years: years when General Motors spoke for American industry and George Meany for "the working class," when a popular topic in typing pools and toolcribs was the impact of that new technological marvel, the ball-point pen, and when "career role" meant a long run on Broadway.

And it is probably the way *you* have been thinking once you got beyond narrow-scope, short-range questions such as:

How do I get ready for that interview next Tuesday?

Should I get my M.B.A. from Berkeley or from UCLA?

What is the vacation plan at Immobile Dynamics? The holidays?

It is not necessarily bad to think about your career path or to contemplate trying another. But neither is it the best way to go about planning and building a career—now. Today the *forces of change*, technological, economic, social, and political, are reshaping, radically and rapidly, the world of work. They are changing the *what, where, why, when,* and *whether* of work. And the *how* and the *who* of it! The chances are, therefore, that your future will be better served by your making your *career veer* another way, by becoming a *cluster specialist,* a change of career *role* that may or may not involve a change of career *path*.

The person who becomes a cluster specialist will, regardless of current collar color, enjoy measurable and enviable advantages, all those advantages we examined in Chapter 7—those "edges" that are simply not available to traditional specialists and traditional generalists. Restated briefly, these are:

1. You will not live in fear of the consequences of knowing more and more about less and less.
2. You will not live in fear of the consequences of knowing less and less about more and more.
3. You will satisfy your basic need for variety in the work you do.
4. You will satisfy your basic need to apply your brainpower, aptitudes, and attitudes, rather than repetitive know-how, in the work you do.
5. You will benefit from future change by knowing how and when to modify your established cluster to seize new opportunities.
6. You will be a cost-effective, utilitarian person, highly regarded and handsomely rewarded in the new order.

Now I suggest another reason: Becoming a cluster specialist can be fun! It can be fun because it is *different*. After all, almost any workaholic can, with seniority, make the customary career path advances: from vice president of commercial lending to senior vice president of commercial lending, from first officer to captain, from assistant professor all the way to associate professor.

It can also be fun because *you* are in charge of your career, personally planning and doing whatever is necessary to make things happen for you.

But what *is* necessary, and how do you get started on those critical steps? How do you go about establishing your first cluster, the location of which is that "very personal somewhere" described in Chapter 7? How do you begin?

You begin, strangely enough, by examining *who* you are (the U factor, again), and *where* you are (your present situation: job, work history, and so on). And you repeat, over and over, the definition of a cluster specialist: "the man or woman who works effectively, at reasonable technical depth, in a small number of technologies, crafts, or markets *having one or more unifying relationships.*" As you repeat the definition, you will remind yourself of the meanings of its words and phrases:

1. "Man or woman" means just what it says. There is absolutely no difference between the sexes in their abilities or opportunities to cluster successfully (there are, of course, some differences between *individuals*).

2. "Who works effectively" implies that the person's work performance is *somewhat above* the norm, better than the performance of most people doing the same or similar work.

3. "At reasonable technical depth" admits freely that the cluster specialist does *not* have the expertise of the traditional specialist—in the latter's narrow field. But it also says that the cluster specialist has *far* more expertise in that particular field than does the traditional generalist, overly extended and scrambling to "cover" many fields. Finally, this phrase implies that the cluster specialist, being nimble, will acquire, rather quickly, whatever special skills or knowledge may be needed.

4. "In a small number" means, of course, more than the *one* of the traditional specialist and fewer than the *many* of the traditional generalist. The proper number for you will depend on matters that are *personal to you*. But for most people the optimum number will be two, three, or four.

5. "Of technologies, crafts, or markets" reveals several of the ways by which one can build a personal cluster by:

   (a) Bridging similar *professional* activities, such as the *cardiologist* whose practice also involves treadmill testing/evaluation and geriatric medicine; or the *economist* whose consulting fields are agriculture, organic chemicals, and commodity markets; or the *attorney* whose practice is restricted to domestic relations, trusts for minors, and probate matters; or the *psychiatric nurse* who is also licensed as a family counselor and drug-abuse therapist.

(b) Bridging similar *craft* activities, such as the *stationary engineer* who develops the plant's cogeneration plans, methods, and measurements; or the *toolroom machinist* in a small, nonunion shop who doubles as a process planner, developing the setups and operational procedures for dozens of lower-skilled operators; or the *pipefitter* whose industrial repertoire includes the smallest of plumbing and the largest of steamfitting work; or the *executive secretary* in a small company who also edits the company newspaper and writes the nontechnical copy for the firm's product brochures.

(c) Bridging similar *markets,* such as the *industrial security consultant* whose clients consist of government agencies, research hospitals, and university laboratories; or the *word processing supervisor* who, evenings and weekends, instructs employees of other firms in the rudiments of office automation; or the *manufacturer's rep* who markets heavy-duty appliances to prestigious restaurants, hotels, and country clubs; or the *financial analyst* who monitors, for his brokerage firm, the product developments and changes in top management of twelve biotechnology and medical imaging corporations.

6. "Having one or more unifying relationships" has been shown in the preceding examples. In each case the person was pursuing two or three somewhat different, yet related activities, whether "in house" or "moonlighting."

Another, perhaps even better way to illustrate properly related clusters is to point to several common but *improperly* constructed clusters.

## CASE 1

Carlton Clout obtained his B.S.E.E. degree (microelectronics) at age 22. He then spent two years at an exclusive (and expensive) graduate school of business because he had been assured that an M.B.A. is most potent when it is from a top-echelon university and follows a technical undergraduate program. (He obtained the M.B.A. because "everyone knows" that it is the prepaid ticket to the top of the pyramid.) He entered the real world as a financial planner for a pharmaceutical firm and, two years later, became an acquisition analyst for a major bank. The following year young Carlton moved to a large oil and gas company as assistant treasurer. Two years later he became chief financial officer of a privately held clothing retailer. He had expected to replace the aging CEO but "resigned" after six months, rebuffed by the company's culture and rebuked by its outside auditors. He is now 31 and has been "consulting" (this means job hunting) for almost a year. What went wrong here? Well, almost everything! Examples:

• His technical degree has never been used, even indirectly. At 22 he had sound knowledge of electronics theory but no skills as an engineer. Nine years later he still has no engineering skills, and his technical knowledge bank is outdated, shrinking, and of little market value.

- His industry experience (pharmaceutical, banking, oil and gas, and retailing) is fragmented, so unrelated that it has almost no meaning for prospective employers.

- He has changed jobs, companies, and industries so often that he has little seasoning in any of them.

- There are no unifying relationships throughout his career. True, he has been a "number thumper" on every job. But this is relatively weak as a unifying force in today's world of electronic spreadsheets, precalculated tables, modeling tools, and similar software programs.

- Clout had acquired no expertise in accounting (on the job or in school) before becoming chief financial officer, a high-risk gamble for him and for his fourth employer.

- While scrambling upward, he alienated key managers in all four companies. So when reference checks are made . . .

## CASE 2

Phyllis Phast, age 27, has been with Sophisticated Spatulas since graduating (barely) from teacher's college five years ago. Hired as receptionist, this only child of Sophisticated's largest stockholder was soon promoted to secretary in the advertising department. Despite her problems with the language and her uncanny ability to forget names and faces, she was again "promoted," first into customer relations and then into credit and collections, where her weaknesses in arithmetic were called into play and usually demonstrated.

During her five years (and nine moves) with the company, fellow employees were puzzled: They could not detect the reason for all those transfers! Was she being moved about because someone saw her as an outstanding performer, or was the personnel department gleefully punishing the supervisors for whom she worked? The basic reason, of course, was to satisfy Mr. Phast, the major stockholder. His desire was straightforward and understandable; he wanted his daughter prepared for a career in business. Phyllis, who sometimes confused her physical attributes with intelligence, insisted that she be "broadened" through a lengthy series of brief, rotational assignments. Which she received.

Now she has a problem. It seems that just before Daddy passed over the Great Dividend Divide, he unloaded all his Sophisticated stock and bought municipal bonds issued by Rapid City, South Dakota. Now on her own at age 27, Phyllis has a lot of job titles to point to but not much to say about any of them. (But with all those tax-free bonds, she should worry about her lack of cluster!)

---

# A WEIGHTY PROBLEM

If you are a traditional generalist, you will have to lose some weight. To become a cluster specialist you must get rid of some of that excess baggage you have been lugging around for all these years, those seldom-used trappings to which you point with pride now and then just to prove that you are not a traditional specialist.

Let's say that you are an attorney in Keokuk, Iowa, dealing with bankruptcies, personal injuries, union petitions, divorces, SEC registrations, partnership dissolutions, real estate offerings, and farm foreclosures. And you are often in court, representing clients accused of insurance fraud, slander, breach of promise, public misconduct, and piracy on the high seas. Whew!

When you have a moment, you might begin sorting out the pieces of this jumble (and the pieces of the drawn-and-harried you). Your purpose will be to decide which three or four pieces of that chaotic smorgasbord should be retained and emphasized, thus moving you closer to the definition of a cluster specialist.

The same process is in order for other chubby, wheezing traditional generalists:

> *The entrepreneur* whose convenience shop sells astringents and applesauce, barley and bourbon, china and chopsticks, dusters and diapers, erasers and euphoniums, fetters and . . .
>
> *The tax consultant* who supplies advice on the legal and accounting nuances of tax situations in Alabama, Zaire, Alaska, Zambesi, Arizona, Zanzibar, Arkansas, . . .
>
> *The manager of administration* responsible for overseeing office services, secretarial hiring, records retention, building maintenance, labor relations, industrial security, and public relations—plus purchasing, parking, cafeterias, and employee recreation activities

But if you are at the opposite extreme—a traditional specialist, your goal is to fatten up by broadening your base consistent with the description of your new role—cluster specialist. By doing so, you will no longer depend solely on your expertise in repairing Edsel grilles (or designing treads for spacemobiles, or refereeing three-dimensional tic-tac-toe tournaments, or translating Sanskrit into Navajo).

So much for examples, except to say that these were just that, examples constructed to start you thinking about *your* first cluster and how to capitalize on *your* work experience and U factor.

Perhaps, to get started as effectively as possible, we should plan *together,* you and I, the team approach. But we must recognize the obvious problem: I know nothing about you except that you are now reading these words. I cannot even assume that you bought this book because you were interested in building a rewarding career. For all I know, it was given to you by a doting relative who prayed that it would keep you off the streets. Or it could have been donated by a "friendly" rival at the office who thought it might cause you to resign and take up tenor sax, thereby giving him a clear shot at the big prize—that district manager's job in International Falls, Minnesota.

So here is a workable solution to our dilemma: You supply the general information pertinent to your situation, and I will contribute those things that appear to be most responsive to that situation. Let us again use the method we used in Chapter 10—a form of catechism. In this exercise I will respond to the questions that I believe you might ask if we were to meet socially. My answers on these pages will be similar to what they would be if we were to chat for a few minutes at a party, with each of us trying to understand (and to be understood), despite the obvious barriers imposed by insufficient information about each other. In these pages, as at the party, I cannot study your résumé, nor can I learn anything about the most important (and certainly the most interesting) U factor that you will ever encounter— *yours*.

Yet we must do our best, so here goes! I will start with the gentleman near the hors d'oeuvre table. Yes, sir?

**QUESTION 1** Is there a standard process that most people should use as they go about building their first cluster?

**ANSWER** There are several things that most men and women should do. First, though, let's call out those things that almost everyone should *not* do as they begin changing their career role to that of the cluster specialist. Most men and women should avoid:

- Thinking of this move as a "second career." That catchy term implies an abrupt and radical change in what a person does for a living—the civil engineer who trades slide rule and correlation coefficients for palette and potter's wheel, or the Chicago clergyman who, at age 50, doffs the cassock and moves to Tibet, vowing to become a Himalayan travel guide.

- Rushing into the conversion of a hobby into a business; this seldom turns out as well as expected (the perils of this approach were treated in Chapter 10).

- Confusing career *path* with career *role* as they make the career veer. The veer occurs when the person builds that first bridge from his established role (traditional specialist or traditional generalist) to what will be the new role—cluster specialist. The career veer may, or may not, also involve a change of career path.

- Becoming so concerned about finding the "ideal" job, or that "industry of the future," that they overlook the more important aspects of career planning: the U factor, organizational culture, and work experience.

The standard list of things *to* do includes those key suggestions made throughout the earlier pages:

Understand the U factor, then plan how to best exploit it.

Understand the culture of the organization—yours, and that of the one you might join, then plan how to take advantage of culture—rather than becoming another of its victims.

Understand your job, and the world of work that surrounds it—not only as they exist today but as they are likely to become in the years ahead.

Then decide from *which elements* of your work experience the first bridge should be built, and to *what.*

And now a question from the young lady in the green dress!

QUESTION 2   I am an accountant with a Big Eight CPA firm. As an audit supervisor I sometimes lead the work of one or two junior accountants. Next year I will be promoted to audit manager and several years later I may, if I am very fortunate, be elected to partnership in the firm. My responsibilities have increased quite a bit in the four years I have been with the firm, and they will continue to grow as I progress. So what *is* my job? You say it is critical that I understand my work, but it will always be evolving, so I doubt that I ever know what its next form may be. So how am I to understand my work?

ANSWER   I believe that your work has changed for several reasons. The main one concerns your own progress since being hired off-campus by the accounting firm. You began as a *staff professional,* although your duties in that first year were sometimes routine tasks that could have been performed by someone with only half your training in accounting principles. The firm's main purpose was to drill you, to make sure that you learned *exactly* how *it* wants those elementary accounting tasks performed and recorded. Now you have begun to change career paths; it seems that you are sometimes leading small ad hoc teams and will soon become a *supervisor of workers.* This means that although you are still doing a lot of auditing and accounting work, more and more of your time is devoted to overseeing the work of other professionals. And if your work and your potential continue to please the powers that be, less and less of your time will be spent directly on the real work of accounting. Such is the saga of most *staff professonals* who become *supervisors of workers* or *managers of resources,* whether the field be accounting, advertising, economics, engineering, law, medicine, nursing, or the ministry.

   I agree that your work has changed. But how much, and in which ways?

I believe that, in one respect, your job is similar to almost all other jobs in the business world. Every job, every position, no matter how complex or how simple, is merely a collection of duties and decisions. It may be a very particular collection of duties and decisions such as those required of the president of the United States, or those performed only by the president of the Cook County Republican Boosters Club. Each of those jobs has its duties and its decisions, and not much else. One could, I suppose, argue that one job has this privilege and the other job has that hazard, but their duties and decisions are predominant.

Another way to look at this concept is to realize that if you were to hold either of those prestigious positions, you would be trying to please those who pay your bills. The same is true if you are a schoolteacher, robotics technician, CEO, maid, sales manager, computer programmer, welder, commercial artist, switchboard operator, or machinist. Almost regardless of your occupation, you are *selling your services to someone*. In each case an employer is paying your salary and providing your benefit plans *in exchange* for the satisfactory performance of your duties and decisions. (A similar statement applies when you are a volunteer worker, perhaps performing some *pro bono* income tax work in the inner city—except that you *donate* your services and receive, in return, "satisfiers" other than money.) Even the entrepreneur/owner is not exempt from the rigors of this ages-old marketplace. He or she also has duties to perform and decisions to make. Good performance on these leads to a product or service that is then exchanged for money with that ultimate employer—the customer.

The entrepreneur must perform well or go out of business. Similarly, most people on the other four career paths either perform to the satisfaction of their employers or eventually lose their jobs. So your job performance . . .

**QUESTION 3** Do you mean that my understanding of my performance is an important part of my work as an accountant?

**ANSWER** Yes, m'am! And just as all jobs are composed, essentially, of some mixture of duties and decisions, job performance is determined by some combination of four basic elements:

1. *Knowledge,* or information about the work to be done
2. *Skill,* or proficiency in executing the tasks
3. *Aptitude,* or ability to garner the required knowledge and to develop the essential skills
4. *Judgment,* or wisdom in applying knowledge, skill, and aptitude to the work to be done

These are the four basic elements that determine performance on *every* job. Naturally, the relative importance of one element to another element will vary from job to job and, to some extent, from person to person on the *same* job. (I realize that a case could be made that other elements, such as interest, attitude, perseverance, or divine intervention, play a part in performing work. For our purposes, however, we shall consider them as subsets of the basic four.) Although these basics are work-related elements, all four reflect portions of the U factor, especially aptitude and judgment.

Any job, therefore, regardless of its title, salary grade, organizational level, or work content, is a special collection of duties and decisions to which you apply the four basic elements. But each job has its own mixture of those elements. For example, I would estimate the relative importance of the elements in your job, as it is today, to be weighted something such as this: 35 percent knowledge, 30 percent skill, 20 percent aptitude, and 15 percent judgment. Later, as a partner with the firm, the ratio is likely to be about 20 percent knowledge, 30 percent skill, 10 percent aptitude, and 40 percent judgment.

QUESTION 4 But I just received my CPA! Why will my skill percentage remain constant, while knowledge and skill drop so much and judgment climbs so sharply?

ANSWER The pivotal element here is judgment. You will, as a partner, be sitting in judgment of the work performed by many nonpartners and of their progress in the firm. You will accept, reject, and modify their audit findings and recommendations to your clients. Often you must determine if, when, and how forcibly to disagree with a client, and on rare occasions whether your firm must issue a qualified opinion in a client's annual report to its shareholders. Or, worse yet, you may have the unpleasant task of recommending that your firm resign from a long-standing, profitable account; you may have concluded that the client's actions violate your ethical code and bend, if not break, the law.

These are *judgment* calls that flow from *seasoning,* from all those practical, on-the-job successes and failures yet to be experienced by accountants junior to you. You must supply the judgment that they will acquire (you hope!) a bit later in life.

Yet you will rely on those newer people for current technical knowledge and skill as they take evening classes and cram to earn the CPA designation. You don't have time to keep up with the multitude of changes, but junior professionals are expected to keep acquiring knowledge and to hone constantly their technical skill. These neophytes are also expected to show aptitude for *learning.* They must learn the various ways of researching knotty problems and promising opportunities. You will look to them to "bruise the books" and to "modem in" as they interrogate the nation's electronic data bases—those enormous, centralized repositors—where technical information is updated *daily.*

So that will leave you with the same 30 percent skill emphasis that you now have, but the type of skill will be surprisingly different. Right now, most of the skill requirement of your job is technical: verifying receivables, confirming inventory and tooling, testing the integrity of the purchasing cycle, reconciling bank statements, and so forth. As a partner, most of your skill requirement will pertain to bringing new clients to your firm and to directing and evaluating the career progress of professionals lower in the organization.

I believe the middle-aged gentleman in the corduroy sport jacket has a question. Yes, sir?

**QUESTION 5**   Now wait a minute, mister! I am *not* middle-aged; I am only 53 years old! Anyway, I am a lawyer by education and work experience, and for the past ten years I have been a *supervisor of workers* in a large aerospace company. As an associate general counsel, I direct the activities of five lawyers, two patent attorneys, and ten paralegal and clerical personnel. My unit supports the company's defense electronics businesses. My peer, the only other associate general counsel, supervises a similar unit; it is dedicated to the firm's aircraft and rocket businesses. Two years from now our boss, the vice president and general counsel, will finally retire. I fear that my peer, who is only 49 years old, will then become my new boss. We don't get along too well, so I have been thinking about taking early retirement at age 55 and starting my own law firm—one that consults with small, government contractors on matters such as contracts and pricing, renegotiations, and patent disputes. Would that be a good career veer for me and, if so, how do I build my first bridge?

**ANSWER**   I cannot recommend that you stay with, or retire from, your present employer at age 55. That decision will be based on many personal considerations—things that only you can assess.

Your idea of starting your own law firm is certainly an entrepreneurial thought, and I believe that you have already identified that first bridge. Actually, your career veer will be minor—you are already a cluster specialist! As I understand your plan, you will cluster in those few portions of the law (and of the business world) in which you have expertise. Although you will change career paths, you will probably avoid lurching into the horror chambers of a second career. So, not knowing any more about you than you have just told me, I have only four thoughts for you as you plan your new venture: continue doing your best for your present employer, expand and cultivate your contacts in those small firms, save your money, and reread Chapter 10!

The woman near the coffee table has been very patient; now your question, please?

QUESTION 6 I am the receptionist for a residential real estate agency. I think I have a reasonably good knowledge of myself—I understand the U factor. My interest is in sales, my long-range goal is to become the top salesperson in my company, and I know how to get there! I am already taking evening classes in real estate and sales techniques at a community college. I read all the manuals in the office and sometimes I get to tag along as the manager shows houses to prospective buyers. I like my company and am eager to . . .

ANSWER Pardon my interruption, but I don't believe you have a question—certainly not a problem! It sounds to me as if you are already doing all the right things. You appear to be on a track that will be good for you, and I wouldn't want anything I might say to detract from the good . . .

QUESTION 7 But my question is not about me! It is about *other* blacks—*other* minorities. What do you think most minority men and women need to do to prepare themselves for satisfying careers in the new economy?

**ANSWER** I believe that, in general, minority men and women should make the same U-factor appraisals, culture examinations, and work history analyses as do their nonminority counterparts. I am not aware of special "do's and don'ts" that apply only to minorities.

We all know that discrimination persists in many workplaces, despite the law and despite the efforts of many fair-minded nonminorities. Judging people *superficially,* solely on the basis of race, sex, age, health, religion, and similar generalities, is, in my opinion, not only morally wrong, it is stupid.

On the other hand, we have seen some instances where employers have erred the other way—where large organizations, private and public, have been too eager to play the EEO "numbers game." They have zealously hired and promoted a minority to a job *far* beyond his or her ability to perform. And that, in my opinion, is also morally wrong, and stupid. It is a shortsighted policy, not in the best interest of anyone: the organization, the minority, or the person who *should* have gotten the job. It is even more unfair to *qualified* minorities—people who may not get a chance in the future because of that one bad experience. The "bad taste" may linger long after the grievances and lawsuits have been forgotten.

I don't think I can focus on the "get ready" needs of minorities per se. But I can do something that might be helpful—not only to certain minorities but to all men and women who, for whatever reason, are among those unfortunate people referred to as "disadvantaged." [Note: Just to make sure that you and I will deal with the same definition of the term, I decided to look it up in my *Webster's Ninth New Collegiate Dictionary*. There I learned, to my surprise, that the term has been in the language since 1879. (The more things change, the more . . . .) Anyway, here is the defintion: "lacking in the basic resources or conditions (as standard housing, medical and educational facilities, and civil rights) believed to be necessary for an equal position in society."

All those conditions relate to career success, with the most obvious being education, the purpose of which is to prepare us to function effectively as adults. And *that* often carries with it the requirement to function effectively as an income generator—a wage earner. The terms *wage earner, education,* and *functioning effectively as an adult* imply an acceptable level of literacy— a reasonable ability to use the language and to make it work to one's advantage. Of course, it is possible that in the years ahead people will not be expected to be literate at all. Perhaps there will be intelligent nanocomputers, tiny devices embedded in our tie tacks and brooches, that will read, write, speak, and listen to each other. By short, silent, squirt of signal on a secure frequency, your nanocomputer will deposit in your brain selected bits of what my nanocomputer relayed to yours from *my* brain, then *your* brain will silently signal your . . .

Perhaps. But I think not. The chances are that tomorrow, even more so than today, successful people will be *skilled communicators,* at work and in leisure pursuits. They will be adept at reading, writing, listening, and speaking, and many of them will be facile in more than one language. But many people will have limited communication capabilities, and they will be in trouble tomorrow.

During my several decades of recruiting and consulting with corporations on personnel matters, I have seen federal and state education and training programs for the disadvantaged come and go—some tolerably good, some unbelievably bad. And they keep coming, for reasons such as this. California has designated fifty-eight of its high schools (mostly in large, urban areas) as "low-performing" schools because their students' average

score is in the bottom 25 percent of the standard state-
wide reading test. A study has revealed that:

- About 80 percent of the youngsters entering these
  high schools read at the fourth-grade level.
- Most of them remain functionally illiterate as
  long as they stay in school.
- Many of them are habitual truants and drop out
  before graduating.
- Most of those who graduate do so without the
  basic skills they will need to function effectively
  in the adult world.
- Teachers soon tire of the struggle to teach science, literature, and social studies to pupils who
  can barely read.
- Not all big-city schools are created equal. In
  some urban schools the average score is at an
  acceptable level, although most students are minorities and from destitute families!

I believe that many of the people who will be in
trouble tomorrow are rapidly heading that way today.
Yes, ma'am?

**QUESTION 8**   You answered my question—partly. You said
that minorities should prepare for future careers in
much the same way as nonminorities. And you seem
concerned about the future of those Americans of all
races who are disadvantaged. So what should *they* do
today to get ready for tomorrow?

**ANSWER**   The worst, yet most truthful answer is: "I don't
know." As I noted in an early chapter of the book, the
socioeconomic problems of our nation's uneducated
(and partly unemployable) are complex—and beyond
the scope of my book. So I don't offer a list of all the
things disadvantaged men, women, and children should
do to prepare. We could point to you as an example—a

minority-group member who appears to be doing the right things to prepare herself for future opportunities: studying the U factor, setting goals, attending night classes, and so forth. You may have been disadvantaged earlier in life, but not today! You seem *self-reliant*—to realize that although "they"—the government, a company, or a labor union—*may* provide a program, *you* are the one whose attitudes and actions will determine career success. Self-reliance is a *must*; you have it, and you are on your way!

You are also a skilled communicator, and I suspect *that* may be the other basic building block for success, today and tomorrow. This ability—to exchange ideas, to question, to learn, to unlearn, to explain, to convince—can open many locked doors.

And now your question, sir?

**Question 9**   I am a high school science teacher with a bachelor's degree in education and all but my thesis for my Master's in education. I like science but I, too, am tired of the struggle that you mentioned. I'm not sure who is to blame for this mess—the kids, their parents, TV, our permissive society, the school system, or I. All I know is that I am underpaid, overwrought, and I want out! My wife's uncle owns a hunting and fishing lodge in northern Saskatchewan, and he needs a partner—someone to handle the business parts of the lodge while he takes care of the field trips. So my wife and I have been thinking; perhaps she should quit her job at the advertising agency at the end of this school year, and we could then . . . Say, why is everyone giggling and pointing at me? Why are they laughing?

**Answer**   I suspect that most of them have had similar spasms—before they read the book and thought about becoming a cluster specialist. From what little I know about your situation and your plan to change it, I think that you are burning rather than building bridges. If you must leave the teaching profession, why not consider industry? You say that you still like science, so you might bridge from your long suit—physics, let us say— into an engineering assistant or lab technician job in a high-technology company. In addition to helping experienced engineers on interesting technical tasks, you might be able to bring your teaching skills into play by instructing sales personnel and customer reps in how to use and service the new models. To get started in industry you might have to reenter evening classes for a semester or two; later you might decide to go all the way for a bachelor's degree in physics or mechanical engineering. Then when you and your wife visit northern Saskatchewan for a two-week vacation, you can convert the lodge's power plant from DC to AC, install central heating, and redesign the sewage system!

It is getting late, and our host may wish . . . Yes, m'am?

QUESTION 10 My husband and I started a small company five years ago, making electronic devices in our garage. He did all the engineering, manufacturing, and selling while I took care of the books, wrote the ads, boxed and labeled shipments, and made the collections—the *business* side of the business. I have been running the company for the past two years, with the help of three experienced men I hired from other electronics firms. Last year we grew from $500,000 to almost $1 million in sales, all to customers right here in this region. We still make the same family of products we started with— filters that prevent static electricity from damaging computer memories.

My engineer thinks that in addition to continuing to update and improve our filters, we should be developing new concepts in other product lines. He is particularly keen on getting us into X-MOS chips, laser cogenerators, reflective absorbers, and other far-out products. My sales manager believes that we should stick with filters. But he wants to expand our sales effort into other parts of the country and to broaden the line to include protective filters for end products other than computers. My production supervisor says that we need to expand and modernize our manufacturing facilities and install a quality control robot.

My banker disagrees with all three! His recommendation is that we consolidate our gains and become *really* profitable, thus increasing our share values, if and when we offer stock to the public. He says that we can increase our profitability greatly, just by becoming more efficient at the things we are already doing.

I enjoy being an owner/entrepreneur, but my instincts tell me that my little company is approaching a critical intersection. My question is this: Should we keep forging straight ahead, or should we change direction? And if so, in *which* direction?

**ANSWER** First I must warn you that I know nothing—*zero*—about electronics. I wouldn't recognize a filter or an electron if one were to slither from that chandelier and splash into the punch bowl. But I do know a thing or two about entrepreneurial ventures, and my impression is that your situation is a classic—typical of the ventures that start small and bootstrap a good idea into a successful business, mainly by keeping things simple and satisfying the customers.

I agree that your company is now at the crossroads and that important decisions must soon be made. You realize, of course, that I cannot make them, but I have several observations that you might wish to consider:

- You—your company, rather—is probably too close to some of the same perils that surround the traditional specialist. You have only one product line, and it serves only one purpose—to protect computer memories. Your only customers are computer manufacturers and, really, only those with plants in this region. You might benefit by playing the "what if" game:

> What if memory designers begin placing *their* filters inside their memories?
>
> What if someone invents a totally new type of memory—one that requires no filter?
>
> What if a competitor from another region decides to blitz your region with loss-leader filters?
>
> What if static electricity is banned by the Environmental Protection Agency?

It seems that some "fattening up"—building a cluster of one sort or another—is in order.

- Some of the clustering options you will consider may be relatively inexpensive, reasonably safe, and have moderate potential for future growth and profitability. Other options, more speculative, may cost more to get into but, oh!—they are exciting! They might drive you directly into debtors' prison, or they could position your company to become the next Apple.

- Your three functional supervisors express the same general thoughts that their counterparts express in other companies. Most engineers thrive on developing new products; manufacturing people usually push for better space and more modern equipment; and sales managers are generally eager to open new territories and to broaden the established product line.

  Each of these functional heads probably tries to do what he thinks will be in the best interests of the company. But his functional training and experience tend to restrict his vision—to channel his thinking processes—to prevent him from seeing and understanding the broad, business picture.

- Your three supervisors have many different ideas and concepts about what the firm should do. (As a practical matter, I doubt that the firm could try all of them, even if it wanted to and had a line of credit ten times its present ceiling.) So which of the three is more nearly correct? Or does the banker have the best plan of all?

What we are wrestling with is a typical executive management decision. Dozens of similar decisions are made each week by a *manager of resources*—an executive with profit and loss responsibility who listens, very carefully, to the conflicts, the contradictions, the divergent views. He tests the testy contenders with tough questions and sometimes sandbags the sycophants with false clues. He then makes the decision and moves rapidly to the next problem (which he probably classifies as an opportunity).

Apparently, you may have made quite a few sound decisions during the two years you have been CEO of the venture. Now you must make the most important decision you will probably ever make as the CEO: Should you, or should you not, *remain* as CEO?

*Most entrepreneurs remain in charge too long!* Henry Ford, Adam Osborne, Lore Harp, Eddie Rickenbacker, and hundreds of thousands of other gifted founders were absolutely superb in the early stages of their firms' growth. Most entrepreneurs eventually harm that which they love most—their creation—because they are convinced that no one can help it as much as they can.

I am in no position to suggest what your decision should be in this matter—whether you should recruit a seasoned general manager, the "right" CEO for your situation, or whether you should stay on as CEO until those nanocomputers arrive on the scene. But I can tell you that this is *the* question. All those other issues about expanding, modernizing, and diversifying are peripheral issues and should not even be addressed until that CEO decision has been made.

Just one more question, ladies and gentlemen. It is almost time to . . . Yes, sir?

**QUESTION 11** I am a *manager of resources* and have been in the room-air-conditioner business all my life—or until three months ago, when I retired after thirty-three years with the same manufacturer. I started as a sales rep, right out of high school, and stayed in sales and marketing supervisory positions until I was promoted to Division General Manager five years ago. Now, after only three months of golfing, fishing, and gardening, I am ready—more than ready—to retire from retirement.

I did very well as a *manager of resources,* but I don't think I want that level of responsibility again, not at age 52 and with a strange company. My question is this: Should I hang out my shingle as a consultant? If not, what else should I consider? I'm anxious to get going again, and the sooner the better!

**ANSWER** I think one portion of the U factor is showing—vitality! But I could be wrong; maybe it is merely impatience, or restlessness, or the need for excitement. Or some combination of the four.

I mention this partial (and perhaps incorrect) glimpse of the real you to illustrate a point: The U factor, which differs from you to her, and from her to him, and from him to me, is *central* to a very important cluster—yours. That is what makes becoming a cluster specialist such a personal thing. Let's make up a hypothetical situation. While we are in the mood for make-believe, let us say that it happened in Washington, D.C., where strange things have been known to occur.

Two electrical engineering graduates, age 22, were hired on the University of Maryland campus by the same federal agency. During their twenty years with this organization these men received the same training, held the same types of jobs, and earned identical salaries. They left the agency on the same day, each age 42. How similar, how different, might their future work be?

We might assume that both will stay relatively close to those things with which they have become familiar: engineering processes, technologies, counterparts in industry, technical societies, administrative routines, and—of course—the Potomac. And they may do just that. But because we know almost nothing about the inner men, it is also possible that they will not. They may, while admiring each other's twenty-year pins, decide to go to work for the Thessolonian embassy in New York City, or to enroll in a correspondence course in travel agentry. More likely, one of them will remain close to his habitat because comfort, stability, and security are large elements of the U factor. And, for all we know, the other will not. Maybe he has been, and always will be, a bit of a maverick. Maybe he remained in government service only because he was gathering data for a textbook on incongruity. And maybe he stayed in the Washington area so that he could be close to its fountainhead. Now he has all the data he needs, and he wants to move to a quiet place where he can write without being distracted by the niceties of inner-city living. Fortunately, an old college buddy has a hunting and fishing lodge somewhere in northern . . .

So I think we can detect, sir, your need for speed—that strong urge to get back into the action. And that's great if you can slow down long enough to identify and evaluate your alternatives—the options available to you, based on the U factor, your work experience, and the types of culture you believe you should and should not enter.

Looking only at your work experience, I see certain things you should be able to bring to the consulting table: your knowledge of the room-air-conditioner business, your expertise in sales and marketing, and your five years' successful P&L experience as a division general manager. I believe I can identify several first-cluster possibilities for you. You have the responsibility to find and assess all of them, but here are a few for starters:

1. On *general management* problems for producers of the one product that you know thoroughly—room air conditioners

2. On sales, marketing, and distribution matters on a small group of related items—room air conditioners, evaporative coolers, dehumidifiers, and heat pumps

3. On *dealer training* programs covering *all* types of major appliances, large and small, for use in the home

4. On *market research* activities for *all consumer* items

You may have noticed that when one aspect of a cluster is *broad,* such as general management, the other aspect of that cluster is *narrow*—in this case, only one product. Conversely, when the first aspect is narrow (such as market research), the other aspect is very wide—*all* consumer products. And that is the ideal way for all clusters, regardless of one's career path, to be constructed. Another desirable design feature is to have *one* "lead" specialty, the one field in which your expertise is, and will continue to be, greatest. A case in point is the second cluster suggested above. There you consult on sales and marketing matters involving four related products, but your lead specialty, based on your work experience, will probably be room air conditioners. But suppose that in several years your expertise is no longer in demand—that room air conditioners have been replaced by nanocomputers—those tiny gadgets on tie tacks. There, again, the cluster specialist has the advantage over people still clinging to the old career roles. The cluster specialist will always have one or two other closely related fields of strength on which to rely. More important, the experienced cluster specialist has conditioned himself to be *alert for change*—to anticipate those new developments that may present problems *and opportunities* for the existing cluster. He or she can take advantage of the *new,* long before competitors realize that the *old* has joined the wringer-washer and the IBM 360.

Another and somewhat different option is for you to become a dealer. For years you have trained others how to sell to the end user, but you have yet to do it yourself. It might be fun and, with your background, most producers would look favorably upon your chances of making a franchise really hum. Still another cluster to consider is becoming a manufacturer's rep. Here you might set it up in either of two ways. You could sell a small line of component parts for a variety of electromechanical appliances, or you could concentrate on a large line of such parts for one appliance (or, at most, two or three).

I suspect that you may have more options to consider than patience to evaluate them. And that could be a potential problem—why begin making serious mistakes at age 52? Why not wait another thirty years or so? But your potential problem also contains a ration of opportunity. You *do* have interesting options for clustering, any one of which could keep you so busy that an occasional round of golf would be fun again.

And now, ladies and gentlemen, we will have the *final* question, and I have reserved it for our host—the dapper gentleman in the white dinner jacket. But I must admit, sir, that it is difficult for me to imagine that you—a super-successful entrepreneur—the owner of this lovely mansion behind locked gates—could have a career question or problem. But these final minutes are yours, sir.

QUESTION 12   Well, I do have a question, and it is linked with the whole story of how I got where I am today.

Most of you may not know it, but I used to be a machinist in the auto industry. I built jigs, fixtures, and other tooling for the production lines, but in my spare time I was always fooling around with new and different ways of doing things. I dropped dozens of my ideas into the suggestion boxes, and the plant manager usually liked them. And they would reward me—$100 here, $50 there—you know how those things work.

Then one Saturday it happened! I was in my garage, working on the exhaust system of my old van, when I stumbled onto the *big* one. I discovered how to make an internal combustion engine run on what I termed the "repetitive, regenerating, recycling process," and I invented the three-stage reverse coupling device that operated the process. I can't tell you anything more about the process or the device because I was sworn to secrecy when I sold all my rights to one of the Big Three for $25 million. That was eight years ago, and they have since resold it to a Middle East oil consortium for $750 million, so you will never be able to enjoy the remarkable benefits of my first great invention.

I then began thinking about numerous other inventions, things desperately needed by our society that I could prevent from ever seeing the hood of your car or the inside of your home. So I quit my job at the assembly plant, took a three-day vacation, and opened the first shop of its kind in the world: Impeded Inventions, Inc.

My first impeded invention after the one that would have taken the place of gasoline was the "paste pusher-puller." This little electronic molecular rearranger not only extracted *all* the paste from a tube of toothpaste, glue, and so on, it would also reinject all paste that had been accidentally squeezed from the tube. You can imagine what a furor this created when I demonstrated it to . . . well, to one of the largest corporations in America. Those executives recognized it at once for what it was—the threat of the century—and bought me out, through a mysterious Bahamian bank, for $35 million tax-free dollars.

Then came the "restorative staple remover"—it automatically refilled those two little holes as the staple was removed. After that came my solution to one of our nation's most complex problems: "The check is in the mail!"

But enough of this background. I am not happy as a multimillionaire, super-successful entrepreneur, wearing white dinner jackets and living behind locked gates! I miss the fun of working with the guys in the toolroom and on the production lines. I have tried to get my old job back, but I have no seniority. And other companies are afraid of me. They think I will come up with another invention—one they will have to impede by buying me out. My question is this: How can I return to the *worker* career path?

**ANSWER** Well, yes . . . Well, it *is* awfully late, and many of you have a great distance to drive. Perhaps I, as the expert here in career counseling, should consult on this question with my host, *privately*. In that way, he and I could . . .

# CASE DISCUSSION

## CASE DISCUSSION 1:
## Bradley Monson

1. *Should he consider leaving ICC?* Yes, but calmly.
   He must also continue good work and improve ties
   with his new boss.

2. *Why? Why not?* Because he senses that he is near-
   ing a major career crossroads. Either he will or will
   not be promoted to vice president and controller in
   two or three years, and his relationship with Reedy
   either will or will not be positive. Besides, Monson
   should see just what is "out there."

3. *If "yes," to which industries and which cultures
   should he move?* He should consider stable, mature
   situations—ones most apt to appreciate his likes
   (especially his needs for a structured environment
   and for recognition and reward), and his highs
   (particularly his technical strengths and leadership skills). Greater Pittsburgh has many such
   situations.

4. *Should he discuss his concerns with Reedy? With
   the chief financial officer?* Yes. Yes. He has little to
   lose and, perhaps, much to gain by having frank
   discussions with these two decision makers. He
   should also be prepared to talk with the CEO, especially if Reedy appears to vacillate. But even if
   Monson were to be assured by all that he would be
   promoted in several years, he should begin expand-

ing external business contacts, mainly among CEOs and CFOs. Assurances have a way of dissolving into intentions after a year or two; besides, he might find a situation superior to what ICC would offer. In the meantime, he should *not* forsake his ICC vested retirement (available in two more years) to join that entrepreneurial venture—look again at the U factor.

I suspect that, on balance, Bradley Monson may be better appreciated at ICC than he realizes and that his "fans" will grow as more time goes by. His new boss may or may not be successful and, whether he is or not, certain members of management (and the outside auditors) will surely prize Monson's strengths. So, who knows? Someday our man may fill ICC's top financial job.

## CASE DISCUSSION 2:
Phillip Larghretti

1. *How should he respond to the comments of Titanic's consultants?* Quickly, and consistent with their wishes. After all, they were hired by Titanic's CEO and, presumably, have his respect. Larghretti neither understands nor trusts their quantitative approaches, but such is now the name of the game in his company. He needs to buy some time—time to plan and evaluate career options—and the purchase price is to submit the requested plan and in proper fashion. This is his best short-range tactic, even if he must secretly hire a wet-eared M.B.A. student to help him assemble the plan.

2. *Can he adjust sufficiently to the new methodologies—enough for him to be considered a potential replacement for his boss?* Probably not. His boss, also "old school," will most likely be replaced (and soon) by an executive whom the CEO believes will

direct Fathomless according to a detailed business plan. Such direction is not Larghretti's long suit.

3. *Can he adjust enough to stay where he is?* This is much more likely, but far from a certainty. For years, Larghretti has been running sales organizations, *successfully,* by "gut feel" and "instant instinct." His adjustment problems would be more attitudinal than intellectual. Larghretti could soon learn to "throw the numbers around" sufficiently well to please the powers that be—if he really wanted to. Maybe an acceptable solution would be for him to recruit an assistant whose profile counterbalanced his own. Thus the new man or woman would supply the missing theory and interests while, concurrently, absorbing Phil's practicalities.

4. *Should he even try to adjust?* Yes, at least for two or three years while another part of him explores outside possibilities with competitors, with food brokers, and with the bankers regarding a startup venture in frozen foods. Also, those two years could see some interesting developments within the company: The consultants could be drummed out in dishonor while Phil earned a vested pension! And the CEO might come to appreciate Larghretti for what he is: an *excellent* sales manager who can produce great results if not burdened by sophisticated methodologies. (If I were that CEO, I would ask Larghretti to help me find and recruit his new peer—a "new school" marketing vice president with whom *he* would be comfortable. I would stimulate them to plan and act as a team, and I would make sure that Phil's total income was far greater than ever—provided that he and his sales force met the sales targets that he had helped establish.)

Phil Larghretti will not change the Titanic culture, but he *can* change his attitude and modify his behavior sufficiently to become even more successful at Fathomless than in years past. And, in so doing, he just might learn a thing or two, and those consultants might learn from him.

## CASE DISCUSSION 3:
## Margot Lansky

1. *How should she handle her relationship with Loshin?* First, Margot must decide whether to leave SIL-MOS now or to remain for at least two more years, thus earning a vested pension. If the decision is to leave in the next few months, she should be thinking about the outside world rather than expending emotional energy trying to relieve that strained relationship. She should, of course, do everything reasonable to avoid worsening matters, but her primary concern should be the identification and evaluation of attractive career options.

   If, however, she elects to stay with SIL-MOS, both she and Loshin need to make a dedicated, sustained effort toward improving their working relationship. This effort must be based on open, two-way communication in which each raises questions, discusses issues, and suggests solutions—solutions to which both parties contribute. To do less would be unfair to both, and to SIL-MOS. It could also be damaging to all concerned; relationships, once they have begun to move in a negative direction, tend to accelerate, drawn toward that black hole labeled DISASTER!

2. *How much, if anything, does she "owe" SIL-MOS for the fast track and partial tuition it has provided her?* For the fast career track, nothing! Her *performance* earned those promotions and pay increases. The answer to the partial tuition issue is not as apparent. It dwells deep within the framework of each person's view of offerings and obligations, investments and indebtedness. SIL-MOS probably expected to benefit from its "investment" in her legal

education, but it received no such guarantees. (The laws permitting indentured servitude were repealed in those early years when computers consisted of only two parts: slate and graphite.)

And the company *has* benefited during the three years since she completed evening law classes and passed the California bar. Her value to the company has zoomed, mostly because she has been working as a cluster specialist. As such, she taps skills in three related fields—product design, competitive analysis, and patent law—a powerful cluster of pertinent strengths that has helped SIL-MOS keep ahead of Japanese and domestic competitors. And let us not forget that cluster-generated coup that saved SIL-MOS three-quarters of a million dollars; that feat would seem to take care of the continuing education of a hundred talented professionals.

But this is a subjective decision—one to be made by the person directly involved—one that the rest of us should not prejudge or second-guess. (But if I were Margot . . . )

3. *Where will Margot be happiest and most productive?* The easy answer is *somewhere other than SIL-MOS.* Her U factor almost demands, for several reasons, that she move to another company: Her progress has plateaued, her learning opportunities are fewer than in earlier years, and she will soon begin to smart under Loshin's increasingly close supervision. True, she could remain, hoping to replace Loshin or the engineering vice president before their anticipated retirement dates. Or she might aspire to a new executive position resulting from SIL-MOS's future growth, internal or by acquisition.

I believe that Margot's sights are set higher than on any of those rather remote possibilities and that she has made the decision to leave, and *soon.* So that brings us to the more difficult answers—answers to the *what, where, and when* of the outside world.

Generally, she should avoid bureaucratic, hierarchical, stodgy organizations that manage by *committee action*. Also, she should peer warily at organizations that regardless of size, stress *decision by consensus, Theory Z,* or other forms of participative management. These democratic but slow-moving cultures have many pluses and are ideal for some people, but not for Margot—for long. Her rapid mental processes, incisive insights, and need for closure would often be dented, deflected, and derailed by group impediments. She would then become at least as frustrated as she would if she were to remain at SIL-MOS—Loshin now feels threatened by her prowess, so his gaze is flinty and his supervisory controls are closing around her. (A man or woman with her U factor is not happy when forced to play slide trombone in a telephone booth!)

Her credentials would enable her to join a large, high-technology firm as director of development engineering or as chief patent counsel. Or she could readily be appointed vice president of engineering by a firm similar in size and product scope to SIL-MOS. These would not necessarily be bad moves for her; neither do they seem to be the best available options. Here are several situations that appear to have superior long-range values for this talented young woman:

- As general counsel for a dynamic, high-technology company somewhat larger and broader than SIL-MOS. This could preserve her career role of cluster specialist—design engineering, competitive analysis, and patent law—and expand that cluster by adding a fourth zone: corporation law. A move such as this *could* be the final move for Margot. She could exploit her cluster specialist role thoroughly, becoming ever more expert in her four *zones of authority*. Then as more and more change occurs in her world, she might decide to drop one of the four, perhaps replacing it with another, or perhaps delving deeper and deeper into the three remaining zones of her cluster.

- As a principal (soon-to-become-partner) in a large, general management consulting firm such as a McKinsey, A. T. Kearney, Booz-Allen, or A.D. Little. Or she could join, in the same capacity, a large public accounting firm such as Arthur Young, Arthur Anderson, or Ernst & Whinney. (These and other Big Eight firms offer, in addition to their audit and tax practices, management advisory services that have little, if anything, to do with accounting.) Or she could join, in the same capacity, a major law firm—one that serves the particular needs of high-technology industries, including patent work.

There are three reasons why these consulting options may not be "right" for her. First, most such firms are huge partnerships, dedicated to consensus management and brimming with their own brand of bureaucracy. Second, in each firm *one* type of practice (such as audit or litigation) tends to predominate, thus relegating other practices to lower status. To paraphrase George Orwell: "All partners are equal, but some are more equal than others." Third, each firm would shrink her established cluster. She would not be allowed to practice law, even patent matters, in a Big Eight or general management consulting firm. Conversely, her two engineering zones—design and competitive analysis—would not be fully exercised in a law firm. But wait! There are several good reasons why one of these consulting options could be ideal—could be just what the career counselor ordered for Margot:

- It would broaden her knowledge of the business world. She would be exposed to critical differences in industries, products, companies, and cultures. (She *is* provincial.)

- It would provide stimulating peer relationships. She would interact daily with dedicated professionals of all ages and backgrounds—men and women just as bright, eager, and talented as she. (And a bit of humility would not hurt this young woman!)
- She might learn to like the "big partnership" world, adjusting to its methodologies, yet retaining her individuality and eventually becoming a top producer. (Possible, but unlikely; recheck that U factor!)
- It would help her move higher into the corporate world. Her consulting experiences would provide a substantive training ground for upper-management responsibility. (And, almost as important, that's the way her consulting background would be viewed by the hiring CEO.)
- It would prepare her for starting her *own* practice! This is probably the most important reason for her to serve a two- or three-year apprenticeship with a "name" law firm or consulting house. If she could play trombone for that long, those few years could serve as the ideal springboard into her own entrepreneurial venture—one that she could shape and reshape around her cluster—a venture that would exercise her talents to the fullest and would allow her to express her individuality as she saw fit. (Well, *almost*. She would still have to remind herself that her clients, no matter how stupid they might sometimes appear to be, are paying her fees—fees that could enable her to retire on the Riviera the same year that Leonard Loshin cashes, gratefully, his first Social Security check.)

*NOTE:* In the remaining case studies the reader, rather than the author, supplied the questions. Those case discussions will therefore be structured somewhat differently from the first three. In particular, they will be less lengthy than the case just discussed, which was explored in some depth for two reasons:

1.  To increase your awareness (after the relatively simple treatments of the first two cases) of the depths to which almost any case can be examined.

2.  To set the stage for *your* plumbing the depths of the remaining six cases. I will present my thoughts, but you will be expected to do some thinking about these plateaued people. Remember, the key points in any of these nine cases could apply to *you* or to *someone in whom you are interested.*

## CASE DISCUSSION 4:
Peter Haagen

Haagen will probably have difficulty moving into another corporation at his present level of compensation and "perks." Despite his record of success after success in three companies, the limiting factor is that all his experiences have been in or near the manufacturing function. Even now, as president of a profitable $150 million division, he does not have true profit and loss responsibility—the marketing and sales of his products are the responsibility of headquarters personnel. In reality, Haagen is a well-paid, glorified *supervisor of workers* rather than a true *manager of resources.*

But he is obviously ambitious, talented, and capable of broader responsibilities. My general recommendation is for him to remain at Immaculate Perception for at least two or three years. While becoming pension-vested, he should improve his mobility quotient in several ways:

- By gaining experience in marketing and sales, either by having those functions assigned to his division, or by transferring to corporate headquarters on some sort of rotational executive development assignment.

- By developing positive relationships with managing partners of several international management consulting and executive search firms; they would relish the Haagens' international backgrounds (and Mrs. Haagen's desire to live in a major European city).

- By developing positive relationships with bankers and financial analysts active in his industries, including those with ties to international and foreign-based corporations.
- By rekindling old relationships within LePont and Priest Laboratories and with alumni of those companies.
- By encroaching, *gently,* on the territory of the new executive vice president (the recently appointed "Mr. Outside") by expanding personal contacts among customers, suppliers, and competitors.

## My Questions for You

1. Mrs. Haagen, who does not like living in Chicago, would be content with life in San Francisco or in Washington, D.C.—cities that are not centers for industries in which Peter has worked. Should he try to move into a related industry in one of those locations?

2. Should he become an entrepreneur? If so, in which field? How should he go about it? In which city?

3. Should he try to change career roles—become a *manager of resources,* by moving to a true CEO position, even though it would mean running a company only two-thirds the size of his present division? And with a commensurate reduction in pay and benefits?

4. How can Haagen best capitalize on his superb three-zone cluster—industrial engineering, production troubleshooting, and factory management—without becoming a CEO?

## CASE DISCUSSION 5:
### Harold Nakahara

Nakahara's mobility is limited but certainly not nonexistent. His age and lack of degree are partial restrictors, as are his unwillingness to relocate or to try (again) as an entrepreneur. Most important, Harold no longer has an influential sponsor to help boost his career progress.

So this aerospace/defense electronics executive has a major problem—one that he is not aware of—avoiding impetuous action! Granted, he believes that he has lost face, and it is understandable that he feels the need to redeem himself. But that redemption need not take the form of a sparkling promotion either within Iris Interdiction or with another defense contractor.

Nakahara's enhanced stature could flow from the already sound relationship he has established with his new boss—that bright, young Ph.D. from Pantheon. It could result from long (after) hours advanced-concept work they perform together. Perhaps this is a special long-shot "black" project, secretly funded by the CEO. (Remember, the CEO is pleased that the two have such a good relationship. He is enthusiastic about the blending of the old and the new, the practical and the theoretical.) In this scenario, each could draw from and build on the skills and savvy of the other, eventually demonstrating the value of symbiotic technical relationships. (Translation: A hidden pair of aces will, when revealed, provide some unexpected results!)

Another Iris-based option would be for Nakahara to become active in one or two industry/professional associations. By representing Iris effectively as he persistently pushes for higher professional standards, Harold will inevitably enhance his stature and reputation.

Generally, I feel that he is properly situated in terms of corporate culture, salary, organizational level, and the nature and scope of his responsibility. I think he should stay with Iris. On the other hand, I respect his emotional status and the fact that, to him, it is a *rational* thought process. His ego needs are, quite properly, very important to him. But so should be the counsel that there are many ways in which he could receive those valuable, positive strokes.

*My Questions for You*

1.   In what other ways could the new boss help Nakahara regain self-esteem?
2.   In what ways could the family help?
3.   In what ways could his fluency in the Japanese language provide needed reinforcement?
4.   How could his interest and skills in training/coaching aid in his readjustment?
5.   If you were to construct an entrepreneurial venture for him, what features would be included? Excluded?

## CASE DISCUSSION 6:
### Billy Joe Woodson

This Georgian seems to have all the essential ingredients for continued success in the business world—*almost*. To continue his progress Woodson need not complete his degree (although that would probably be helpful, both in substance and in face validity). He need not become expert in computers, nor must he uproot his family (thus shattering his wife's legal practice) and relocate to New York. What he needs most is a *specific goal*. And that goal could be fashioned around one of the following:

• Continue, until retirement, in his present position as Atlanta district manager for Tokishubi
• Join a rapidly expanding competitor in the same capacity, with the understanding that as sales and profits increased in his district, he would be made

responsible for the southeastern region, based in Atlanta

- Establish his own business by becoming a manufacturer's rep, selling and servicing several related families of office copiers and supplies

The first two options are readily available to Woodson; the third demands both restraint and flexibility. Restraint is required because he should not leave Tokishubi precipitously; he needs to learn a few more things before risking his own assets. Flexibility is important because, short-range, Woodson may just find himself doing several things that he would prefer not doing, such as working part-time each week in New York City.

My suggestions for implementing the third option include:

- Groom an assistant, a responsible person on whom Woodson can rely to help manage the Atlantic district, and in whom Pat O'Myhe, Tokishubi's national sales manager, has confidence
- Strike an agreement with O'Myhe regarding the job about to be offered Woodson—national sales training manager—its main mission being to plan, produce, and update a lengthy series of interactive, video training discs
- View the next two or three years as an opportunity to get ready for the main event—his own business!

The agreement with Tokishubi would deal with matters such as salary, expense account, work schedule, schedule for completion of the videodisc series, his grooming a replacement for himself as national training director, and so on. This agreement, properly fashioned, could be in the best interests of both parties. Woodson, while vesting, would learn a new training and communication technique, one he could later apply in almost any setting. More important, he would absorb much of the *business* aspect of selling and servicing copiers as he toiled in the city's concrete canyons each Tuesday, Wednesday, and Thursday. He would, we presume, preserve most of the critical elements of family life (and expand Georgia business contacts) during the four days and nights he worked in Atlanta. He would help develop his assistant district manager, thus providing a built-in potential replacement should the entrepreneurial urge prevail. He could also be planning that possible new venture, considering many things, including whether or not he should have a counterbalancing partner, a man or woman strong in the financial aspects of entrepreneurship.

Tokishubi could also benefit from a part-here/part-there deal with Woodson. His training, coaching, and personal selling skills would be captured on the new videodisc system, preserved for use by all Tokishubi employees. His commuting expenses—travel and lodging—would, for two or three years, be much lower than the costs of a permanent transfer and relocation. Further, the company would be reasonably assured of having *two* qualified replacements for Woodson, should he be lured elsewhere.

## My Questions for You

1. What are the dangers of such an arrangement for Woodson?
2. Why is he apt to succeed as an entrepreneur? To fail?

## CASE DISCUSSION 7:
## Malcolm Maclean

You may recall that this is the only case in which the plateaued person and I are not in agreement about the U factor. Although I concur with MacLean's view of his likes and dislikes, we differ distinctly as to the highs and lows.

In particular, Malcolm sees himself as a skilled manager, a team player, an inspirational leader, and a good developer of subordinates. I consider him to be a brilliant but self-centered person—an individualist, almost a "loner." I think he may be effective as the technical leader of small teams; in that narrow context I can see him as a (sometimes) inspirational leader and somewhat of a *technical* developer of subordinates.

MacLean considers his lows to flow from his relative lack of experience in certain sections of the business world. Again, I must disagree. Generally, I regard such voids as being, at worst, temporary barriers to career progress. His real problem, I believe, is a negative cluster of three interrelated lows:

- Weak "people skills"
- A superior/snobbish attitude
- A disregard for the interests and viewpoints of other people, whether subordinates, peers, or superiors

Our differences of opinion become even greater as we try to visualize his future. MacLean, who entered the business world as a *staff professional,* is now a *supervisor of workers.* He directs several subordinate supervisors and, through them, the work of several dozen *staff professionals* and *workers.* He sees himself becoming a *manager of resources,* CEO of a major financial services corporation—as soon as he obtains the needed experience.

I see the converse. In fact, I believe that he will revert to *staff professional,* the career role that is probably best suited to his particular collection of strengths and weaknesses. I would expect this reversion to the status of a highly creative individual contributor to occur several years in the future. As users of information systems and services become less awed by the mystique of the computer and its software, they will sound an increasingly strong voice in the creation and maintenance of those systems that support their line-management efforts. MacLean is not at his best in these give-and-take sessions with nontechnical people; in fact, such confrontations tend to evoke his worst traits. His best, I believe, can be called upon from a highly technical cluster, one that taps his great strengths in mathematics, computer science, and systems engineering. This cluster would be situated far upstream from current software development and would contain no formal management responsibilities. I can see MacLean functioning very well in some remote, backroom environment—a high-tech "tinker room"—from which he would emerge every several years—trumpeting his latest breakthrough in embedded software, artificial intelligence, or thought-actuated word processing.

*My Questions for You*

1. How can MacLean get to know "the real MacLean?"
2. Will he ever overcome his urge to *manage*? Why? Why not?
3. If he does, what will enable him to do so?
4. He seems to be doing quite well where he is. Why shouldn't he remain there on a relatively permanent plateau? Can he?
5. In what ways are he and Margot Lansky alike? Dissimilar?

## CASE DISCUSSION 8:
### Katherine Steiner

Katherine has established a kind of "double cluster." First, she has put together a trio of specialties: market research, sales promotion and advertising, and product management. Better yet, she has applied her considerable skills "on both sides of the desk"—as an advertising agency consultant serving major corporations, and as an executive *within* the corporate structure. Further, she has gained valuable skills, experience, and exposure in her teaching and her seminars for professional societies.

She is well prepared to move in a number of directions, all of which should permit her to capitalize on her clustering while remaining in Chicago and preserving her established quality of family life. Her most obvious options include:

- Remaining at Gramble and Machter, at least for the present. She has not been told that she will not replace her boss, so there is still the chance that she will receive that big promotion. Besides, she admits that she respects both of the men candidates and could work very well for either of them. There are other reasons for not leaving: She enjoys her work, she likes the company, and the company likes her.

- Joining a major competitor, at a sizable increase in pay but with essentially the same responsibilities she now has. (This sort of move can be soothing, sometimes, for the bruised ego, and it can also set the stage for future promotion within the new company. It can, however, also project the executive into a corporate culture that is "wrong" for the U factor.)

- Joining a smaller competitor, as *the* person responsible for marketing and sales. (This could be an attractive option, especially if the culture were "right" for her. But it could also be dicey; remember, she has no actual sales experience, and there are few places to hide in a small organization.)

- Returning to the agency side, in one of four situations:

  1. To a large agency, in charge of all food accounts
  2. To a medium-sized agency, heading all packaged-goods accounts

3. To a small agency, responsible for all operations, including all accounts, research, and creative and production work

4. To her own agency, in charge of everything

Of the four primary options, the first strikes me as her best, mainly because it provides her with so much more flexibility than do the others. Her cluster, track record, and talent could lead to several opportunities during the next several years within Gramble and Machter. But even if these did not materialize, or if she found them unattractive, she would have used that period to analyze and compare the intricacies of the other options. (And although she may have relatively little need for a vested pension, she might as well earn it while evaluating her career choices.)

I suspect that she may eventually elect to have her own firm. To enhance her chances of success in that venture, she should do several things first: return to a well-known agency, become even more active in professional seminars, and strive to expand contacts among prospective clients. (And read Chapter 10!)

*My Questions for You*

1. Suppose that she *is* offered her boss's job and accepts it. Should she discard her other options? Why? Why not?

2. Suppose that, *not* being promoted, she decides that she should spend more time at home. How does this affect the four options?

## CASE DISCUSSION 9:
## Joseph Newman

This is, perhaps, the least complex of the nine cases of careers in limbo. I believe that Newman should adopt a career plan that is shaped along these lines:

- Accept certain conditions as being reasonably descriptive of his situation. These might include:

Despite his recent *faux pas* and his preoccupation with the more traditional aspects of the personnel function, he is still well liked by his boss and by Baronett's CEO.

His presence will be needed at Baronett for many years, although his sphere of responsibility will be smaller.

He and his new peer-to-be will not be rivals; neither will become successor to the senior vice president.

The new person and he will be expected to work *together,* helping each other and learning from each other's strengths.

- Determine to remain with the company, at least until he vests in two years.

- During those two (or more) remaining years, expand his contacts on both sides of the bargaining table in his four-industry cluster (steel, auto, chemicals, and retailing).

- Intensify his arbitration, teaching, and seminar activities. Study, discreetly, the earnings and work/travel schedules of successful, full-time arbitrators, attempting to determine his desire and adaptability for such a "business."

- Decide, during the next two years, whether he will remain with Baronett until normal retirement (but still doing some part-time teaching and arbitrating) or whether he will, at age 60, move to his special corner of entrepreneurland.

## My Questions for You

1. What are some of the things Newman should do to help his new peer be successful?

2. What are some of the things that Newman should say, within and beyond Baronett, about the reason for his change of status?

3. Suppose that, one year from now, the search for his new peer has been declared unsuccessful and has been terminated—that Baronett did not like the candidates it could have hired and could not attract the ones it wanted to hire. Should Newman volunteer to perform those new activities? Why? Why not? Or should he attempt to recruit a qualified assistant to head up this new work? Or should he hire a consultant to help him get these new programs in place?

4. What would be some of the advantages and disadvantages of his leaving *now* to accept the equivalent of his boss's job in a major competitor of Baronett's?

5. In what ways are he and Phillip Larghretti alike? Dissimilar?

6. What led you to believe that this was a simple case?

# EPILOGUE

Some books, some of them by gifted writers, have a final page or two in which the author attempts to sum up the major points made throughout the book.

This book has no such summary.

In this book, the points themselves are best thought of in the context within which they were presented in the earlier pages. My main points were usually embedded in case histories, in anecdotes, or in my frequent attempts to apply the light touch to some rather heavy topics.

So if you wish to refresh your memory on a certain point, you must, I fear, rummage through a major section or two of the book—all over again.

And such was my intention.

# INDEX

Abbott Laboratories, 133
Acceptance rules, 156–165
Accountability, 184
Acquisition analysis, 2
Acquisitions, corporate, 139–140
Action rules, 156, 165–168
Adler, Polly, 181
Aerojet-General, 188
Aerospace industry, 2, 99
Air pumps, 24–26
American Can, 2
American Dream, 179
Analysis, acquisition, 2
Apple Computer, 10
Aptitudes, necessary, 2, 112, 122
Arizona, 17–18
Ash, Mary Kay, 180
Assessments of new organizations,
    155–178
AT&T, 4
Attitudes, necessary, 2, 112, 122
"Automated" offices, 42
Automation:
    in factories, 32–39, 46–47
    in offices, 1, 40–54
Automotive industry, 9, 17, 39
Avco Corporation, 133–134
Avis, 139

Banking industry, 28–29
Bell, Alexander Graham, 188

"Blackstack" economy, 8, 65
Borman, Frank, 157
Boyle, Robert, 24
Bright, H. David, 40
British Petroleum Company, 140
Brousseau, Kenneth, 169
Burford, Anne, 157
Burns, Robert, 144
Burroughs, 140, 141
Business:
    changes in, 1–2, 8
    failures in, 11, 190–195
    new, 11–12
    small, 188–199
Business doctors, 158–163

CAD (computer-aided design), 33, 35,
    37
CAE (computer-aided engineering),
    33, 35, 37
California, 1
Callender, Marie, 180
CAM (computer-aided manufactur-
    ing), 35, 37
Capitalism, 28–29
Capone, Al, 181
Carborundum Corporation, 140
Career paths:
    and cluster specialists, 110–111,
        124–125

Career paths (*cont.*)
decision making in, 202–212
and rate of change, 1, 4
Career roles:
and cluster specialists, 110–111,
121–125
decision making in, 213–217
and rate of change, 1, 4
Career veer, 4, 213
Careers:
and change, 1, 5, 8, 16–18, 123,
148–149
dual, 15–16
in future, 1, 5, 31–55
half-lives of, 97–99
new opportunities for, 2
in past, 21–30
in present, 7–20
Carnegie, Andrew, 180
Caterpillar Tractor, 132–133
Ceramic engineers, 99
Change and careers, 1, 5, 8, 16–18,
123, 148–149
Chemicals industry, 1
Churchill, Winston, 157
Cluster specialists:
building clusters, 221–242
case histories of, 112–121, 217–219
decision to become, 213–217
defined, 110
in general, 4–5, 109–112, 121–124
types of, 124–129
Clusters, building, 221–242
Coal industry, 24, 27, 29
Cody, William F., 184
Coldwell Banker, 139
Colonial period in America, 23, 26–30
Communications industry, 3–4
Companies, leading, 2
Company economic factors, 2
Competition, worldwide, 13, 37, 64
Computer-aided design (CAD), 33,
35, 37
Computer-aided engineering (CAE),
33, 35, 37
Computer-aided manufacturing
(CAM), 35, 37
Computers:
corporations that produce, 140–142
in factories, 32–39

historical background on, 26, 28
and new technologies, 1, 10–12,
19–20
Connell, John, 42
Consolidated Foods Corporation,
135–136
Control Data, 140
Corporations:
acquisitions and mergers, 139–140
assessments of, 155–178
culture of, 131–153
in general, 9, 14, 150–152
Cost reduction and cluster specialists,
123–124
Counseling, employee, 2
Cultural values in general, 131–133
Culture, corporate, 131–153
Culture clashes, corporate, 139–144
Customs, 8–9

Deal, Terrence, 168
Dean Witter Reynolds Inc., 139
Decision making, 201–242
Defense industries, 2
DeLorean, John, 181
Depressions, economic, 66
Disney, Walt, 181
Doctors, business, 158–163
Dual careers, 15–16
Dun & Bradstreet reports, 11

Economic factors:
and careers, 1–4, 8
depressions, 66
and employment, 58–67
recessions, 3, 59–61, 100
recoveries, 2–3, 59–60
Economic forces, 9–11
Edison, Thomas, 180–181
Einstein, Albert, 157
Electrical engineers, 99
"Electronic" offices, 42–43
Electronic supervisors, 36
Electronics industry, 2, 10, 17, 19–20,
99
Employee economic factors, 2
Employees:
case histories of, 67–95, 112–121
and clustering, 124–129
decision making by, 202–204

Employees (*cont.*)
  migrations of, 18
  and restructuring, 60–63
  shifts of, 33–34
  training, 2, 12
Employers:
  cost reduction by, from clustering,
    123–124
  and restructuring, 61–63
Employment, 12–13
Engineering industry, 98–99
England, 23–30
Entrepreneurs:
  being own boss, 179–200
  and clustering, 127–128
Entrepreneurship, 182
Esmark, 139
Executive search firms, 150–152
Executives, 150–152
Experience, 185–188
Exxon, 139

Factories, future, 32–40, 46–47
Failures, business, 11, 190–195
Farm machinery industry, 2
Financial services, 1–2
Firestone, Harvey, 180
Fisher-Price Toys, 139
Flexibility, 54–55, 111–112, 185
Flexible manufacturing system
    (FMS), 32–39, 46–47
Florida, 18
FMS (flexible manufacturing system),
    32–39, 46–47
Ford, Henry, 181
France, 24–26, 28
Franklin, Benjamin, 180–181
Future, careers in, 1, 5, 31–55

General Dynamics, 188
General Electric (GE), Company, 18,
    37, 98, 140–143, 145–147
General Motors (GM), 37, 213
Generalists, 2, 4–5, 106–107, 110,
    219–220
Germany, 24, 26, 38
Governmental forces, 9
Great Depression, 66
Grisanti, Frank, 158
Guericke, Otto von, 24, 26

H&R Block, 139
Habits, 8–9
Halas, George, 181
Half-lives of careers, 97–99
Harp, Lore, 157
Harris, 18
Heckel, Jack, 188
Hero of Alexandria, 23–24
Hewlett-Packard, 18
Hilton Hotels Corporation, 134
Honeywell, 18, 140, 188
Howard K. Sams, 139
Huygens, Christian, 24

Iacocca, Lee, 162
IBM (International Business Ma-
    chines), 4, 18, 140–142, 145
Illinois, 1
INA Health Care Group, Inc., 134
Independence, need for, 184
Industrial economic factors, 1
Industrial Revolution, 26, 30
Industries, leading, 2
Information society, 8, 55
Instrumentation industry, 17
Insurance industry, 28–29
Integrated offices, 44
Integrated systems in factories, 33
International Business Machines (*see*
    IBM)
International Harvester, 2
Inventions, 19–20, 26–29, 189–190
Iron industry, 26
ITT, 139

Japan, 32, 35–38
Jobs in greatest demand, 2
  (*See also* Careers)
Jobs, Steve, 10, 180
John Deere, 2
Johnson, Howard, 180
Journeymen, 101
Junior employees, 61

Kennecott Copper, 140
Kennedy, Allan, 168
Kentucky, 38
"Knowledge bank" half-lives, 99
Kroc, Ray, 180

L. L. Bean, 134
Leeuwenhoek, Anton van, 28
Leibniz, Gottfried Wilhelm von, 28
Levinson, David, 14
Lincoln, Abraham, 157
Ling, James, 181
Locke, John, 28–29
Lockheed, 179

McCardle, Archie, 157
Machine tool industry, 37–38
McKay, John, 157
Managers:
  and clustering, 127
  decision making by, 208–212
  in general, 13–15
  professional, 146
  and restructuring, 64, 66
Manufacturing industries, future, 32–39
Marie Antoinette, 157
Martin, Billy, 157
Martin, James, 8
Martin Marietta, 18
Massachusetts, 17, 26, 29
Max Factor, 139
Meany, George, 213
Mechanical engineers, 98
Mechanical workers and clustering, 125
Mergers, corporate, 139–140
Merrill Lynch & Company, Inc., 136
Metals industry, 1, 17
Michigan, 1, 17
Migrations, worker, 18
Milacron, 38
Minnesota Mining & Manufacturing Corporation, 135
Modernization of plants and equipment, 12
Motorola, 18

Naisbitt, John, 8
National Education Corporation, 39–40, 134
NCR, 140, 141
Netherlands, 24, 26, 28
New Hampshire, 1, 16–17
New Mexico, 17
New York, 27, 29

Newcomen, Thomas, 25–26
Newspapers, 2
Newton, Isaac, 27, 29
North American Aviation, 147
North Carolina, 28
Northrop, 179
Norton Simon, 139

$O^2P$ factor, 145
Obsolescence, technical, 99
OCR (optical character recognition) devices, 47
Office managers, 13–15
Office Technology Research Group, 42
Offices, future, 1, 40–54
Ohio, 1, 17, 38
Optical character recognition (OCR) devices, 47
Organizational economic factors, 2
Organizations:
  assessments of, 155–178
  culture of, 131–153
Osborne, Adam, 181
O'Toole, James, 168–169

Palmieri, Victor, 158
Palucci, Jeno, 180
"Paperless" offices, 43
Papin, Denis, 24–26
Parts assembly, 33–34
Pascal, Blaise, 26, 28
Past, careers in, 21–30
Paths, career:
  and cluster specialists, 110–111, 124–125
  decision making in, 202–212
  and rate of change, 1, 4
Peer pressures, 9
Penney, J. C., 180
Pennsylvania, 1, 28–29
People proficiency, 55
Perseverance, 185
Pillsbury, George, 180
Pillsbury Company, 133
Pinkham, Lydia, 184
Planning, strategic, 2
Plasticity, 54–55, 111–112. 185
Playtex, 139
Political factors, 9–11

Ponzi, Charles, 181
Posner, Victor, 181
Preparations, necessary, 2, 54–55
Present, careers in, 7–20
Prices, 9
Procter & Gamble, 132
Product design, 33–34
Professional staff:
  and clustering, 126
  decision making by, 206–208
Proficiency, people, 55
Prosperity, selective, 3, 59–60

Quaker Oats, 139

Railroad industry, 3–4, 17
RCA, 140, 141
Recessions, economic, 3, 59–61, 100
Recoveries, economic, 2–3, 59–60
Regional economic factors, 1
Restructuring:
  of employees, 60–63
  of management, 64, 66
Retraining, 12
Retrovision, selective, 10
Reuther, Walter, 39
Rhode Island, 17–18
Risks, willingness to assume, 184
Robotics:
  in factories, 32, 36, 38–40
  in offices, 53
Rockefeller, John D., 184
Rockwell International, 2, 147
Roles, career:
  and cluster specialists, 110–111,
    121–124
  decision making in, 213–217
  and rate of change, 1, 4
Routine, office, 47
Rubber industry, 17
Rubenstein, Helena, 180

Sales personnel and managers, 13
Sanders, Colonel, 180
Savery, Thomas, 25–26, 29
Scotland, 24, 26
Search firms, executive, 150–152
Sears, Roebuck, 139
Selective prosperity, 3, 59–60
Selective retrovision, 10

Self-reliance, 184
Self understanding, 144–145, 184–186
Senior employees, 61–62
Seniority, 61–62
Shaklee Corporation, 135
Shifts, employee, 33–34
Shipping industry, 27–28
Sigoloff, Sandy, 162
Silk industry, 28
Silverman, Fred, 162
Skills, necessary, 2, 40, 112, 122
Small Business Innovative Research
    Act (1982), 188
Small businesses, setting up, 188–
    199
Social forces, 8–11
Somerset, Edward, 19, 23–26
South Carolina, 28
Specialists:
  cluster (see Cluster specialists)
  decision to become, 97–107, 213–
    217
  and small businesses, 196–199
  traditional, 2, 4–5, 19, 102–107,
    110, 220–221
Sperry Corporation, 18, 134
Staff, professional:
  and clustering, 126
  decision making by, 206–208
Standard Oil of Ohio, 140
Steam engines, 19, 23–26, 29
Steel industry, 3–4, 17
Storage Technology, 18
Strategic planning, 2
Success, 1, 5, 31, 37, 55, 122–124
Supervisors:
  and clustering, 125–126
  decision making by, 204–206
  electronic, 36
Supply and demand system, 9
Swift Foods, 139

Taxes, 16, 27–30
Tea industry, 27
Technical obsolescence, 99
Technological forces, 9–11
Technologies:
  and computers, 1, 10–12, 19–20
  and inventions, 19–20, 26–29, 189–
    190

Technologies (*cont.*)
  leading, 2, 4, 8
  and new jobs, 12–13, 18
Telecommunications industry, 3–4
Texas, 17
Textiles industry, 1, 17
Tobacco industry, 27
Tools, manufacturing, 33–34, 37–38
Traditional specialists and generalists,
    2, 4–5, 19, 102–107, 110, 219–
    221
Training:
  necessary, 2, 39–40
  retraining, 12
  vocational, 40
TRW, 18, 179
Twain, Mark, 191
Twentieth Century-Fox, 139
Tymshare, Inc., 135
Typewriters, 43–44, 48, 51–52

U factor, 144–145, 184–186
Understanding of self, 144–145, 184–
    186
Unemployment, 12–13
Unions, 9, 16–17, 63–65
United Auto Workers, 39
Univac, 140–141

Vacuums, 24–26
Veer, career, 4, 213
Vesco, Robert, 181
Virginia, 27
Vocational training, 40
Voice recognition systems, 53

Wages, 9
*Wall Street Journal*, 2
*Washington Star*, 2
Watt, James, 19, 24–26
Wells, Mary, 180
Westinghouse, George, 180
Wilson, Bob, 162
Wisconsin, 38
Wood industry, 27
Word processors, 43–44, 52–53
Workers:
  and clustering, 125
  decision making by, 202–204
  migrations of, 18
  and restructuring, 61–63
World Future Society, 176
Worldwide competition, 13, 37, 64

Xerox, 188

Yamazaki, 38